THE SENTIMENTAL EDUCATION OF THE NOVEL

Frontispiece to *Valida, ou la Réputation d'une femme* by Sophie d'Epinay Saint-Luc, 1835.

THE SENTIMENTAL EDUCATION
OF THE NOVEL

Margaret Cohen

PRINCETON UNIVERSITY PRESS   PRINCETON, NEW JERSEY

Library of Congress Cataloging-in-Publication Data

Cohen, Margaret.
The sentimental education of the novel /
Margaret Cohen
p. cm.
Includes bibliographical references and index.
ISBN 0-691-00648-2 (cloth : alk. paper)
1. French fiction—19th century—History and criticism.
2. Sentimentalism in literature. 3. French fiction—Women authors—History and criticism.
I. Title.
PQ653.C54   1999
843'.709353—dc21   98-37765 CIP

This book has been composed in Sabon

The paper used in this publication meets the minimum requirements
of ANSI/NISO Z39.48-1992 (R1997) (*Permanence of Paper*)

http://pup.princeton.edu

1 3 5 7 9 10 8 6 4 2
Printed in the United States of America

Contents

Illustrations

Acknowledgments

THE INITIAL RESEARCH for this book was funded by an NYU grant during the summer of 1988. I completed the archival work during 1991–1992 when I was supported by an American Council of Learned Societies grant for recent recipients of the Ph.D. and an NYU Presidential Fellowship. An NYU summer grant in 1997 enabled me to revisit the archive once my argument was in place.

Throughout the composition of the book, superb readers have helped me sort through my ideas. My argument never would have taken shape without Franco Moretti, Richard Terdiman, and Margaret Waller, my readers at Princeton University Press, or without the insights of April Alliston, Anne Higonnet, Gloria Kury, Sharon Marcus, Molly Nesbit, and Kristin Ross. Discussions with Peter Brooks, Jann Matlock, Sandy Petrey, and Christopher Prendergast were invaluable as I first formulated my questions about realism. Emily Apter, Carolyn Dever, Fabienne Moore, and Vanessa Schwartz offered astute and timely critical advice.

Thanks go to my colleagues in Comparative Literature at NYU for their support of the project, notably to my Chairs Timothy J. Reiss, Jennifer Wicke, and Daniel Javitch. I rely on Sarah Harrell's superlative research. I am also endebted for research help to Jacquelyn Walsh, Jennifer Rappaport, Tyler Rollins, and Mary Lou Gramm. The staff in the Département des Livres Imprimés at the Bibliothèque Nationale, in particular Marie-Hélène Pons, Véronique Meunier, and Marie Jo Chehere, facilitated access to books during my trip to France in 1997. Mary Murrell is everything one could hope for in an editor.

My friends and family have lived with the ups and downs of the writing process and know my debts to them. *Hors catégorie*: Dan, Sam, and Max Klotz.

THE SENTIMENTAL EDUCATION OF THE NOVEL

Reconstructing the Literary Field

OUT OF THE CENTURY'S CHAOS

Before 1830, the novel in France was *"pleasant entertainment for lazy gentlefolk [honnêtes paresseux],"* to cite the noted critic, Charles-Marie de Féletz, himself quoting a celebrated seventeenth-century formulation.[1] After 1830, the genre became an authoritative form of social and cultural analysis imbued with the highest literary prestige.[2] "Racine and the coffee house are outmoded; asphalt and pavement will pass from fashion; but the novel will remain," declared a reviewer in 1838 impressed with the novel's new prominence, and history has vindicated his literary judgment.[3] Jules Michelet testified to the novel's increased authority in depicting social relations when he considered how to portray the class that had emerged as a political force with the Revolution in *Le Peuple* (1846). Dismissing statistical analyses and economic histories for their "partial and artificial results," Michelet turned rather to "writers, artists": the leading French novelists whose powerful works, in his estimation, now shaped international as well as national perceptions of French society.[4]

Throughout the twentieth century, the French novel's transformation from polite entertainment into ambitious social analysis has been equated with the realist codes that have played such a vital role in French literature and culture as well as in literature and culture throughout the world. It has also been equated with two great authors, Balzac and Stendhal, inventing their brilliant poetics in a heroic struggle to make sense of the economic, social, and political upheavals resulting from the French Revo-

---

[1] Charles-Marie de Féletz, *"Eugène de Rothelin,"* in *Mélanges de philosophie, d'histoire et de littérature*, 6:138. All translations are mine unless otherwise indicated. The phrase is from Pierre-Daniel Huet's *Traité de l'origine des romans* (1669). Féletz's review was first published after *Eugène de Rothelin* (1808) appeared. It was then republished in the six-volume *Mélanges*, which commemorated Féletz's election to the Académie Française.

[2] For details on the novel's transvaluation in France around 1830, see Erich Köhler, "Gattungsystem und Gesellschaftsystem," in *Romanistische Zeitschrift für Literaturgeschichte*, no. 1 (1977); Karlheinrich Biermann's *Literarische-politische Avant-garde in Frankreich*; and Margaret Iknayan's *The Idea of the Novel in France*.

[3] Emile Pages, "Bulletin bibliographique."

[4] Jules Michelet, *Le Peuple*, 60.

lution. "Balzac dragged a world out of the century's chaos," asserted Heinrich Mann in an extreme version of a mythic narrative that has informed studies of realism attentive to the material factors shaping literary texts from Lukács and Auerbach on.[5]

When Balzac described these factors from the vantage point of his own present, however, he told a less heroic tale. "You will see that men, passions, and needs are at work underneath all these beautiful imaginary things. You will inevitably get mixed up in horrible struggles pitting work against work, man against man, faction against faction," Lousteau warns Lucien concerning the competition shaping literary creation when *Illusions perdues* depicts the underside of literary history.[6] Let Lousteau's warning serve as epigraph for the revisionary narrative offered here. This study asks how the modern novel in France took shape in response to the local conflicts of literary production as well as sweeping social transformation, returning Balzac and Stendhal to the literary contexts of their time.

My attention to the *intraliterary* dynamics shaping arguably the most influential novelistic codes ever invented goes beyond the worthy imperative to take account of the terms a historical moment uses to represents itself. When Balzac relates literature to the "horrible struggles" of literary production, he also, I think, offers a promising solution to an underdiscussed but crucial question confronting contemporary literary studies. This question is how to write literary history in the wake of poststructuralism. From its inception, poststructural theory has taken shape as an attack on traditional literary history, thoroughly discrediting its organizing concepts.[7] At the same time, however, the contours of a new literary history have remained surprisingly unexplored within the poststructural paradigm, where literary critics interested in history have focused on general questions concerning the relation between history and literature rather than scrutinizing the history of literature per se.[8]

---

[5] Heinrich Mann, *Flaubert und George Sand*, 5.

[6] Honoré de Balzac, *Illusions perdues*, 270. Subsequent page references will appear parenthetically in the text.

[7] Paul de Man's *Blindness and Insight*, in particular the essay "Literary History and Literary Modernity," as well as Michel Foucault's *Archaeology of Knowledge* and "What Is an Author?" are seminal poststructural texts that include a challenge to literary history in their attacks on humanism.

[8] On the challenges confronting literary history in the wake of poststructuralism, see the essays collected in *The Uses of Literary History*, edited by Marshall Brown. Lawrence Lipking observes the recent critical turn from questions of literary history to questions concerning the relation of literature to history in his contribution to the volume. This turn is evident whether critics pursue the deconstructive interest in the philosophical interrelations between the categories of literature and history or the materialist interest in how literature partici-

Perhaps as a result, the most rigorous and influential poststructural analyses are sometimes haunted by the discredited categories of traditional literary history despite themselves. No body of work makes this more apparent than poststructural materialist analyses of the modern novel that date its flowering in France to "the first great realisms" of Balzac and sometimes Stendhal.[9] In doing so, materialist critics not only periodize literary history in terms of the same masterpieces and canonized aesthetics sanctified by an earlier generation of critics, they leave unexamined the notion of the masterpiece itself. Where these notions figure, other discredited notions have not been entirely left behind. If we accept literary history as a collection of masterpieces, the assumption follows that literature itself flows through "homogeneous, empty time," in contrast to the conflictual process materialism understands as characterizing history on the level of the whole social formation.[10] And if we unquestioningly equate realism with the modern novel, we give the form a retrospective teleology, perpetuating a narrative of literary history as progress.

As such blind spots illustrate, the last residues of traditional literary history are in how critics conceptualize the literary aspects to literary texts. To rethink these aspects in a fashion doing justice to the materialist strain of poststructuralism, my study proposes that we may well heed *Illusions perdues*, understanding literature as a web of social relations made up of formal and informal institutions ranging from academies and publishing houses to avant-garde movements and literary genres. I revisit the emergence of realism in France to ask, specifically, how realist codes were shaped by the novelistic contexts in which they appeared. Did Balzac and Stendhal in fact invent realism in literary isolation, or were realist poetics responding to other contemporary novels and novelists along with the century's chaos? To answer the question, it is necessary to embed the foundational realist works in the landscape of the French novel during the first decades of the nineteenth century. This landscape must be reconstructed, for the triumph of realism has relegated it to all but complete oblivion.[11]

The Sentimental Education of the Novel is thus a literary history written from the archive. Archive, first of all, in the sense of the dusty documents neglected in libraries. The practices shaping the genesis of French

---

pates in history conceptualized as transformations on the level of the whole social formation.

[9] Fredric Jameson, *The Political Unconscious*, 104.

[10] Walter Benjamin, "Theses on the Philosophy of History," 261.

[11] Only a handful of specialists remember anything more about these "lean years" for the genre than a few exceptional works by Chateaubriand, Constant, and Staël, as well as some historical novels from the late 1820s. I take the phrase "lean years" from Margaret Iknayan's *The Idea of the Novel in France*, which evinces what continues to be the dominant view of the state of the French novel between the Revolution and realism. See Iknayan, 138.

realism are in novels which had to be remembered and then located before they could even be read. And archive as Foucault defined the term seeking to direct historical inquiry away from individual works to the discursive structures that support them, although I am interested in a significantly different archive from the critics who have given this notion a defining role in North American literary studies of the past twenty years. As new historicism illustrates, the archive has overwhelmingly been equated with non-literary discourses traversing the social formation. The archive is, however, not synonymous with the non-literary. Literature has an archive of its own. The books we now remember are only a fraction of the literary past, as Franco Moretti observes in recent important work on how the literary archive might provide crucial raw material for the renewal of literary history. Literary studies has much to learn from the shift that occurred in the discipline of history from a historiography of exceptions to a historiography of norms, dominated by conventions, "repetitive, slow—boring, even. . . . But then, are we so sure that boredom is boring?"[12]

From my archaeology, Balzac and Stendhal will emerge as literary producers among other producers, seeking a niche in a generic market promising both economic and cultural return. We will see that realist novels were not unequivocally celebrated masterpieces in their own time nor was the realist aesthetic the inevitable teleology of the modern novel when it first appeared. Rather, Balzac and Stendhal made bids for their market shares in a hostile takeover of the dominant practice of the novel when both started writing: sentimental works by women writers. And they competed with writers who challenged the prestige of sentimentality using other codes that contemporaries found equally if not more compelling.

Modeling literature as conflictual social production, my study takes shape in a burgeoning field at the intersection of materialist—in particular feminist—literary history, the history of the book, and a sociology of cultural institutions. These methodologies are completely revising how we understand the historicity of the literary artifact, although their transdisciplinary coherence has yet to be articulated in sustained theoretical form. To conceptualize the literary struggles shaping textual codes, I make use, notably, of Pierre Bourdieu's theorization of literature in the spirit of Balzac, even if Bourdieu does not acknowledge how much he learned from *Illusions perdues*.[13]

---

[12] Franco Moretti, *Atlas of the European Novel 1800–1900*, 150.

[13] Bourdieu's *The Rules of Art* is so useful for this study, I am suggesting, because its theoretical model is in fact a historical description of the literary moment under consideration here. It remains an open question how Bourdieu's model applies to the institution of literature as it is configured in other places and times. Would there be, for example, the same

Bourdieu offers his account as a challenge to marxist criticism for the direct correspondence it establishes between social formation and text. If a literary text responds to social conflicts, Bourdieu points out, it is shaped by literary as well as social factors, or rather by social factors that are themselves literary, for it responds within a horizon of literary codes and institutional constraints that confront a writer at a particualar literary historical moment.[14] This situation is further complicated by the fact that a writer is not alone in what Bourdieu calls the literary field, a term he uses to designate a network made up both of official institutions and informal but nonetheless conventionalized social relations. A writer's practice is overdetermined by his or her competition with contemporaries responding to the same codes and constraints, as writers take positions in relation to each other, striving for literary recognition and/or economic success.[15] Bourdieu's model thus effects a major transformation in how critics have long organized the literary past. The identity of a literary historical moment is defined not by the canonized masterworks but rather by struggles involving a broad range of writers, readers, and texts.

Bourdieu himself, however, is most interested in the canonized texts and aesthetics when he shows how his theory might be applied. His argument for the invention of the high/low distinction in Second Empire France turns on such authors as Flaubert and Baudelaire along with such works as *L'Education sentimentale* and *Les Fleurs du mal*. His account has further been justly criticized for its reductive readings of how poetics encode literary struggle. And it does not pay much attention to gender as a category of social analysis, although it certainly makes a theoretical place for the importance of collective identity in shaping a writer's access to economic and cultural capital. In these limitations, Bourdieu's model

---

aggressive competition among writers in a literary field where literary circles and publishing houses are not centralized as they were in nineteenth-century Paris?

[14] Bourdieu writes, "To reintroduce the field of cultural production as an autonomous social universe is to get away from the *reduction* effected by all forms, whether more or less refined, of the 'reflection' theory which subtends Marxist analyses of cultural works." Pierre Bourdieu, *The Rules of Art*, 202. Semiautonomous would be more accurate than autonomous, since the literary field is overdetermined by its relation to other fields within the social formation, as Bourdieu himself makes clear. Tony Bennett offers a similar critique of the pervasive materialist tendency to place social events outside literature in his appropriately titled *Outside Literature*. His chapter on the marxist lineage theorizing the novel is particularly relevant for my study, which heeds his caution that "account must . . . be taken of the specific institutional frameworks conditioning the deployment of literary texts in order to assess the regions of sociality to which, at the time, they were concretely connected and within which they operated" (110).

[15] Bourdieu's concept of position-taking should not be confused with the less precise notion of influence. While influence indicates any textual practice marking a text, position-taking designates only that intertextual dialogue involving a writer's bid for his or her market share.

gains much if it is fused with the feminist practice of literary history, which has been decisive in uncovering neglected works and aesthetics and which elaborates their contours with the most sophisticated textual analysis.

Both these dimensions to feminist literary history inspire my decision to revisit French realism, specifically, in order to rewrite the discredited notions of traditional literary history through attention to the literary field. Feminists working on the history of the novel have been instrumental in showing the conflicting representational modes which constitute a literary historical moment, contextualizing realist poetics as only one among an uneven range of novelistic forms. To take the case of nineteenth-century France, the first critics suggesting that realism emerges in a conflict with other powerful and coherent aesthetics, are, to my knowledge, Naomi Schor, arguing for "recanonizing" Sand's novels as an instance of the once prestigious but now devalued idealism, and Margaret Waller, revealing that Stendhal aimed his first novel against the sentimental works of Claire de Duras.[16]

The fusion of Bourdieu's theory with feminist literary history also offers feminist studies a great deal in return. Notably, feminist studies has much to gain from Bourdieu's notion that the literary field plays a determining role in how social relations shape literary texts. To demonstrate these gains, I use Bourdieu to answer a question which has long vexed French feminist literary history: why were there no French women realists? In the course of excavating the novelistic practices surrounding the emergence of realism, I have discovered that the absence of women writers from the nineteenth-century realist canon is accurate: Balzac and Stendhal's female contemporaries overwhelmingly steered clear of realist codes. Their avoidance of realism did not, however, mean their insignificance or ab-

---

[16] See Naomi Schor's *George Sand and Idealism* and Margaret Waller's *The Male Malady*. The critique of the account equating realism with the modern novel has been even more pronounced among feminist critics of the English novel, who have thoroughly dismantled the "rise of the novel" narrative that long held sway in the English context with the same authority that the agon with the Revolution dominates the historiography of the novel in France. April Alliston, in particular, makes explicit the problematic assumptions concerning literary historical process shaping "the rise of the novel" narrative from Watt to McKeon in her *Virtue's Faults* as well as her "Female Sexuality and the Referent of Enlightenment Realisms," in *Spectacles of Realism*, edited by Margaret Cohen and Christopher Prendergast. My study is also inspired by the revisionary feminist narratives of the English "rise of the novel" in its attention to the archive and to forgotten literature considered from the standpoint of the field. While feminists working within the French tradition tend to revise the great man/great text version of literary history by recuperating the works of individual authors, the most significant feminist interventions in the English context conceptualize forgotten literature as a range of aesthetic and social practices. See, for example, the different kinds of textual archaeologies offered by Laurie Langbauer's *Women and Romance*, Catherine Gallagher's *Nobody's Story*, and Alliston's *Virtue's Faults*.

sence in the contemporary novel. Rather, we will see women writers, George Sand among them, prominent in forging a form that was realism's principal competition across the 1830s and 1840s and that I call the sentimental social novel to emphasize its continuity with early-nineteenth-century sentimentality.[17]

French feminist critics on both sides of the Atlantic have long grounded women writers' antipathy to realism in their social subordination. This explanation has been offered, for example, by theorists of *écriture féminine*, an aesthetic which, in fact, takes shape as a tacit response to women writers' absence from the classic realist lineage. "Not the novelists, allies of representationalism [*solidaires de la représentation*]," Cixous stated emphatically when she surveyed the literary tradition looking for harbingers of women's writing, suggesting the novel, by which she meant the realist novel, as the great literary expression of the phallo-logocentric order.[18]

Taxing Cixous's theories with essentialism, the most important American feminists working on French literature during the 1980s nonetheless followed her lead in explaining women's antipathy to realism by women's dominated social position. When Schor discussed why Sand, the most famous French woman novelist of the nineteenth century, wrote idealist fiction, she identified nonrealist codes as "the only alternative representational mode available to those who do not enjoy the privileges of subjecthood in the real."[19] Similarly, Nancy K. Miller clarified implausible moments within *La Princesse de Clèves*, long placed at the inception of the realist lineage, by pointing to women's dominated social position. This position, she argued, makes them hostile to a historical moment's reigning notions of plausibility and verisimilitude that are the products of the dominant, that is, masculine, culture.[20]

The shortcomings of such an explanation emerge vividly if we glance even briefly at the literary history of that other nation famed for first producing the realist novel. In England, as in France, women were legally, politically, as well as economically second-class citizens and realism was thoroughly implicated in the phallocentric social order, yet the form could

---

[17] Surveying forgotten novels across the nineteenth century, I have found very few realist novels by women before the Third Republic. After 1880, women start writing realist works on a regular basis. For an overview of women novelists' generic practices in the nineteenth century, see my "Women and Fiction in the Nineteenth Century," in *The Cambridge Companion to the Modern French Novel*, edited by Timothy Unwin.

[18] Hélène Cixous, "The Laugh of the Medusa," 250.

[19] Schor, *Sand and Idealism*, 54. This essay was first published in a 1988 *Yale French Studies*, no. 75, entitled *The Politics of Tradition: Placing Women in French Literature*.

[20] See Nancy K. Miller, *Subject to Change*, in particular the chapter on *La Princesse de Clèves*.

not have existed without authors such as Jane Austen, Charlotte Brontë, Elizabeth Gaskell, and George Eliot. This study suggests that to understand women's absence from the genesis of modern French realism, we must take account of the same specifically literary dynamics missing from the great materialist narratives of the form. While French feminists have related poetics directly to the construction of gender on the level of the whole social formation, the impact of gender on texts is, in fact, mediated by the construction of gender within the social relations of literary production.[21]

REALISM IN LITERARY-POLITICAL CONTEXTS

Arguing that realist codes took shape in response to nonrealist fiction by Balzac and Stendahl's "consoeurs" and competition, my excavation revises reigning accounts of the emergence of the modern French novel in several important ways. It opens by showing that the novel did address the Revolution during the first thirty years of the nineteenth century. The sentimental works dominating these decades confront one of the great impasses of revolutionary ideology: how to accommodate both negative and positive notions of rights. In both political thought and practice, it proved extremely difficult to devise a form of government protecting the citizen's negative rights to life, liberty, and happiness as well as the citizen's positive rights to participate in decisions concerning the welfare of the collective. Sentimental novels, in compensation, created an idealized aesthetic community where the difficulties could be played out and overcome. These novels, by such acclaimed authors as Isabelle de Montolieu, Sophie Cottin, Stéphanie de Genlis, Adélaïde de Souza (a.k.a. Flahaut), and Juliane von Krüdener, along with Germaine de Staël, were both the critical successes and the bestsellers of their time.[22]

However, in the years leading up to the Revolution of 1830, and above all in its aftermath, early-nineteenth-century sentimentality lost its persuasive force. The urgency of the conflict between negative and positive rights waned in light of other emerging social contradictions. The most pressing for the novel is, I will suggest, the problem of unequal social division, which took on new importance following the July Revolution. While 1830 legitimated the ideals of 1789, it simultaneously installed a regime that continued the Restoration's government by the privileged classes.

---

[21] Leyla Ezdlini makes a similar point in her suggestive essay "*La Canne de M. de Balzac*: Parody at the Intersection of Politics and Literature," *L'Esprit Créateur* 33, no. 3.

[22] These works thus challenge the assumption common in both traditional and revisionary literary histories that noncanonical texts were necessarily popular or mass literature.

Throughout the July Monarchy, the contradiction between all subjects' symbolic access to liberty, equality, and fraternity and the practical concentration of rights, power, and property in the hands of middle and upper class men played a central role in shaping public debate, in literature as in other social fields.

The events surrounding 1830 also gave an outmoded cast to the compensations sentimentality offered for social impasse. Sentimental problem-solving relies on an Enlightenment distance between aesthetics and politics in a distinction that was strategic as well as ideological, for political censorship was powerful during both the Empire and the Restoration, when sentimentality dominated the novel. Across the 1820s, however, writers and intellectuals nourished the oppositional perception that written opinion should play an active political role.[23] At the end of the Restoration, this perception intensified in response to Charles X's increasingly repressive censorship, and the liberal public sphere proved sufficiently powerful to catalyze a second French Revolution.

Materialist critics have long viewed "the [realist] novelists of the nineteenth century" as "the children of the French Revolution," to cite Sandy Petrey, eloquently paraphrasing Hugo.[24] From the vantage point of the literary field, however, the realist goal to represent the panorama of social life appears not as a delayed response to 1789 but rather as an immediate response to 1830. "The French have the right to print and to publish their opinions, within the bounds of the law. Censorship will never again be established," the Charter of 1830 proclaimed in a statement that was no less significant for the fact that it was not to be respected.[25] One of its

[23] No position makes this perception more evident than Romanticism, which was then taking the cultural world by storm. The reigning literary historical accounts of Romanticism generally make a distinction between the more personal yearnings for liberty characterizing the Romantics before 1830 and the overt politics of "the generation of 1830" when, as Max Milner puts it in the Arthaud history of French literature, "French Romanticism will reveal its true nature, which is, on balance, less aesthetic than philosophical, ethical, and social." Milner, *Le Romantisme I (1820–1843)*, 60. Milner himself observes, however, that "one great originality of French Romanticism is . . . the role played by politics in its beginnings" (55). As the periodization of Milner's study indicates, Romanticism has long offered the dominant grid for conceptualizing literature's engagement with politics during the years at issue here. My archaeology shows, however, that the designation Romanticism obscures more than it reveals when applied to novels from the first half of the nineteenth century. Notably, we will see the designation flatten out differences in the poetic strategies writers use to politicize literature. It also obscures women's prominent role in honing a novelistic form that not only engages the question of freedom before Romanticism but in fact constitutes the prehistory of the movement.

[24] Sandy Petrey, *Realism and Revolution*, 50.

[25] Cited in Nicholas Harrison, *Circles of Censorship*, 31. Harrison provides a concise summary of the flux around censorship in France throughout the first half of the nineteenth century. When Balzac discusses a novel of the Empire in *La Muse du département*, he men-

decisive consequences was to transform the social situation of literature. With the July Revolution, writers were authorized to intervene in political culture, and the most ambitious works across the literary spectrum pursued literature's new power to accede to public affairs.[26] This power was, moreover, of importance in realist and nonrealist novels staking a claim to literary and cultural authority.

If history dissipated the persuasions of early-nineteenth-century sentimentality, the form remained sufficiently prestigious so that novels with serious literary and cultural aspirations took sentimental codes as their starting point.[27] Not all these novels, however, carved up the sentimental legacy in similar ways. While the dominant materialist accounts of realism reduce the literary factors shaping Balzac and Stendhal's practices to the historical novel pioneered by Scott, this study argues that both novelists forged fundamental features of realist poetics in a hostile takeover of the sentimental form. Thus, such an important code as the bildungsroman plot placing the individual in insolubly fractured relation to the collective turns out to derive from sentimentality. But when works like *Le Rouge et le noir* and *Le Père Goriot* appropriated sentimental codes, they transvalued these codes' significance. In the sentimental novel, the plot of fracture, for example, paves the way for a tragic struggle of principles. In realist novels, principles are discredited as sentimental illusions and the plot of

---

tions censorship as a great divide between literature of the present (*La Muse* is set in 1836) and literature of the earlier nineteenth century. "During this period . . . there was censorship, and one must be as indulgent for the man [*l'homme*] who underwent the scissors of 1805 as for those who went to the scaffold in 1793," comments a character, framing censorship not only as a bygone institution but also as a practice which shapes novelistic poetics. Balzac, *La Muse du departement*, 241.

[26] As E. J. Hobsbawm observes, "There has rarely been a period when even the least 'ideological' artists were more universally partisan, often regarding service to politics as their primary duty." Hobsbawm, *The Age of Revolution*, 324. On the open relation between the political and cultural fields during the July Monarchy, see also Biermann's *Literarische-politische Avant-garde in Frankreich*; Richard Terdiman's *Discourse/Counter-Discourse*; André-Jean Tudesq's *Les Grands Notables en France*; Bourdieu's *The Rules of Art*; and François Furet's *Terminer la Révolution*, vol. 2. The "l'art pour l'art" position emerging in the early 1830s reacted against the overwhelming importance of political and social issues in post-1830s literature.

[27] One telling indication of sentimentality's power at this time is how the French novel appeared to foreigners. When the English critic, Henry Southern, surveyed the French novel in 1832, he was more interested in abstracting the general contours of the form than in the diversity of contemporary position-taking. Southern wrote, "The difference between a French and an English novel of the present day is sufficiently marked. The novels of this country turn chiefly on material distinctions. . . . On the other hand, in a French novel, it is difficult to say whether a man drives a pair or lives in a garret: if distinctions are made, they are those of sentiment, language, or manners. The grand business of French fiction is the feeling excited by certain situations and relations of life." Southern, "French Novels," in *A Victorian Art of Fiction*, 1:131.

fracture opens the door to realist compromise, to the protagonist's amoral struggle to succeed.

Gender turns out to be a powerful symbolic weapon in Balzac and Stendhal's campaigns to assert the importance of their new practices. Both Balzac and Stendhal associated the invention of realist codes with the masculinization of a previously frivolous feminine form in their polemic and in their poetics. Their strategy exploited the fact that the prestigious sentimental works in the first thirty years of the nineteenth century were written by women and that women were prominent sentimental social novelists, as integral to the cultural life of the July Monarchy as the form they employed. These women ranged from the utopian socialist reformer Flora Tristan to the Countess Merlin, whose aristocratic salon was a rite of passage for "those who had musical ambitions or talents"; from Louise de Constant, sister of Benjamin, to the professional and eminently successful Virginie Ancelot, known both for her novels and for the popular plays she wrote with her husband; from Hortense Allart, critic, novelist, "romantic muse" to Chateaubriand, Lammenais, Béranger, and Sainte-Beuve, to the Baroness Aloïse de Carlowitz, whose translations of the German Romantics received prizes from the Académie Française.[28]

One such prominent woman was widely considered quite simply the most important novelist of the time, as Michelet indicated when he enumerated literary models for *Le Peuple*. Terming Balzac "a genre painter, admirable in his genius for detail," Michelet came to him only after "classic and immortal novels revealing the domestic tragedies of the rich and well-off classes."[29] Michelet's editor plausibly identifies these novels as the first works of Sand, but that Michelet described them in terms of a practice rather than an author is telling.[30] Sand was one of many novelists who made serious bids for literary and cultural recognition using sentimental social codes.

July Monarchy women's association with the sentimental social novel went beyond their visibility among its practitioners. Whenever they pursued the novel's new power to intervene in public life, whatever their

---

[28] Anne Martin-Fugier, *La Vie élégante*, 315. I take the term, "romantic muse," from Léon Séché's *Hortense Allart de Méritens*, 7.

[29] Michelet, *Le Peuple*, 61.

[30] Paul Vialleneix writes, "Michelet is doubtless thinking of George Sand's first novels, to judge by his interpretation of them at the time of *L'Amour* and *La Femme* (1858–1859)" (*Le Peuple*, 61). Reconstructing the generic context shaping Sand's practice also adds another layer of significance to Michelet's praise. When Michelet qualifies Sand's works as classic and immortal, he may be referring not only to their own importance but to the fact that they exemplify a classic and immortal form of the novel. As will become clear in the next section, Michelet is foregrounding Sand's sentimental affiliation, for the core of the sentimental plot is domestic tragedy in a wealthy setting.

social standing, they overwhelmingly employed the sentimental social form. Why should Balzac and Stendhal's consoeurs have evinced such antipathy for the realist position? This study speculates that it may well have been because realism was "a compromised position [*une fausse position*]" for contemporary women, to use the terms of one female novelist from the time.[31] Realist codes did not appeal to women writers, I argue, because of the complex interaction between the construction of gender in specifically literary and more broadly social contexts.

Two aspects of this construction are textual: (1) Balzac and Stendhal's aggressive campaigns to masculinize the novel in realist poetics as well as polemic and (2) the pervasive gendering of sentimentality as feminine by writers and critics of all poetic stripes. One more aspect is women's status within contemporary institutions of literary production. During the July Monarchy, a woman could not help but write as a "*femme auteur*"; critics, readers, and publishers alike regarded women writers as women first, writers second. A fourth decisive aspect is at the intersection of the literary field and the whole social formation. If, as François Furet suggests, "July 1830 revives and deepens all the conflicts born of 1789," this is true in the realm of gender as well as class.[32] The question whether Revolutionary entitlement should extend to the Revolution's daughters was hotly debated even while domestic ideology exerted its authority and the *femme auteur*, that public woman, became a lightning rod in disputes around the numerous women who reached beyond the private sphere.

When the archive reveals women's presence in the literary dimension to public life during the first half of the nineteenth century, it challenges us to nuance the important and influential arguments made by feminist historians and literary historians concerning the power of bourgeois domestic ideology during the Revolutionary and post-Revolutionary periods. The emergence of domestic ideology to hegemony beginning with the Revolution has led Joan DeJean, for example, to cast 1789 as "surely an inauspicious date . . . for feminist writing in general," and by implication for female authors, in contrast to ancien régime literary culture, where women played a prominent role both as writers and as arbiters of taste.[33] But while ideologically dominant, the doctrine of the separate spheres took shape in relation to practices which, at least within literary production, were substantially more complex.[34]

---

[31] I take the phrase from Caroline Marbouty's sentimental social novel, *Une Fausse Position* (1844).

[32] Furet, *Révolution*, 146.

[33] Joan DeJean, "Classical Reeducation: Decanonizing the Feminine," 30. Joan Landes makes an argument for women's more general exclusion from the public sphere following the Revolution in *Women and the Public Sphere in the Age of the French Revolution.*

[34] Carla Hesse comes to similar conclusions in statistical research that reveals that women started to enter the literary profession in unprecedented numbers during and after the Revo-

The gains from understanding a cultural formation as a *range* of practices are apparent in the case of the work that most famously sets the
terms of post-Revolutionary literary misogyny. This work is Jean-
François La Harpe's *Lycée, ou Cours de littérature ancienne et moderne*
(1791–1803), that, as DeJean persuasively shows, established the French
tradition as overwhelmingly male and that was tremendously influential
in defining the canon from the latter part of the nineteenth century on.[35]
If we position La Harpe within the literary context of his time, however,
his representation of women writers as "virtual nonentities" takes on a
dynamic significance.[36] La Harpe was drafting his canon during the years
when sentimental works by women writers were being published to critical acclaim, even if the judges of high literary value differed on the novel's
importance as a literary form.[37] If gender is at stake in La Harpe's rewriting of the French tradition, it may well be a reaction to women's post-
Revolutionary literary visibility, which only affirms their importance, albeit in negative fashion.[38]

---

lution. See Hesse, "Women in Print, 1750–1800: An Essay on Historical Bibliography,"
Studies on Voltaire and the 18th Century, 1998.

[35] While La Harpe's *Lycée* includes eleven seventeenth-century women writers, DeJean
emphasizes that he evaluates them negatively. In his eight volumes devoted to the eighteenth
century, he includes only Tencin, de Beaumont, Riccoboni, and Graffigny.

[36] DeJean, "Reeducation," 37.

[37] "Women figure with the greatest distinction among modern novelists," declared Marie-
Joseph de Chénier, for example, in his *Tableau historique de l'état et des progrès de la littérature française depuis 1789* (1816), a work that was as influential in the first decades of the
century as La Harpe's *Lycée* (227). Indeed, the critic François-Adolphe Loève-Veimars set
up La Harpe and Chénier as two opposing poles of taste when he surveyed the critical
landscape of the first decades of the century in the opening to his 1825 *Résumé de la littérature française, depuis son origine jusqu'à nos jours*. The *Résumé* begins by praising Chénier's *Tableau*, asserting, in contrast, that La Harpe must be "redone entirely." I quote from
an 1838 edition entitled *Précis de la littérature française, depuis son origine jusqu'à nos
jours*, 1.

[38] The more we explore the literary archive, the more we get a sense that La Harpe's
work expresses one important view among a range of positions, and a disputed view at that.
DeJean is, for example, specifically opposing La Harpe's pedagogical canon to the genre of
the "worldly anthology," which, as she points out, declines with the Revolution. But the
genre nonetheless persists. In 1808–10, for example, A. A. Barbier and N. L. M. Desessarts
publish the *Nouvelle Bibliothèque d'un homme de goût*, which updates Abbé Louis-Mayeul
Chaudon's *Bibliothèque d'un homme de goût* from 1772. Appealing to a public of worldly
adults, Barbier and Desessarts present "opinions that perceptive critics have formulated not
only about the masterpieces of ancient and modern literature, but also about all the works
that, without equaling them, can comprise a select library" (1:i). These authors confirm
DeJean's argument that La Harpe attacks the worldly canon, for they explicitly aim their
work against him. "His [La Harpe's] opinions on modern authors are even more reprehensible [than his opinions on ancient authors] in their prejudice and bias," they remark in their
preface (1:ii). While Barbier and Desessarts do not specify what aspects of La Harpe's opinions they find "reprehensible," their views certainly differ when it comes to the novel. Like

GENRE IS A SOCIAL RELATION

Sentimentality's powerful role in shaping the subsequent history of the French novel bears out a celebrated insight of Marx foundational for Bourdieu. While authors make poetics, they do not make them just as they please. Rather, they make them in relation to the established discourses in which they seek to intervene—in the case of the struggles described here, the significant positions defining the novel. During the first half of the nineteenth century, these positions were differentiated in generic terms. My project to excavate the forgotten poetic struggles shaping the emergence of realism thus engages the paradigm, or rather, the problem, of genre.

The notion of genre is, as Jameson observes, "thoroughly discredited by modern literary theory" because it has historically been delineated with a complete lack of critical rigor.[39] Genre would, moreover, seem to have been dealt the coup de grâce by the deconstructive strain of poststructuralism, with its negative notion of textuality. From the deconstructive perspective, to align the novels of Balzac, Stendhal, or Flaubert with the codes of realism is to miss what is most interesting about them, which is how they undermine convention, how they question and subvert the realist representations they simultaneously offer. Deconstructive theory has also

La Harpe, Barbier and Desessarts put the novel at the bottom of the generic hierarchy, but they agree on little else. Notably, they assign women writers a prominent role in the history of the form, including thirty-nine female novelists and only nineteen male novelists in roughly the same page ratio. The female novelists they single out are la Rocheguilhem, Villedieu, Lafayette, d'Aulnoy, Gomez, La Force, Bernard, Murat, l'Héritier, Durand, Fontaines, le Marchand, Lussan, Tencin, Graffigny, Villeneuve, Lintot, Madame le Prince de Beaumont, Robert, d'Arconville, Elie de Beaumont, Riccoboni, Puisieux, Fagnan, Fauques, Saint-Phalier, Belot, Benoist, Saint-Aubin, la Guesnerie, Saint-Chamond, Brohon, Sommery, Beauharnais, Genlis, Cottin, Souza, and Montolieu. Their list of male novelists consists of Le Vayer de Boutigny, Boursault, Prévost, Le Sage, Hamilton, Marivaux, Crébillon fils, Duclos, Saint-Foix, Diderot, Voltaire, J.-J. Rousseau, Restif de la Bretonne, de la Clos, D'Arnaud, Montjoie, Pigault-le-Brun, Ducray-Duminil, and Fiévée.

Pierre Augustin Eusèbe Girault de Saint-Fargeau's *Revue des romans*, subtitled *Recueil d'analyses raisonnées des productions remarquables des plus célèbres romanciers français et étrangers contenant 1100 analyses raisonnées, faisant connaître avec assez d'étendue pour en donner une idée exacte, le sujet, les personnages, l'intrigue et le dénouement de chaque roman* [Collection of critical analyses of remarkable productions of the most famous French and foreign novelists containing eleven hundred critical analyses, which explain the subject, characters, plot, and denouement of each novel in enough detail to give an exact idea of it], suggests that the worldly anthology was alive and well as late as 1839. Offering to guide an adult public reading for self-improvement and pleasure, the *Revue des romans* also continues the worldly tradition in valuing highly women's contribution to the novel.

[39] Jean-Marie Schaeffer offers a detailed critique of traditional genre theory in *Qu'est-ce qu'un genre littéraire?*

usefully dismantled the project of classification underwriting traditional articulations of genre.[40]

It would nonetheless be a great loss to throw out genre because traditional literary history has failed to do it justice. The concept may reveal nothing about textuality, but it reveals much about literature as a social practice, for genre is a social relation, or, as Jameson puts it, a social contract.[41] The poetic record of the writer's and reader's expectations shaping a text, generic conventions convey crucial information about a text's position within the literary exchanges of its time and illuminate how it engages its audience. Attention to genre thus counteracts a vulgar sociology of literature that identifies a text's social dimension on the level of content as well as complicating the Foucauldian equation of a text's social significance with its participation in nonliterary discourses. As Jameson observes, the problem of genre "has in fact always entertained a privileged relationship with historical materialism," mediating between individual works and "the evolution of social life."[42]

In approaching genre as a social relation, moreover, we escape from the opposition between individual text and class that has troubled genre theory from its classical inception.[43] To use Bourdieu's terms, genre is a position. Genre designates the fact that writers share a common set of codes when they respond to a space of possibles, a horizon formed by the literary conventions and constraints binding any writer at a particular state of the field. Or better, when they resolve the space of possibles, for this space of possibles is dynamic, taking the form of "problems to resolve, stylistic or thematic possibilities to exploit, contradictions to overcome, even revolutionary ruptures to effect"; it constitutes a literary problematic that interacts with factors on the level of the whole social formation to shape textual poetics.[44] When recast as a position, genre, or, in the case of the positions at issue in this study, subgenre, becomes constitutively intertextual as well as intergeneric: a systemic, synchronic relation.[45] The

---

[40] See, for example, the essays collected in *Glyph* no. 7 (1980), notably Jacques Derrida's "La Loi du genre."

[41] Jameson, *Political Unconscious*, 106.

[42] Ibid., 105.

[43] On the problems with this opposition, see Derrida's "La Loi du genre," as well as Schaeffer's *Qu'est-ce qu'un genre littéraire?*.

[44] Bourdieu, *Rules*, 235. Bourdieu writes, "the interplay of homologies between the literary field and the field of power or the social field in its entirety means that most literary strategies are overdetermined and a number of 'choices' hit two targets at once, aesthetic and political, internal and external" (205). Bourdieu employs the term "choice" in structuralist fashion: to describe a member of a community's selection of one possibility from among a set of possibilities.

[45] When Jonathan Arac elaborates the project of literary history in the wake of poststructuralism, he suggests taking "as the fundamental unit of intelligibility not the author but

codes that make up a subgenre not only have an internal coherence as the resolution of a problematic but also take on their identity relationally, against other important resolutions of the problematic.

Once genre is viewed as a position, differences among individual examples of the genre become important when a text transgresses its dominant (in the structuralist sense) generic horizon. In violating the codes that are its point of departure, it engages in what Bourdieu calls position-taking, as its author solicits the reader against rather than with an established practice imbued with symbolic prestige and/or market appeal. As Bourdieu points out, individual position-takings cohere into positions when they become recognized by their contemporaries; when the very use of them becomes symbolically and/or economically freighted. Evidence for a position is primarily textual and established through analysis: proof of its existence is that the critic finds a number of texts sharing a set of codes. The opinions of contemporary writers and readers help illuminate the relevant distinctions among practices, the practices' social and aesthetic significance, and their literary and cultural status.[46] These opinions are, however, not scientific descriptions but rather themselves part of the evidence to be interpreted.

The Sentimental Education of the Novel thus uses realism, that loose baggy monster, in local fashion: to identify the position-taking of several writers around 1830 quickly cohering into a position, a symbolically charged set of codes responding to a problematic that defines a particular moment in the novel. As I have mentioned, this problematic involves the demise of the sentimental subgenre dominating the novel in the first part of the century as a result of specifically literary, as well as extraliterary, transformations surrounding the July Revolution. Realist codes are one powerful way writers seek to renew the French novel starting in 1830. The sentimental social novel is the primary alternative solution writers employ throughout the 1830s and 1840s.

---

the generic system." See Arac, "What is the History of Literature?" 26. Genre is, however, only relevant to the extent that it orients writers' practices in their own present, as it does in the literary historical moments I am describing. In a field where genre is an important literary institution, it can, moreover, orient practices which do not define themselves in generic terms. Thus, no position makes the importance of genre in the first decades of the nineteenth century more evident than Romanticism, for if genre were not so powerful, the Romantics would not find it so definitional to wage a full-scale war on the concept.

[46] When Bourdieu addresses the question of intentionality, he states, "It suffices to read literary memoirs, correspondence, personal diaries and perhaps especially the explicit position-takings on the literary world as such . . . in order to be convinced that . . . self-awareness, always partial, is yet again a matter of position and trajectory within the field, and that it thus varies according to agents and historical periods" Bourdieu, *Rules*, 272.

If Bourdieu situates a position at the intersection of intra- as well as extraliterary problems and contradictions, he leaves the dynamics of its problem-solving vague. In the case of a position that is a subgenre, we can clarify the extraliterary dimension to these dynamics with the help of materialist critics redeeming genre from its traditional abuse. In such powerful accounts as Jameson on romance, Moretti on the bildungsro-man, and Nancy Armstrong on the domestic novel, generic codes give us crucial information about a text's ideological appeal. In Jameson's Al-thusserian formulation, romance originates as "an imaginary 'solution' to" a "real contradiction" fissuring the values of the feudal nobility.[47] For Moretti, the classical bildungsroman resolves a basic tension in modern liberal-democratic society between the primacy of individuality and the processes of normalization essential for society to function smoothly.[48] In related fashion, Armstrong sees domestic fiction as offering an ideal of middle-class love and gender difference that "creates personal fulfillment where there had been internal conflict and social unity where there had been competing class interests."[49] If we fuse the materialist model with Bourdieu, a subgenre becomes a set of poetic strategies that offer a persua-sive fictional solution to urgent contemporary social contradiction even as they resolve a problematic specific to the literary field.

When Jameson, Moretti, and Armstrong define genre, they are inter-ested in the development of their respective forms. The diachronic dimen-sion to the concept is preserved when it is identified as a position within a synchronic system. If a position is sufficiently compelling, it can survive and mutate across different states of the literary field, as the nineteenth-century history of realism well illustrates.

Bourdieu points out that there are two kinds of practices most im-portant for writers as they craft their works: the dominant position(s) defining the problematic when they first start writing, and the other re-sponses to this position that are a writer's greatest contemporary competi-tion. *The Sentimental Education of the Novel* describes both kinds of positions in its excavation of forgotten generic forms. The first chapter traces the poetic and ideological coherence of early-nineteenth-century sentimentality, the most valued practice of the novel when Balzac and Stendhal entered the literary field. The next chapter reconfigures the emer-gence of realism as a displacement of sentimental codes. The book then excavates the sentimental social novel, which was the other important set of codes novelists elaborated to renew the novel contemporary with the

---

[47] Jameson, *Political Unconscious*, 118.
[48] See Moretti, *The Way of the World*.
[49] Nancy Armstrong, *Desire and Domestic Fiction* 51.

emergence of realism. Each generic description is broken down into sections that generally correspond to the subgenre's defining codes.

My study concludes by addressing the remarkable intersection of generic position and subject position in the case of women renewing the French novel around 1830. Literary history offers few cases where gender and genre line up so neatly: why should Balzac and Stendhal's consoeurs have overwhelmingly steered clear of realism when it first emerged? In speculating on this question, I complicate the book's previously rather abstract approach to the writer as producer. Following Bourdieu, I suggest that writers use poetics which both befit and benefit the social determinants of their subject positions, in particular those determinants that affect their situation within the dynamics of literary production.[50]

The final section sets itself a more speculative task than the preceding generic descriptions, for it seeks to explain what was not rather than excavating what was. I have accordingly framed it in more open-ended fashion, as a suggestive case study. To foreground the factors that may have made realism a compromised position for Balzac and Stendhal's consoeurs, I resurrect the literary career of a writer who used this term to diagnose the situation of the contemporary *femme auteur* more generally. Caroline Marbouty was initially a friend of Balzac, but her relations with him became strained after she published a sentimental social novel that he attacked in *La Muse du département*. Marbouty then riposted with the sentimental social novel, *Une Fausse Position*, which rewrote Balzac's account of the literary field in *Illusions perdues* from the perspective of the woman writer.

HORS D'USAGE

In excavating the imbricated battles around gender and genre that we now call the emergence of the modern French novel, this book works with literature that is out of circulation, *hors d'usage*, as the French national library puts it in giving one of the many reasons why a reader might be having difficulty obtaining the book she requested. Books *hors d'usage* are not really lost for a contemporary readership, at least they were not lost in the Bibliothèque Nationale, rue Richelieu, of the early 1990s. There, they simply required additional levels of scholarly justification be-

---

[50] As Bourdieu observes, "the strategies of agents and institutions engaged in literary or artistic struggles are not defined by a pure confrontation with pure possibles. Rather, they depend on the position these agents occupy in the structure of the field" *(Rules*, 206). As we will see, gender plays a defining role in how the woman writer at the time of Balzac negotiates the formal and informal institutions of the literary field.

cause their grimy yellow and blue paper covers disintegrated to the touch; books of such minimal interest over the years that no one had thought to keep them up, let alone read them.

But physical access is not the last nor certainly the least of the difficulties in working with literature *hors d'usage*. Defining an archive is, of course, no self-evident matter and demands the usual unquantifiable interaction of serendipity and sleuthing through which the critic stumbles across an unsolved scholarly question. Once one sits down to read the books, however, the problems have just begun. If my generic resurrections take the form of abstracted descriptions, these descriptions convey little of how illegible I initially found both sentimental and sentimental social novels when I approached them with realist expectations. Literature *hors d'usage* exposes the illusion that a close reader can generate the aesthetic logic of any text. Close reading, as it is generally practiced, depends on a naturalized set of aesthetic expectations derived precisely from a history of reading the works that have not fallen out of circulation.

The great challenge confronting any excavation is to denaturalize these expectations and take forgotten literature on its own terms. What are a work's distinctive poetics; what are these poetics' aesthetic logic and ideological force? Without understanding that forgotten works are shaped by a coherent, if now lost, aesthetic, one simply dismisses them as uninteresting or inferior in terms of the aesthetics that have won out. This mistake has been made, for example, by critics who have previously noticed early-nineteenth-century sentimentality, which was either denigrated because it was not realist or redeemed as realism despite itself.[51]

The key to a particular work's integrity is the contemporary problematic in which its poetics take shape. As Bourdieu observes, "any cultural producer is irremediably placed and dated in so far as he or she participates in the same *problematic* as the ensemble of his or her contemporaries."[52] Defining the problematic unlocks a text's aesthetic and ideological stakes. Once we relate a text to a problematic, we can perceive its distinctive codes as solutions rather than as aberrations from our current aesthetic criteria.

To reconstruct the problematic from an exhaustive survey of everything being published at the time would, of course, be a hopeless task, even if the problematic covered only a small area of the literary field, as it does in this study concerned with transformations in the novel. But we can,

---

[51] Maurice Bardèche's *Balzac romancier* exemplifies how critics have denigrated sentimentality for not being realist, although it also performs the invaluable work of keeping some memory of the subgenre alive. Joan Stewart's *Gynographs*, meanwhile, reads sentimentality as realism crimped by a stilted, artificial poetics.

[52] Bourdieu, *Rules*, 236.

nonetheless, gain a purchase on it by resurrecting several of its key aspects. It is crucial to establish what other texts a forgotten text resembles. Does it belong to a position which was, as in the case of my study, a subgenre? If not, how does it diverge from the important positions of the time? Often, the position shaping the forgotten text will also have been forgotten, and it becomes necessary to read around in the archive, looking for other texts in the position starting from such untheorized resemblances as similar titles and shared thematic concerns.[53] Such reading is not yet close reading, for close reading depends on a sense of when and how a text both reproduces contemporary poetic norms and diverges from them. Rather, it is what Sharon Marcus describes as reading for patterns; it entails looking for repetition on the level of textual structures and developing a checklist of salient codes.[54]

To isolate the coherence of a forgotten text, it is also useful to identify remembered positions and position-takings responding to the same problematic, even if the forgotten text differs from them substantially. The absence of description in sentimental social novels is striking, if initially puzzling, when contrasted with the extensive descriptions in the foundational realist works that are their contemporaries. Similarly, the repetitive sentimental social plot appears all the more distinct when contrasted with the suspenseful hermeneutics of the realist read. Because the remembered positions and position-takings have been theorized, they are useful in identifying not only the specificity of the forgotten practice but also its aesthetic and ideological stakes. As we will see, materialist analyses of the social contradictions shaping realism offer a shortcut to the extraliterary contradictions shaping sentimental social poetics.

One more important step in defining a problematic is to understand the dominant practices from the immediately prior literary historical moment that help set its terms. Because these practices were once dominant, they may, in addition, have the advantage of being remembered and analyzed today. Since I first excavated the sentimental social novel when I began my research, I needed to return back through two previous moments in the French novel to come upon such a practice. When I realized that early-nineteenth-century sentimentality set the terms of July Monarchy struggles to dominate the novel, I only got deeper into the archive, for it, too, had been completely forgotten. Once I started to conceptualize early-nine-

---

[53] Traditional literary histories can be useful at this stage of the process, for they sometimes mention forgotten works which they describe largely on the level of thematics. Surveys of literary production from the time can also serve as guides to the make-up of forgotten positions. In reconstructing the contours of early-nineteenth-century sentimentality, for example, I found booksellers' catalogs from the Restoration useful because they organized works in generic categories, even if these categories were completely unscientific.

[54] Sharon Marcus, "Disciplining Cultural Studies."

teenth-century sentimentality in relation to pre-Revolutionary sentimentality, however, I gained access to a rich critical bibliography which illuminated the coherence of later sentimental literature *hors d'usage*.

Another type of text useful for establishing the coherence of forgotten literature came from outside the problematic I was reconstructing. Both the literary and social issues at stake in forgotten works are sometimes preserved in contemporary aesthetic theory, even if this theory does not seem to address them directly. Hegel's account of classical tragedy, notably, will prove helpful in reconstructing the logic of sentimentality, since it describes a poetics responding to the same political impasses as sentimental texts. Like *Antigone* according to Hegel, sentimentality turns out to offer a tragic resolution to the problem of freedom in the wake of the French Revolution.

As should be clear from these numerous moves, reconstructing the coherence of even one forgotten aesthetic is a lengthy project. I return to the already mentioned problem of charting a course through the vast number of books out there once one ventures into literature *hors d'usage*. With each book requiring so much labor to be rendered legible, the literary archaeologist has to give up any ambition to a thorough reconstruction of the past. Delimiting the field of inquiry is as important as recovering forgotten material; indeed, without such delimitation, there would be no recovery.

It is thus imperative to pare questions in the archive down to the bare minimum. How this occurs will depend, of course, on the story being told. Since I have no axioms to offer about narrowing the field of inquiry, I will simply describe how I approached my own, in particular since the description will allow me to raise questions at the edges of my project that I was forced to bracket in order to start making sense of even a little segment of the great unread. When I first began this study, I focused all my reading on the two questions leading me into the archive: were there alternatives to realism when it emerged, and were there novelistic codes making sense of the Revolution before realism? I subsequently limited the first question to an excavation of realism's primary competition throughout the July Monarchy, once I saw that the sentimental social novel had the potential to clarify the hitherto unexplained problem of women's absence from the great nineteenth-century realist lineage.

In limiting my field of inquiry, however, I did not enumerate all the transformations in the novel we now remember as the emergence of realism in France. To do full justice to this literary historical paradigm shift, it would be important to embed realism in a generic mix including not only the sentimental position, which was the most respected form of the early-nineteenth-century novel, but also the comic novel (*le roman gai*) and an indigenous French Gothic (*le roman noir*), two early-nineteenth-century positions with great popular appeal. The subgeneric system began to shift when Scott was imported around 1820. His novels, initially popular successes, then received critical acclaim, and the favorable reception of Manzoni's *The Betrothed* increased the historical novel's prestige. The importance of the foreign historical novel in turn sparked a short-lived French historical novel in the late 1820s informed by Manzoni and Scott as well as Cooper, who was considered Scott's American imitator, along with the other two early-nineteenth-century positions coexisting with sentimentality, the *roman noir* and the *roman gai*.[55] This indigenous historical novel inaugurated French writers' serious challenges to the domination of the sentimental form. It is indicative of the struggles I described that Balzac used historical codes when he first sought to leave his mark on the novel with *Les Chouans* (1829).

Following 1830, realism and the sentimental social novel quickly supplanted the historical novel as the most persuasive ways to renew the genre, although realist poetics certainly absorbed key historical codes, as critics have noted from Lukács on.[56] The historical novel also made its own brief appearance in the competition for how the novel should assert its new public authority in the wake of July 1830, but declined in prestige after reaching its apogee with Hugo's 1831 *Notre-Dame de Paris*.[57]

With the historical novel relegated to a subordinate status, realism and the sentimental social novel reigned as the most valued practices of the novel during the remainder of the July Monarchy. A full account of their reign would discuss contemporary challenges to both practices, notably the art for art's sake position exemplified by Gautier's *Mademoiselle de Maupin*. It would, in addition, describe how this reign was complicated when the subgeneric system started to shift once more in the 1840s. Now the destabilizing impetus came from below. It took the form of that tremendously popular subgenre somewhat imprecisely called the *roman feuilleton* (many kinds of novels were published in feuilleton format, not just the *roman feuilleton*), exemplifed by Sue's *Mystères de Paris* and the novels of Dumas.

No discussion of the difficulties in working on literature *hors d'usage* would be complete without a question I have frequently heard in the

---

[55] The historical novel's role in early-nineteenth-century struggles around the novel was complicated by the fact that the concept predated Scott in France. Sentimental and Gothic novels with historical subject matter were sometimes identified as historical novels by booksellers and critics of the Empire and early Restoration, and sentimental novels with historical subject matter continued to be written throughout the life of the historical novel.

[56] See, of course, Georg Lukács, *The Historical Novel*.

[57] On the historical novel's decline in prestige during the remainder of the 1830s, see Iknayan. One reason the historical novel declined in importance after 1830 was, I suspect, its indirect approach to social conflict. When censorship is relaxed, political issues can be confronted in the present rather than distanced in a historical past.

course of writing this book. Isn't it boring reading sentimental novels, both friendly and hostile critics of the project have asked—in other words, wouldn't you really rather be reading Balzac—as if we all agreed that these works were intrinsically uninteresting, even if I could dress them up with critical arguments. The question foregrounds one great problem working on literature *hors d'usage*, which is the continued skepticism concerning its literary value. Attention to forgotten literature is too often treated as antiquarian fussing over texts that deserve to be forgotten. Another version of this skepticism is the charge that critics working in noncanonical literature reveal nothing about the literary dimension to literary texts, reducing literature to history.

There was nothing like the process of mastering a forgotten aesthetic, however, to unsettle my confidence that literary value is a self-evident attribute of a text. When I first started reading literature *hors d'usage*, I found it mystifying. After I reconstructed the problematic shaping forgotten works, I started to appreciate the diversity and elegance of their solutions. Once having gotten my aesthetic bearings, that is to say, literature *hors d'usage* was no longer an undifferentiated night of aesthetic relativism in which all texts were gray. For literature out of circulation (as for literature in circulation, moreover), a good work, a work that deserves to be studied for literary reasons, provides a forceful response to the contemporary problematic, whether the work takes shape within a position, honing its codes with maximum clarity (the Aristotelian view of literary excellence), or whether the work breaks with the dominant practices in significant and inventive ways (the preferred modernist text).

Literary evaluation, is, as Barbara Herrenstein-Smith suggests, "one of the most venerable, central, theoretically significant, and pragmatically inescapable set of problems relating to literature," although the canon wars have thrown traditional ways of appreciating literary excellence into irremediable disarray.[58] In recent years, the difficulty making arguments about literary value has led some critics who were at first supportive of dismantling the canon to turn away from noncanonical literature in the name of literary pleasure, which is to say canonical works legible in our time. Working in literature *hors d'usage*, it becomes clear, however, that current obstacles to literary evaluation derive not from the noncanonical but rather from the fact that so little about it is known. Too often, noncanonical texts are fragments of lost solutions or answers to questions we no longer hear. If we could reawaken the struggles among conflicting aesthetics reified in the tradition's procession of cultural treasures, we would have a deeply historical way to renew the project of literary evaluation.

---

[58] Barbara Herrenstein-Smith, *Contingencies of Value*, 17.

CHAPTER I

Conflicting Duties: Sentimental Poetics

WHAT ELSE IS LOST IN *ILLUSIONS PERDUES*

One cold morning in September 1821, Balzac's "great man from the provinces" screws up his courage to peddle his literary wares in Paris. Strolling to the publisher's district by the quai des Augustins, Lucien peruses the newly invented publicity device of the poster, advertising works like *Le Solitaire* by the Vicomte d'Arlincourt and *Léonide* by Victor Ducange. When Lucien finally enters the boutiques of the booksellers, he is shocked by the "brutal and material aspect" of literature which they reveal (219). He is summarily dismissed by two hustling booksellers who are in the process of threatening Ducange's editor with their interest in Ducange's rival, Picard. Lucien does succeed, however, in getting a hearing from "an odd old man" named "Father Doguereau" (219). When Lucien tells Doguereau he has written a novel "in the genre of Walter Scott," the publisher comments, "I would have preferred a novel in the genre of Madame Radcliffe," but he then offers to take a look at the manuscript (220).

Balzac frames *Illusions perdues* as a ruthless exposé of Restoration literary production and the work has long been praised for its "force and truth."[1] But when it comes to the Restoration's novelistic landscape, Balzac is fabricating some literary history of his own. Compare the tastes of Doguereau to the historical figure who was his prototype, the publisher and bookseller Alexandre-Nicolas Pigoreau, whom Balzac knew in his youth. The year Lucien visited the quai des Augustins, Pigoreau published his influential *Petite Bibliographie biographico-romancière* advising the Restoration book trade on the authors most in demand. Updating his work throughout the 1820s, Pigoreau consistently placed the same authors at the pinnacle of popular taste: "Without wanting to belittle the merit of men, do any of them in our day prevail over Madame de Genlis, Madame de Staël, Madame Cottin, Madame Flahaut?"[2] These authors

---

[1] Antoine Adam, introduction to *Illusions perdues*, xxvii.

[2] Alexandre-Nicolas Pigoreau, *Troisième Supplément à la petite bibliographie biographico-romancière*, v. The 1828 *supplément* to the *Petite bibliographie* gives a good sense of how Pigoreau ranked the leading sentimental novelists vis-à-vis Radcliffe and Scott. Claiming to offer a comprehensive map of the most popular novels, Pigoreau advised: "Principal attention should be given to the works of Madame de Genlis, Madame de Montolieu, Ma-

all wrote in a distinct subgenre, which the contemporary book trade termed the sentimental novel, neither the "genre of Madame Radcliffe" nor the "genre of Walter Scott."[3] Indeed, while Pigoreau gave Scott, too, high marks for popularity, he ranked Radcliffe's novels substantially lower in audience appeal.

Is Balzac displaying an innocuous lapse in memory when he rewrites Pig to Dog? As Balzac himself proclaimed, however, the realist god is in the details. In twentieth-century sociological studies, Pigoreau's preferred authors—Genlis, Staël, Cottin, and Flahaut (more commonly known as Souza)—consistently top Restoration popularity charts along with another sentimental novelist, Isabelle de Montolieu. Working with printer's records, Martin Lyons, for example, finds that the single best-selling novel at the beginning of the Restoration was Sophie Cottin's *Claire d'Albe*, closely followed by her *Elisabeth, ou les Exilés de Sibérie*.[4] Approaching popular taste from the side of reception rather than production, Françoise Parent-Lardeur distinguishes favorite Restoration authors based on the catalogues of private lending libraries in Paris.[5] Parent-Lardeur's study

---

dame Cottin, Madame de Souza, Madame Armande Roland, Madame de Staël, Madame Renneville. A choice should be made among productions of Madame Guénard, Madame Choiseul-Meuse, Madame Barthélemy Hadot. The novels of Ducray-Duminil, Monjoye, Picard, and Dinocourt should not be forgotten. To the French novels should be added good translations of the English novels of Madame Radcliffe, Maria Regina Roche, Mistriss [sic] Bennet, the two Miss Porters, Miss Burney, Miss Edgeworth. Above all, add the novels of Walter Scott, those of his American imitator Cooper; the novels translated from German of Lafontaine; Goëthe [sic], and Madame Pichler should not be left out." Pigoreau, *Dix-septième Supplément à la petite bibliographie biographicio-romancière*, 38–39.

[3] On the relation between the categories of the Restoration book trade and authors' subgeneric practices, see Bardèche, *Balzac romancier*.

[4] In *Le Triomphe du livre*, Lyons compiles lists of nineteenth-century best-sellers, based on the *Bibliographie de France* and material from provincial archives as well as on printers' official declarations before a book's publication. Lyons addresses the most popular novels of the early nineteenth century only indirectly since (1) he tracks books produced for purchase rather than books people wanted to read and (2) he is interested in all books being printed rather than specifically in novels. In the years 1821–25, for example, Lyons lists no recent novels among the great best-sellers. But Lyon's lack of attention to the early-nineteenth-century novel makes his mention at such works all the more significant. Lyons finds that *Claire d'Albe* was the most popular novel in the years 1816–20. At this time, Cottin's work enjoyed a minimum known print run of 19,000 copies that, Lyons estimates, may have been as high as 25,000–30,000 copies. Lyons numbers *Elisabeth*'s minimum known print run during the same years at 14,500 copies, placing the novel's estimated print run between 20,000 and 25,000 copies. In 1826–30, four works by Scott are the novels that top the best seller list. According to Lyons, all have both a known and estimated print run of 20,800 copies.

[5] Most reading for pleasure during the Restoration took place through these libraries. The relatively expensive price of novels put them out of reach of all but the wealthiest, and public libraries did not yet exist.

is emphatic that novelists "in the genre of Radcliffe" are runners-up to the leading sentimental novelists, Doguereau's/Balzac's tastes notwithstanding:

> An exhaustive summary of the authors the lending library directors [*maîtres de lectures*] select as 'the most well known' or 'the most in favor'—according to the long lists of works printed in their catalogues (in 30/80)—, revealed the following names: at the top, Madame de Genlis and Walter Scott; then, Mesdames de Montolieu, Guénard de Méré, de Flahaut de Souza and Cottin; Messieurs Pigault-Lebrun and Auguste Lafontaine; Madame Barthélemy Hadot and Anne Radcliffe; Fenimore Cooper, Ducray-Duminil, Madame Gottis, the Count d'Arlincourt; Messieurs Victor Ducange, de Dinocourt, Paul de Kock, Picard; and finally Madame de Choiseul-Meuse.[6]

In the private lending libraries, both Radcliffe and France's authors of a homegrown Gothic, d'Arlincourt, Ducray-Duminil, and Dinocourt, are indisputably less in demand than the sentimental novelists, Genlis, Montolieu, Souza, and Cottin.

When Balzac's Doguereau classifies works by genre, he accurately reflects the practices of the Restoration book trade. For publishers and lending library directors, these classifications were marketing tools.[7] The book trade's generic categories also corresponded to three distinct practices of the novel that remained stable throughout the first quarter of the nineteenth century. These practices were the sentimental novel (*le roman sentimental*), the comic novel (*le roman gai*) and the Gothic novel (*le roman noir*).[8] As Parent-Lardeur's findings show, all three subgenres had substantial popular appeal along with the historical novel, which was a foreign import into France in the late 1810s and early 1820s.[9]

---

[6] Françoise Parent-Lardeur, *Les Cabinets de lecture—La Lecture publique à Paris sous la Restauration*, 157, n. 1. "Strange selection which leaves out Chateaubriand (mentioned only one time), Mérimée, Hugo, and still others," Parent-Lardeur comments. "It has been verified, however, that [these works] then enjoyed indisputable fame" (157, n. 1).

[7] In the *Dictionnaire des romans* (1819), for example, Antoine Marc explains that he classifies works by genre to help booksellers . . . satisfy their clients. . . . This work is only meant to recommend all the Books and all types [*genres*] of reading that a client could desire." Cover of Antoine Marc, *Dictionnaire des romans anciens et modernes*.

[8] Bardèche rightly observes, "In novelistic production, three principal categories can be distinguished for which we will keep the terminologies used at the time in catalogues and bibliographies: the novel with a sentimental plot, the Gothic [*le roman 'noir'*] and the comic novel [*le roman 'gai'*]. We only retained these three divisions because all three correspond to a technique. The *personal novel* [*roman personnel*] will not be given a special place . . . it is only a subcategory of novels with a sentimental plot." Bardèche, *Balzac romancier*, 1.

[9] Comic novelists on Parent-Lardeur's list of most popular authors include Guénard de Méré, Pigault-Lebrun, Picard, Ducange, de Kock, and Choiseul-Meuse, as well as the German writer, Auguste Lafontaine.

In Lucien's visit to the quai des Augustins, then, Balzac mentions authors who invoke the entire spectrum of popular novelistic subgenres with one notable absence. Scott represents the historical novel, Radcliffe and d'Arlincourt the Gothic novel, Ducange and Picard the comic novel, but who represents the sentimental novel? Balzac's lacuna is all the more flagrant because the sentimental novel outstripped both the comic novel and the Gothic novel in popular appeal.

The sentimental novel and sentimental novelists are moreover almost entirely absent from *Illusions perdues*. The few exceptions are telling: Staël is parodied as the Corinne d'Angoulême, Madame de Bargeton, and when Balzac does mention a work with a title evoking a sentimental novel, *Yseult de Dôle*, he condescendingly frames it as a "nice work from the provinces" (282). But the novel's reception by the contemporary judges of literary value tells a different tale.

"Women figure with greatest distinction among modern novelists," wrote Marie-Joseph de Chénier in his influential 1816 *Tableau historique de l'état et des progrès de la littérature française depuis 1789.*[10] As the most distinguished novelists, Chénier mentioned Staël, Cottin, Souza, and Genlis, writers known for their use of the sentimental subgenre.[11] Chénier's opinion was characteristic of the years surrounding Lucien's plunge into Parisian literary slime. During the first decade of the Restoration, critics judging literary value considered sentimental novels by women writers to be the most important French novels, although they treated the novel as polite entertainment rather than as a preeminent literary form.[12] What codes, after all, did the ambitious Balzac choose when he first sat down to write a novel around the time Lucien de Rubempré was drafting his *L'Archer de Charles IX? Sténie*, composed in 1819–20, is not a novel

---

[10] Chénier, *Tableau historique,* 227.

[11] The *Tableau* does not mention *Adolphe* and it gives Chateaubriand mixed reviews. *Atala*, Chénier explains, merits discussion because it "caused a stir. It is singular in its conception, its narrative [*la marche*] and its style" (48).

[12] The works Restoration critics frequently put at the pinnacle of the novel included Germaine de Staël's *Delphine* (1802) and *Corinne* (1807); Sophie Cottin's *Claire d'Albe* (1799), *Malvina* (1801), *Amélie Mansfield* (1803), and *Mathilde* (1805); Adélaïde de Souza's *Adèle de Sénange* (1794), *Charles et Marie* (1802), *Eugène de Rothelin* (1808), and *Mademoiselle de Tournon* (1820); Stéphanie-Félicité de Genlis's *Mademoiselle de Clermont* (1802); *La Duchesse de la Vallière* (1804); and *Mademoiselle de la Fayette* (1813); Isabelle de Montolieu's *Caroline de Lichtfield* (1786); Juliane von Krüdener's *Valérie* (1804); and Claire de Duras's *Ourika* (1823) and *Edouard* (1825). Critics sometimes also included Chateaubriand's *Atala* in their pantheon, but more often they did not, for one of two opposing reasons. Either they were ambivalent about *Atala*'s extravagances or they considered the novel so important as to transcend the genre. Once we reconstruct sentimental poetics, it will become clear that Chateaubriand's novels in any case substantiate the primacy of sentimentality, for sentimental codes constitute their dominant (in the structuralist sense) generic horizon.

"in the genre of Walter Scott" but rather a sentimental novel in the genre of Cottin or Staël.[13]

Lucien's nonfictional contemporaries distinguished the novels at the pinnacle of critical taste both by their authors' gender and by genre. When Charles Nodier designated the most important novels since the Revolution in 1817, he defined them in generic terms. "For fifteen years in fact, the novel has relied only on natural affections, tender sentiments, moral and pious thoughts. . . . We must be grateful to novelists for having offered truth a refuge when it was exiled by false politics and false philosophy."[14] Making no mention of individual authors, Nodier implied that their identities were so well known they did not need to be named. A similar assumption underwrites the pronouncements of critics who designated the leading novels of their time simply by gender. Thus, an 1817 review of a sentimental novel declared: "This novel is by a woman, and the scepter of this literary genre has been in women's hands for quite some time; men agree, and in this, they cannot even take credit for gallantry; they are only being fair; which is moreover sometimes more difficult and commendable than being gallant."[15] If critics singled out the leaders among these reigning women, they invariably named the novelists mentioned by Chénier. In 1821, the journalist P. A. Vieillard praised "Mesdames de Staël and Genlis, [who] have seen the names of Mesdames de Flahaut, Cottin, de Montolieu, Gottis, Pannier, and Simons-Candeille gathered around theirs."[16] Similarly, a review by Em. Dupaty asserted:

> Many women, this very day are striving to outdo the fame of the most famous writers. They triumph above all in the painting of tender sentiments [where] . . . [t]heir own memories guide and enlighten them. Therefore, works by women will always be in demand. Our eagerness to read them is, moreover, further justified by the entertaining hours we have spent with the excellent writings by the authors of *Corinne* [Staël], *Mademoiselle de Clermont* [Genlis], *Adèle de Sénange* [Souza] and *Mathilde* [Cottin].[17]

---

[13] When Scott's works first appeared in France, they were popular hits: "It was more than a success: it was a craze," observes Louis Maigron. But, he points out, Scott's first critical reviews are mixed. Louis Maigron, *Le Roman historique à l'époque romantique*, 99. By the mid-1820s, Scott garnered widespread critical acclaim and critics characterized the historical novel as an exciting poetic innovation. While critics initially regarded the subgenre as a foreign import, French writers with high literary ambitions began to experiment with its codes in the last five years of the 1820s, and an indigenous historical novel emerged to challenge sentimentality as the reigning French novelistic form (Vigny's 1826 *Cinq-Mars*; Balzac's 1829 *Les Chouans*; Mérimée's 1829 *Chronique du règne de Charles IX*; Hugo's 1831 *Notre-Dame de Paris*).

[14] Charles Nodier, "*Louise de Sénancourt* par Madame de T...."

[15] Review signed A. of *Auguste et Frédéric*.

[16] P. A.Vieillard, review of *Agnès de France ou le Douzième Siècle, roman historique*, 46.

[17] Em. Dupaty, review of *Les Séductions*, 547.

Vieillard and Dupaty's reviews were written in 1821, precisely when Lucien makes his visit to the quai des Augustins. If, as Balzac proclaimed, "French Society was to be the historian, I was only to be the secretary," why does *Illusions perdues* erase the sentimental novel from the Restoration literary landscape?[18] The question takes us to the crux of realism's bid for literary and cultural prestige. We will see Balzac and Stendhal assert their primacy through a campaign to discredit sentimentality. Collapsing genre into gender, they associate the sentimental novel with weak and stupid femininity even as they appropriate important aspects of sentimentality in forging their own practices. In addition, we will see Balzac and Stendhal's vexed relation to sentimentality help explain why contemporary female novelists disassociate themselves from realist codes. But we cannot understand these literary political struggles based on the sentimental novel's current critical profile. Twentieth-century literary studies has bought into realism's erasure of its origins in what Walter Benjamin calls history written from the standpoint of the victors.

Critics have long disregarded the early-nineteenth-century sentimental novel despite the subgenre's importance in its time. Writers known for their major intellectual status such as Staël and Constant have been studied in detail, but there is little attention to the generic horizon in which they write. What attention there is both caricatures and denigrates the sentimental form. This attitude strikingly unites critics with otherwise opposing intellectual and political agendas.

Maurice Bardèche attacks sentimentality on the terrain of genius and originality. If his *Balzac romancier* performs the invaluable service of keeping the subgenre's memory alive, Bardèche approaches the early-nineteenth-century sentimental novel as an "artificial," insipid form that only makes the "miracle" of Balzac's creation the more glorious.[19] In the most important marxist study of the genesis of Balzac's practice, Pierre Barbéris taxes the sentimental novel with failing to represent the material transformations taking place in society. According to Barbéris, the subgenre *"no longer confronts fundamental problems. . . .* Social reality, fortune, profession, everything that connects man [*sic*] to earth: none of this becomes the stuff of literature."[20] Even Joan Stewart, the only feminist critic to consider early nineteenth-century sentimental authors as a group, redeems their texts by denigrating sentimental practice. Stewart treats sentimentality as a façade that must be stripped away to reveal hidden political and social content, looking for "the subversiveness of texts whose style and surface often appear orthodox."[21]

[18] Balzac, *Avant-propos,* 11.
[19] Bardèche, *Balzac romancier,* 15.
[20] Pierre Barbéris, *Balzac et le mal du siècle,* 1:342; 344.
[21] Stewart, *Gynographs,* 7.

Despite their differing critical investments, Bardèche, Barbéris, and Stewart all share an unquestioned aesthetic prejudice for realism. Their prejudice is that of twentieth-century literary history more generally, which cannot conceive that any important nineteenth-century novels lacked historical specificity, extensive description, a suspenseful narrative, and a parade of unprincipled characters motivated by self-interest and desire. Sentimental poetics have, however, their own distinctive aesthetic and ideological power, although it is illegible from the standpoint of the realist aesthetic.

Like an anamorphic picture, a literary structure puzzling from a habitual perspective takes on coherence if we shift the point of view. To redeem sentimentality's concentrated and abstract plot, its ethically driven characters, its absence of material detail, and its ineluctable narrative movement towards a dénouement evident from the beginning, I invoke the subgenre's similarities to tragedy. That the sentimental novel would have an affinity with tragedy is not surprising given the prehistory of the form. The subgenre emerges from the novels of passion of the late seventeenth and early eighteenth centuries, and these novels are informed by classical French tragedy as well as by heroic romance. In addition, the sentimental novel takes shape in a dialogue with eighteenth-century "*tragédie domestique et bourgeoise* [domestic and bourgeois tragedy]" and shares aspects of its poetics.[22]

Hegel's *Aesthetics* offers the model of tragedy most relevant to the sentimental novel. This model has been pilloried from its inception for casting the political and ethical orders at stake in classical tragedy in Enlightenment liberal terms.[23] But its anachronism is our gain in studying a form whose life just about spans Hegel's own (1770–1831). Updating classical tragedy into a genre addressing the conflict between private and public duties, Hegel identifies it with a fundamental tension in Continental liberalism's conceptualization of citizenship which is, I will argue, at issue in the sentimental novel as well.[24]

[22] I take the phrase from Peter Szondi's "*Tableau* and *Coup de Théâtre*," 324.

[23] For a concise summary of these objections, see Martin Donougho, "The Woman in White: On the Reception of Hegel's *Antigone*," *The Owl of Minerva*, 21, no. 1.

[24] It would thus be more accurate to refer to the subgenre reconstructed in this chapter as the liberal sentimental novel than the sentimental novel, for critics loosely apply the latter term to works running from the novels of passion of the late seventeenth and early eighteenth centuries to mass culture romances of the twentieth century. While the subgenre dominating the early-nineteenth-century French novel does share features with Lafayette and Tencin's novels as well as with Harlequin romances, it also has a distinct poetic and ideological identity. I have nonetheless used the term "sentimental novel" because "liberal sentimental novel" is cumbersome and because I want to retain the standard twentieth-century way of designating these texts. The designation is, for example, used by both Bardèche and Stewart as well as by Béatrice Didier when she briefly discusses early-nine-

Hegel's model of tragedy also serves my analysis because it explains literary genre as social persuasion. Proposing genre as a mode of social expression, Hegel depicts tragedy specifically as the genre that both represents and resolves ethical contradiction in the register of the aesthetic. Hegel thus offers the first materialist account of tragedy, or rather, with his account, Hegel founds the materialist model of genre underwriting my study. When Jameson describes the novel (implicitly the realist novel) as "producing . . . the new secular and 'disenchanted' object world of the commodity system" in response to capitalism's transformation of traditional daily life into a "bewilderingly empirical, 'meaningless,' and contingent *Umwelt*"; when Moretti proposes the "happiness" of the classical bildungsroman as "the very opposite of that imagined by Jefferson and Saint-Just"; when Armstrong reads the English domestic novel as resolving "competing class interests" by representing them "as a struggle between the sexes," these critics all build on Hegel's insight regarding tragic resolution, profoundly historicizing what Hegel understands as ethical contradiction and as aesthetic response.[25] My study, too, historicizes Hegel's account of tragic resolution to explain the persuasions of the sentimental form. In this explanation, I am particularly interested in clarifying sentimentality's unequal yet suggestive relation to the French Revolution.

Sentimentality is a poetics that predates 1789, first emerging in France, to my knowledge, with *La Nouvelle Héloïse*. While the sentimental subgenre dominated the novel from the 1790s through the early 1820s, it was only sporadically, if successfully employed before 1789.[26] Clearly, the sentimental novel was not a response to the Revolution. Is it nonetheless significant, I will ask, that the Revolution coincided with the form's explosion to generic prominence?

Since *La Nouvelle Héloïse* is central to the sentimental paradigm, I could have foregrounded this well-known text in defining sentimental codes. I emphasize sentimental novels from the early nineteenth century instead because they epitomized the most prestigious and popular novels when Balzac and Stendhal started writing and because they are distinguished by a specific tone that is a legacy of sentimentality's passage through the Revolution. That most early-nineteenth-century sentimental novels are, however, now forgotten makes their description no easy task. Only a very few specialists would understand passing references to even one of these works without extensive contextualization.

---

teenth-century sentimental novels in her volume on *Le Dix-huitième Siècle 1778–1820* for Arthaud's *Littérature française* series.

[25] Jameson, *Political Unconscious*, 152; Moretti, *Way*, 23; Armstrong, *Desire*, 49.

[26] Richardson inaugurated the subgenre in England ten years before Rousseau, with *Clarissa*. Charrière's *Lettres de Mistriss Henley* (1784) and *Caliste, ou la Continuation des*

To avoid swamping my argument with a plethora of plots and characters, I employ a strategy familiar throughout the history of genre criticism
from Aristotle and Hegel on tragedy to Todorov on the fantastic and
Barthes on realism: I focus on one text where the features of the genre
appear with particular clarity. At the same time, this strategy has its own
limitations in the case of a subgenre that has been so neglected. Most
readers cannot grasp the relevance of generalizations since they do not
know the texts making up the generic field. To give some sense of its
density, I also include references to other sentimental works.

My *Oedipus* of the sentimental novel is the 1799 *Claire d'Albe*, which
Martin Lyons isolates as the great best-seller of the years 1816–20. I also
select this text because Cottin was among the most acclaimed authors of
her time. In addition, *Claire d'Albe* has the advantage of being short, in
contrast with the 1805 *Mathilde*, which is often cited by Cottin's contemporaries as her best work.[27] Distilling the essence of sentimentality into a
slim epistolary exchange, *Claire d'Albe* offers an economical presentation
of sentimental codes that lends itself to reading and teaching.

CONFLICTING DUTIES

The paradigmatic sentimental plot is a plot of double bind.[28] The sentimental novel catches its protagonists between two moral imperatives,
each valid in its own right, but which meet in a situation of mutual contradiction. Collective welfare, which constitutes one term of the double bind,
is aligned with an unstable cluster of Enlightenment abstractions including the public good, manners, society, reason, and other people's well-
being. Against this imperative, the sentimental novel asserts the imperative to individual freedom, which it associates with happiness, choice,
nature, the private, sentiment, and erotic love.

An adulterous love affair catalyzes the moral double bind in *Claire
d'Albe*. The plot of adultery threatening collective welfare is a familiar

---

Lettres écrites de Lausanne (1787) as well as Montolieu's *Caroline de Lichtfield* (1786) are
popular and well-received pre-Revolutionary examples of the sentimental subgenre.

[27] *Mathilde* is set during the Crusades (it was written over ten years before *Ivanhoe*). The
novel narrates the pure but forbidden love between Mathilde, the virtuous, beautiful sister
of Richard the Lion-hearted, and Malek-Adhel, the noble, sexy brother of Saladin, the Saracen king.

[28] I use double bind to characterize a "damned if you do, damned if you don't" situation
rather than in the psychological sense given to the term by Gregory Bateson. One aspect of
Bateson's analysis is nonetheless suggestive for sentimentality. According to Bateson, the
double bind provokes a crisis in the subject's ability to interpret a situation. The sentimental
double bind, too, provokes an interpretive crisis, as we will see.

scenario in the French novel from its prehistory in medieval romance. What distinguishes *Claire d'Albe* and other sentimental novels representing adultery is that adultery is not simply passion transgressing the law. Both positions in the conflict are given moral dignity.[29]

Cottin's novel tells the story of the young, beautiful, and virtuous Claire, who has married an upright older man, M. d'Albe, in accordance with her father's will. Living on M. d'Albe's prosperous country estate, Claire finds her comfortable life upset when her husband brings home a young cousin, Frédéric, who has become his ward. Frédéric's "supple and agile body" is on a par with his "original mind" and his "frank character," as Claire remarks upon meeting him.[30] Later, Claire's confidante, Elise, charges her with understatement: "Claire did not paint him as he appeared to me: he has the head of Antinous on the body of Apollo" (748). Frédéric and Claire fall in love, and Claire spends the remainder of the novel struggling over what to do.

Claire possesses the principal attributes of sentimental heroism: moral integrity, sensibility, and intelligence. Like other sentimental protagonists, she also wants to act virtuously. April Alliston perceptively observes that "The virtue of eighteenth-century heroines . . . does not consist, like manly virtue, in the performance of good deeds or serviceable actions but rather in the avoidance of fault. . . . The classical *virtus* of agency comes to be replaced by a feminine virtue of suffering."[31] In the sentimental subgenre, virtue is simultaneously the passive imperative to avoid fault and the active imperative to promote the moral order. Appropriately, sentimental virtue crosses gender lines even while sentimental novels with female protagonists outnumber sentimental novels with male protagonists. In similarly ambiguous fashion, sentimental novels describe virtue both in passive terms and with a dynamic language of combat recalling the heroism of the classical "*preux*" (cf. Rousseau's Saint-Preux). When Claire's son asks her "what is *virtue*," she replies, "It is strength, my son . . . it is the courage to carry out rigorously everything we feel to be good, whatever pain it may cause us" (734).

Despite her courage and rigor, however, Claire finds herself caught in a practical impasse. Claire's marital bonds link her to the collective, impli-

---

[29] The search for a morally valid alternative to collective welfare is already palpable in late-seventeenth- and early-eighteenth-century novels of adulterous passion. It is at stake, for example, in the Princess of Clèves's famously implausible confession to her husband of her love for another man. Torn between passion and duty, Madame de Clèves seeks a third term to express her independent identity, although she can only find it with a gesture that scandalizes the norms of her society.

[30] Sophie Cottin, *Claire d'Albe*, 697. Subsequent page references will appear parenthetically in the text.

[31] Alliston, *Virtue's Faults*, 86.

cating her in its welfare. At the same time, her adulterous love reveals to her the conflicting imperative of individual freedom, specifically the freedom to choose one's partner. This freedom is missing from Claire's marriage, which her father arranged.[32] To underscore that Claire's marriage is problematic, Cottin represents her heroine as unhappy at the novel's beginning, although her husband is a caring and worthy man. Claire initially casts the source of her unhappiness in positive terms when she explores her dissatisfaction in a letter to Elise: "*Should* I not also bless my father for *having chosen* such a worthy husband for me?" (694, emphasis added).

Cottin uses the delineation of character to reinforce her text's organizing double bind. The two principal secondary characters each embody one of the opposing moral imperatives tearing Claire apart. M. d'Albe, the character on the side of collective welfare, is passionately devoted to the collective good: "He is like the center and cause of all the good that is done for miles around" (696). Frédéric, the advocate of individuality and independence, is a wild child from the mountains. Frédéric acts according to the spontaneous movements of his soul, unconcerned with how his actions will be viewed by others. Importantly, however, Cottin does not frame this action as immoral or amoral but rather as a natural base for morality. Claire writes to Elise, "I like his original personality, [*caractère neuf*] which shows itself without a veil and without a detour; this raw frankness which makes him lacking in politeness but never kindness, because the pleasure of others is for him a need" (697).

When the first French sentimental novel characterizes its heroine's inability to chart a course of action between affective choice and family obligation, Rousseau's Julie describes herself as torn by "conflicting duties [*devoirs opposés*]."[33] With this phrase, Julie eloquently captures the fact that each term in the sentimental conflict rests on a positively constituted moral imperative. Endowing individual freedom and collective welfare with equal measures of moral dignity, the sentimental novel does not, however, mute their respective dangers. It shows each imperative important in itself and destructive when pursued to the exclusion of the other.

Thus, in *Claire d'Albe*, Cottin shows love pursued without consideration for collective responsibility to result in social collapse. As Claire explains her dilemma to Frédéric,

[32] Cottin reinforces M. d'Albe's alliance with Claire's father by making them friends and having the father, now dead, buried on M. d'Albe's land.

[33] Jean-Jacques Rousseau, *La Nouvelle Héloïse*, 177. Subsequent page references will appear parenthetically in the text.

"Oh Frédéric! if it is true that you love me, learn from me to treasure our love enough never to taint it with anything base or contemptible. If you are everything for me, my universe, my happiness, the God that I adore; if all of nature shows me only your image . . . I am not guilty. . . . is it up to me to extinguish what a higher power has kindled in my breast? But because I cannot give my husband such feelings, does it then follow that I should not keep our sworn vows?" (741)

Refusing to describe her passion according to a traditional Christian scenario of sin, Claire associates it with "a higher power," a notion of divinity formulated in Enlightenment terms. At the same time, Claire stresses that to act on her love would be to destroy "sworn vows," the individual's pledged responsibility to others that founds rational social organization. When Claire eventually chooses Frédéric over the collective, the novel bears out the truth of her words. She dies, and Frédéric, proclaiming himself "free" from all social ties, vows he will soon follow her (769).

Claire d'Albe also, however, draws attention to the potential abuse of collective welfare when pursued at the expense of individual freedom; neither imperative in the sentimental conflict suffices to define morality on its own. In a heroic effort to save her marriage, Claire gathers together her courage and sends Frédéric away. But M. d'Albe is so eager to preserve his family that he does not respect Claire's handling of the situation. He takes advantage of Frédéric's absence to try to destroy Claire's love, telling her that Frédéric has been unfaithful although this is in fact not true. In lying, M. d'Albe himself betrays "sworn vows," which is to say precisely the foundation of the marriage contract he is trying to preserve. Rather than working, his lie precipitates the novel's final catastrophe. Claire and Frédéric only consummate their relationship after Frédéric returns to clear his name.

When I argue for the positive moral value of sentimental passion, I take issue with reigning materialist and feminist accounts of adultery in the novel that understand the situation as an expression of transgressive social energy. In Tony Tanner's influential explanation, adultery allows the emergence of repressed forces of alterity that threaten bourgeois hegemony. Similarly, Nicola Watson frames adultery as the struggle of rebellious female desire against patriarchy when she astutely observes the importance of conflict in shaping sentimental texts: "The action to which she [the sentimental heroine] is subjected and through which she is produced as a sentimental subject is paradigmatically . . . the plot of the conflict between paternal fiat and sexual passion."[34] But the adulterous conflict is so troubling because it reveals the ethical order divided against

---

[34] Nicola Watson, *Revolution and the Form of the British Novel*, 25.

itself.[35] Adultery is simultaneously transgressive and endowed with moral worth.

Cottin's contemporaries also understood sentimental passion as having positive moral significance. Indeed, one anonymous review took the opposite tack from Tanner and Watson when it discussed the collected novels of Cottin, associating the threat to society represented in sentimentality exclusively with the demands of collective duty. According to this review, sentimental love preserves individual liberty against the socially corrosive overemphasis on the welfare of all that French society had recently experienced in the Terror. Cottin's novels, it declared, are particularly suited to a generation disillusioned with the Revolution: "Thus, when the bloody tyranny of the praetorium oppressed the universe, ardent love and ardent Christianity, which, rightly understood, is love itself, consoled budding generations for their catastrophes."[36]

Adultery is one of two scenarios sentimental novels prefer to bring individual freedom into conflict with collective welfare. The other is family obstacles to marriage, and both coexist in the earliest example of the subgenre. In the first part of La Nouvelle Héloïse, Julie falls in love with a man whose position runs counter to the interests of her family. After considerable anguish, she attempts to abolish the conflict between freedom in love and family welfare with sophistical sleight of hand. She chooses freely to be unfree, to twist a notorious phrase from The Social Contract (I will return to the relation between the two texts), acquiescing willingly to a marriage with Wolmar. But the remainder of the novel makes clear that Julie cannot cheat on the demands of the heart. Rather than abolishing the conflict, her marriage raises it to a tragic pitch.

[35] My analysis also complicates David Denby's equation of sentimental morality with individual feelings. For Denby, "Sentimental love, the spontaneous experience of the heart, dictated by nature, is pitted against the social prejudice which sets obstacles of birth and fortune in its way, and the sentimental identification of the text is all on the side of the victims." David Denby, Sentimental Narrative and the Social Order in France, 1760–1820, 13.

[36] Review signed A. of the complete works of Riccoboni and Cottin, 14. Hegel was another contemporary who ascribed moral worth to individual love in his passing remarks on "modern romantic fiction" in the Aesthetics. Hegel writes, "Young people especially are these modern knights who must force their way through the course of the world which realizes itself instead of their ideals, and they regard it as a misfortune that there is any family, civil society, state, laws, professional business, etc., because these substantive relations of life with their barriers cruelly oppose the ideals and the infinite rights of the heart." Georg Wilhelm Friedrich Hegel, Aesthetics, 1:593. Referred to hereafter as A; subsequent page references will appear parenthetically in the text. In his discussion of the novel, however, Hegel does not consider the possibility that this conflict could end badly. Rather, he equates the modern novel with the bildungsroman, assuming that the protagonist will inevitably learn to balance affective rights with social duties. For Hegel, the hero's [sic] struggles

While the sentimental novel's plot schema may seem narrow, it in fact lends itself to a wide variety of "combinations" and "situations," to borrow Balzac's terms for sentimentality's richness on the level of plot, even if he offered it while proclaiming the death of the form.[37] Some of this variation is a matter of décor. Characters and events can have a range of historical and geographical identities, as Cottin's *oeuvre* makes clear. Cottin's works take us from the refined gentry on M. d'Albe's country estate to the warriors and nobility pursuing each other across the searing deserts of the Crusades in *Mathilde*; from the Russian aristocracy in the depths of Siberian winter in *Elisabeth* to the hypocrites, prudes, and rakes of proper Scottish society in *Malvina*.

Novels also vary the sentimental conflict depending on how they cast the protagonist's relation to it. This relation takes shapes between two poles: inclination and duty. Some novels align inclination with individual liberty and duty with collective welfare. In Montolieu's *Caroline de Lichtfield*, for example, the heroine's family marries her to the gruff but noblehearted Count Walstein. "An interesting and unhappy victim of obedience," Caroline inclines to freedom, which she pursues in the form of a love affair with an elegant gentleman who turns out to be Walstein's friend.[38] But there are other possibilities. Richardson's *Clarissa* is remarkable because inclination is on neither side of the heroine's double bind. In *La Nouvelle Héloïse*, inclination is on both sides, which is the case of *Claire d'Albe* as well. It is also the case of *Eugène de Rothelin*, where the hero, Eugène, is torn between his love for his father and his love for a woman who belongs to a family that his father detests. Genlis's *La Duchesse de la Vallière* offers an uncommon variation on the paradigm: the heroine's inclination is on the side of collective welfare. In love with Louis XIV, Louise wants to remain virtuous. She only acts on her love under duress, when Louis uses his royal authority to kidnap her from the convent where she seeks refuge from his ardor as well as her own feelings.

With the character of Louis XIV, Genlis's text also gives a distinctive twist to the fundamental sentimental opposition between individual and collective. In loving Louis XIV, Louise falls for a man collapsing these two abstractions into one another ("L'état, c'est moi"). As this novel illus-

---

"are nothing more than 'apprenticeship,' the education of the individual into the realities of the present, and thereby they acquire their true significance" (*A*, 1:593).

[37] Balzac, "Note de la première édition de *Scènes de la vie privée* [1830]," 1175.

[38] Isabelle de Montolieu, *Caroline de Lichtfield, ou Mémoires d'une famille prussienne*, 1:47. *Caroline de Lichtfield* is one of the few sentimental novels that end happily, thanks to the mediation of Caroline's lover, who did not realize that Caroline was married to Walstein when he first pursued a liaison with her. A devoted friend, who puts the happiness of others before his own, the lover convinces Caroline of Count Walstein's true worth, helping her to reconcile her socially ordained marriage and her heart.

trates, sentimental works generate diverse plots depending on how they align the unstable Enlightenment abstractions clustering around their founding ethical conflict. As in *La Duchesse de la Vallière* too, this variation finds primary expression in the delineation of character. In *Claire d'Albe*, Cottin tempts Claire with a man devoted to individual freedom, sentiment, and nature, while Claire's husband upholds social duty, reason, and culture. In *Corinne*, by contrast, Oswald is dazzled by a woman bringing together individual freedom, sentiment, and a nature that the novel identifies with artistic genius and the height of civilization, while Oswald's socially sanctioned choice is an artless girl belonging to stultifying country society. Meanwhile, Cottin's Mathilde in the novel of the same name discovers individual freedom in the person of a warrior motivated by natural impulses that take the form of sensibility, valor, and an acute sense of social duty. Cottin contrasts the noble Saracen, Malek-Adhel, with the artful courtier to whom Mathilde's brother, Richard the Lion-hearted, has betrothed her. This courtier, Lusignan, feigns social duty in order to pursue individual interest with coldly calculating rationality.

THE DOUBLE BIND OF LIBERALISM[39]

The sentimental novel's plot of virtue struggling with insurmountable moral conflict is an aspect of the form that makes little sense for critics writing from the vantage point of realism. They object to this plot, notably, for reducing to moral absolutes the complex play of power and interest that constitutes human affairs. In his account of tragedy, in contrast, Hegel puts the conflict between two purified moral principles at the foundations of the genre. Hegel's paradigmatic tragedy, *Antigone*, pits Creon, who "honours Zeus alone, the dominating power over public life and social welfare" against Antigone, who "honours the bond of kinship, the gods of the underworld" (*A*, 2:1213). Hegel writes, "the original essence of tragedy consists then in the fact that within such a conflict each of the opposed sides, if taken by itself, has *justification*; while each can establish the true and positive content of its own aim and character only by denying and infringing the equally justified power of the other" (*A*, 2:1196).

On the level of plot, this view of tragedy certainly resembles sentimentality. The combat between the two conflicting imperatives differs, however, in one significant fashion. While the sentimental plot delineates these

---

[39] I take this phrase from Waller's incisive analysis of *Adolphe* which in fact characterizes the politics of an entire subgenre. See *The Male Malady*, the chapter entitled "The Double Bind of Liberalism."

imperatives in powerful secondary characters, classical tragedy embodies these imperatives in its protagonists. In classical tragedy, then, the conflicting imperatives square off directly, in contrast to the sentimental novel where they meet in the conflicted soul of the protagonist whose torment defines her novelistic career. With this modification, sentimentality exploits the novel's formal ability to depict the nuances of interiority.[40]

But this difference in no way affects the similarity between the sentimental and the tragic dénouements. In the tragic dénouement, as Hegel remarks, "the individuals destroy themselves through the one-sidedness of their otherwise solid will and character, or they must resignedly accept what they had opposed even in a serious way" (*A*, 2:1199). The sentimental novel also ends when the characters embodying the conflicting imperatives take them to extremes. Placing collective welfare above everything, M. d'Albe lies in a desperate and misguided attempt to separate Frédéric and Claire. Placing individual freedom above everything, Frédéric then returns to overwhelm Claire with his love. Because the imperatives meet in the soul of the protagonist, she is the one destroyed when they are overdone. In *Claire d'Albe*, Claire dies, exhausted by violence from both sides of the double bind.

If tragedy resembles sentimentality on the level of plot, does plot in each genre convey a similar content? Hegel puts the plot of conflict at the foundations of tragedy because it addresses a fundamental truth about "ethical life." Defining tragedy's philosophical significance, Hegel writes,

> The substance of ethical life, as a concrete unity, is an ensemble of *different* relations and powers which only in a situation of inactivity, like that of the blessed gods, accomplish the work of the spirit in the enjoyment of an undisturbed life. But the very nature of this ensemble implies its transfer from its at first purely abstract *ideality* into its actualization in *reality* and its appearance in the mundane sphere. Owing to the nature of the real world, the mere *difference* of the constituents of this ensemble become perverted into *opposition* and collision, once individual characters seize upon them on the territory of specific circumstances. (*A*, 2:1196)

With its plot of moral conflict, tragedy shows the difficulty of realizing ethical abstractions in ethical practice. In particular, it shows the difficulty of reconciling two poles of ethical life that are at issue in all tragic plots, according to Hegel. Hegel writes, "The range of the subject-matter . . .

---

[40] Hegel isolates an increased emphasis on interiority as an important difference between modern and classical tragedy. While the protagonists of classical tragedy "are firm figures who simply are what they are, without any inner conflict," "the poetic interest" of modern tragedy "lies in the greatness of the characters who . . . display the full wealth of their heart" (*A*, 2:1209; 1206).

may be variously particularized but its essence is not very extensive. The chief conflict . . . is between the state, i.e. ethical life in its *spiritual* universality, and the family, i.e. *natural* ethical life." The conflict between universal and natural ethical life provides the subject matter of tragedy because "the full reality of ethical existence consists in harmony between these two spheres" (*A*, 2:1213).

The tragic plot not only represents this difficulty but resolves it, although this resolution takes the form of destruction and loss. In Hegel's analysis, the tragic dénouement demonstrates that moral imbalance cannot survive for long. Tragedy "affords . . . the glimpse of eternal justice . . . [that] overrides the relative justification of one-sided aims and passions" (*A*, 2:1198). Calling eternal justice the "power supreme over individual gods and men," Hegel also associates it with reason. "Rationality consists in the fact that the power supreme over individual gods and men cannot allow persistence . . . to one-sided powers that make themselves independent and thereby overstep the limits of their authority" (*A*, 2:1216).

"Always historicize," Jameson asserts as materialist imperative in *The Political Unconscious*. Transforming Hegel's analysis in light of Jameson's dictum, we can liberate its significance for the sentimental novel. Sentimentality, too, is persuading its readers that a rational ethical order exists beyond any individual violation through its representation of conflict, excess, and destruction.[41] But the stakes of this persuasion belong to a historically specific ideology rather than constituting the necessary "substance of ethical life." In opposing individual freedom to collective welfare, the sentimental novel addresses a fundamental tension fissuring French liberal political thought from its Enlightenment genesis.[42]

French liberalism is defined by the difficult if not impossible project to integrate negative and positive notions of rights, as Furet and Ozouf have observed of the two distinct notions of "freedom" informing "the French case."[43] In the sentimental conflict, individual freedom expresses a negative notion of rights: rights as the individual's rights to do what she or he wants. Collective welfare, in contrast, expresses a positive notion of rights, rights as the individual's rights to participate in government. Furet and Ozouf ascribe the French interest in integrating negative and positive

---

[41] In suggesting that sentimentality vindicates rationality through loss, I complicate Denby's assertion that sentimentalism belongs "firmly on the optimistic and triumphant slope of the Enlightenment project" (87).

[42] I use the term "liberalism" to designate an ideology that founds rational social order on liberty rather than "the conception of liberalism strictly speaking . . . which aims to protect the natural rights of individuals against all encroachments of power." Furet and Ozouf, preface to *Le Siècle de l'avènement républicain*, 12.

[43] Ibid.

notions of rights to the hybrid inheritance of French Enlightenment political theory. French thinkers absorbed the Anglo-American tradition concerned with protecting the individual's negative freedom. At the same time, they incorporated "the inheritance of absolutism" with its vision of a strong state, as well as "the intellectual tradition of republicanism in Europe since the Renaissance."[44]

In France, liberal ideology is forged by a class that crosses traditional class distinctions. This class is made of the *noblesse de robe* and some members of the *noblesse d'épée* as well as professional, financial, and protoindustrial bourgeois.[45] An emerging social elite in the second half of the eighteenth century with considerable economic and cultural as well as some political power, it comes to full-scale political dominance with the Revolution, albeit in a situation of symbolic and social disarray. In an argument suggestive for the class genesis of sentimentality, Guy Chaussinand-Nogaret proposes that this elite's notion of merit founded on "moral worth and professional ability" starts to take precedence over a purely aristocratic notion of merit grounded in blood and valor around 1760.[46] The sentimental novel substituted its notion of merit as moral worth and intelligence for an earlier literary representation of merit as aristocratic virtus around the same time. *La Nouvelle Héloïse* was published in 1761.

Two examples will illustrate the liberal preoccupation with fusing negative and positive notions of rights across the life of the sentimental novel: one from the inception of the subgenre and one from when it was the dominant novelistic form. For my concerns, there is no better starting point than *The Social Contract* (1762). Appearing just a year after *La Nouvelle Héloïse*, Rousseau's political text opens with a similar predicament. While the notion of human society rests on a commitment to liberty ("to renounce liberty is to renounce being a man"), Rousseau also underscores the potential abuses of individual freedom if it is unrestrained. " 'How to find a form of association which will defend the person and goods of each member with the collective force of all, and under which

---

[44] Ibid.

[45] Distinguishing between aristocrats and bourgeois as members of "distinct sociojuridical categories" in the second half of the eighteenth century, Immanuel Wallerstein observes that "the categories tend to overlap heavily as de facto capitalist entrepreneurs." Wallerstein, *The Modern World System*, 3:100. On the extent to which the nobility absorbed middle-class values, see Guy Chaussinand-Nogaret, *The French Nobility in the Eighteenth Century*.

[46] Chaussinand-Nogaret, *French Nobility*, 39. Chaussinand-Nogaret points out that ennoblement is justified as "the surest means of inspiring virtue" before 1760 (38). After 1760, "ennoblement is simply the official confirmation of the personal merit of those 'who combine virtue and the sentiments which make up the character and source of nobility.' It could not be said more clearly that nobility is not a matter of birth" (38–39).

each individual, while uniting himself with the others, obeys no one but himself and remains as free as before.' This is the fundamental problem to which the social contract holds the solution."[47] The social contract, of course, consists in a "reciprocal commitment between society and the individual" inaugurated by the complete alienation of one's freedom in the general will.[48] Rousseau's critics have long stressed how this notion is riddled with contradictions. In a lucid essay analyzing these contradictions, Louis Althusser makes the suggestive although undeveloped remark that Rousseau may have looked to literature for their resolution.[49]

To illustrate the liberal preoccupation with fusing negative and positive rights when sentimentality dominated the novel, we can also turn to an important political theorist who wrote a sentimental novel. During the Restoration, political polemic threw around the L-word with as much vigor as U.S. political debates of the 1980s and 1990s, and no thinker was more identified with liberal theory of the time than Benjamin Constant. "The double bind of liberalism," is how Waller aptly titles her analysis of Benjamin Constant's *Adolphe*, a text staging the paralysis of a hero torn between freedom and "a deep internalized feeling of responsibility . . . to others."[50] Constant puts a similar conflict at the core of his political theory.

"Our current constitution expressly recognizes the principle of the sovereignty of the people, which is to say the supremacy of the general will over any particular will. This principle . . . cannot be disputed," are Constant's opening lines in his *Principes de politique* (1815).[51] But, he continues, "it does not then follow that the universality of citizens . . . can sovereignly dispose of the existence of individuals."[52] How should a state founded on the positive rights of citizens to participate in government protect individuals' freedom to dispose of their existence as they please? Constant's solution was to propose negative rights beyond the reach of "the universality of citizens." As founding tenet of the *Principes de politique*, he asserts, "Citizens possess individual rights that are independent of any social or political authority, and any authority that violates these rights becomes illegitimate. The rights of citizens are individual freedom,

---

[47] Rousseau, *The Social Contract*, 60.

[48] Ibid., 62.

[49] Althusser, *Montesquieu, Rousseau, Marx*, 160.

[50] Waller, *Male Malady*, 94. Waller makes clear *Adolphe*'s uncommon spin on the founding terms of the sentimental double bind when she foregrounds its suspect gender politics. Constant's hero equates freedom with a rather vague desire for individuality rather than love, while collective welfare consists in "the ties that bind him to others and, in particular, Ellenore, an inappropriate woman" (94).

[51] Benjamin Constant, *Principes de politique*, 269.

[52] Ibid., 271.

religious freedom, freedom of opinion, including its public expression; the enjoyment of property, the guarantee against all arbitrariness."[53]

"Minds possess a natural reason," the preface to Constant's work states, as if the proposition needed no explanation.[54] In affirming the power of reason, the sentimental novel resolves the conflict between negative and positive notions of rights in eminently liberal fashion rather than, as Hegel suggests, vindicating "the eternal substance of things." But if Hegel's schema of tragedy reveals the return to reason at stake in sentimental excess, it is because Hegel's own "substance of things" is not eternal either. Critics have long attacked Hegel's view that classical tragedy vindicates rationality as a modern misreading of antique divinity and fate. They have similarly criticized his account of the tragic conflict as an anachronism; Michelle Gellrich comments that it is premised on the modern notion of "an ethical individual with rights."[55] Indeed, in confronting a conflict between "ethical life in its spiritual universality" and "natural ethical life," Hegel's tragic protagonist encounters a situation that resembles the conflict between positive and negative notions of rights structuring the sentimental novel.[56] Hegel places precisely these competing notions of rights, moreover, at the basis of his own contribution to political theory contemporary with the *Aesthetics*, the *Philosophy of Right* (1821).

"Freedom is both the substance of right and its goal," Hegel declares in the opening to this text, very quickly differentiating freedom from a purely negative notion of rights: "If we hear it said that the definition of freedom is the ability to do what we please, such an idea . . . contains not even an inkling of the absolutely free will, of right, ethical life, and so forth."[57] The substance of Hegel's inquiry concerns how to protect what Hegel calls the individual's "subjective" freedom while allowing the development of freedom in its "objective" form. Hegel locates the key to the problem in the state, which "bestow[s] on the powers of particularity [in this case, individuals] . . . both their positive and their negative rights" (*PR*, 177–78).

---

[53] Ibid., 275.

[54] Ibid., 267.

[55] Michelle Gellrich, *Tragedy and Theory: The Problem of Conflict since Aristotle*, 68.

[56] The terms of the conflict do, however, take different concrete forms in classical tragedy according to Hegel and in sentimentality. In classical tragedy, natural and universal ethical imperatives conflict in a struggle pitting an individual representing the family against the collective. In sentimentality, negative and positive notions of rights conflict in a struggle pitting the individual against the family aligned with the collective.

[57] Hegel, *Hegel's Philosophy of Right*, 20; 27. Referred to hereafter as *PR* and cited parenthetically in the text.

Antigone makes an appearance in Hegel's inquiry concerning the constitution of freedom in order to clarify the role of the family in modern civil society. And when Hegel reads the play from the vantage point of political theory, he updates its tragic collision in frankly liberal-sentimental terms. In the *Philosophy of Right*, as in the *Aesthetics*, Hegel views *Antigone* as exemplifying "the supreme opposition in ethics and therefore in tragedy" (*PR*, 115). In the *Philosophy of Right*, however, this opposition confronts "public law . . . the law of the land" with the law of the private, sentiment, "the law of the inward life," in contrast to the *Aesthetics*, where it confronts universal and natural ethical spheres designated as the state and the family (*PR*, 115).

WOMAN'S DESTINY

In *Antigone*, as in society, the *Philosophy of Right* comments, the "supreme opposition in ethics . . . is individualized . . . in the opposing natures of man and woman" (*PR*, 115). Assigning women the work of private life to free up men for public affairs, Hegel exemplifies the gendering of the spheres common in eighteenth- and nineteenth-century liberalism. Throughout the life of the sentimental novel, liberal thinkers assume that those subjects fit to enjoy positive rights are male, excluding women from access to positive rights and limiting their enjoyment of negative rights as well. Given the liberal depoliticization of women, it may seem surprising that the sentimental novel prefers to address the conflict between negative and positive notions of rights using female protagonists. Julie, Mistriss Henley, Caroline de Lichtfield, Claire d'Albe, Mathilde, Malvina, Delphine, La Duchesse de la Vallière, Mademoiselle de Clermont, Adèle de Sénange well outnumber William *** in *Caliste*, Gustave in *Valérie*, Eugène de Rothelin, Adolphe, and Oswald in *Corinne*.

We can, I think, situate the sentimental novel's preference for female over male protagonists at the intersection of poetics and ideology. One important principle in tragedy is economy of representation. Differentiating the concentration of drama from the leisurely pace of epic, Hegel proposes that in drama, "the epic description of a world-situation in its entirety disappears," and all attention is focused on "the collision which provides [its] essential subject" (*A*, 2:1168). Hegel points out the consequences of this focus for the plot construction of tragedy, which he considers drama in its most concentrated form. Tragedy suppresses "incidental actions and characters in a sub-plot" that might distract from the central dramatic collision (*A*, 2:1167).

The sentimental novel exhibits similar tragic concentration in the situation that enacts its underwriting ideological conflict. A single action, the

choice of a beloved whom authority does not sanction, produces the collision between individual freedom and collective welfare with no need for
further complication. Male and female protagonists alike encounter this
collision in romantic relations despite the vast differences in nonfictional
men and women's careers. Nonetheless, these vast differences give romantic dilemmas their greatest collective resonance when they confront a
woman. For all but exceptional individuals throughout the life of the sentimental novel, "man has his actual substantive life in the state, in learning, and so forth, as well as in labour and struggle with the external
world. . . . Woman, on the other hand, has her substantive destiny in the
family," as Hegel observes when he discusses *Antigone* in the *Philosophy
of Right* (PR, 114).[58] A woman's choice of erotic object unavoidably raises
questions of collective welfare and can never be simply a matter of individual feeling. Whether the choice concerns a future marriage partner or love
outside wedlock, it involves a woman's family and the welfare of her
children, if she has any. In both cases, too, a woman who defies her family
runs the risk of collective ostracism.

I thus explain the sentimental preference for women in inverse fashion
to Armstrong clarifying the role of the female protagonist in the English
domestic novel. Instead of enabling private plots to obscure collective
conflict, French sentimental novels use female protagonists to give private
relations their maximum collective resonance. At the same time, Armstrong's analysis is suggestive for the uncomfortable way in which the
French sentimental focus on feminine destiny skirts the political. "By virtue of their apparent disregard for matters [of business and politics]," she
writes, "plots turning on the sexual contract offered the means of passing
off ideology as the product of purely human concern."[59] In resolving the
tension between negative and positive rights with ethical narratives re-
moved from political subject matter, French sentimental novels similarly
avoid material that would foreground the vast gap between the aesthetic
restoration of rationality and the "one-sided aims and passions" ruling
public affairs (A, 2:1198).

When the sentimental novel uses female protagonists as paradigmatic
liberal subjects, it assumes that the domestic sphere is a microcosm
of collective life; that women's careers can grapple with problems that
threaten the very makeup of the res publica. Such an assumption is, however, fragile, given the disparity between the ideological function

---

[58] Cottin makes a related observation in *Malvina*: "[N]ovels are the domain of women:
they begin to read them when they are fifteen; at twenty, they live them out, and they have
nothing better to do than write them when they are thirty . . . it belongs to women to capture
all the nuances of a feeling which is the history of their life, while it is barely an episode in
the life of men." Cottin, *Malvina*, x–xi.

[59] Armstrong, *Desire*, 42.

of Woman and women's juridical, political, and social status. Indeed, women writers may play such an important role in the sentimental novel because this disparity makes women particularly sensitive to both the distinction between negative and positive rights and the contradictions it can produce.

If a novel draws attention to the discrepancy between Woman's figurative ability to resolve political conflict and women's actual social standing, it can disrupt the sentimental return to reason. The discrepancy can, in fact, itself generate the plot of collision, as we shall see in sentimental social novels of the July Monarchy, which adapt sentimental codes to undermine liberal constructions of gender. The discrepancy is, moreover, already exposed and exploited in some exceptional sentimental plots where protagonists encounter obstacles in love deriving from the specifics of their social situations. Thus, Staël's heroines meet with objections from their beloveds' families because they engage in actions unacceptable for a woman (Delphine's divorce and Corinne's refusal to stay in the private sphere), although these actions would not taint a man. Depicting the powerful consequences of gender difference, Staël's works draw attention to the unthinkable problem elided in the liberal conflict between individual freedom and collective welfare: the problem of social inequality.[60]

A LIGHT TOUCH

Distinguishing the concentration of tragic representation from the panoramic focus of epic, Hegel epitomizes this difference with a single poetic code. In tragedy, as in drama more generally, "the epic *description* of a world-situation in its entirety disappears" (*A*, 2:1168, emphasis added). The effacement of description characterizes the sentimental novel as well. Sentimental novels delineate setting and the material aspect of characters only with a few attributes that are often commonplace. The action in *Claire d'Albe* takes place in a château that is "huge and comfortable" (694). Claire is introduced as "beautiful and attractive" while Frédéric is embodied in his "supple" and "agile" body (692; 697). When Saint-Preux first speaks of Julie, he mentions simply that she is "beautiful" before

---

[60] Waller makes a similar point about *Adolphe*, underlining that Adolphe's impasses advance his position while Ellenore's end in her death. As Waller suggests, the hero and heroine's asymmetrical careers reveal that if all citizens are created equal, they do not all have equal access to rights. For another version of this argument, see Carla Hesse's reading of Charrière's *Trois Femmes* in "Kant, Foucault, and *Three Women*," in *Foucault and the Writing of History*, ed. Jan Goldstein. Hesse astutely isolates the nucleus of sentimental collision when she analyzes Charrière's stories as representing a conflict between virtue and happiness.

praising her soul: "No, beautiful Julie; your charms had dazzled my eyes; never would they have distracted my heart without the more powerful charm which animates them" (6). Neither Saint-Preux nor Julie introduce their liaison with details on the locations where it unfolds. On the cover of her sentimental social novel, *Deux Originaux* (1835), B. Monborne places a line from Alexander Pope that well captures sentimentality's descriptive restraint: "It is enough to be able, with *a light touch* / To place shadow here and there, light."[61] The practice was also described as "the delicate touch."[62]

Critics with a bias towards realism have long denigrated sentimental novels for their failure to describe material specifics in detail. Bardèche's objections to their "conventional characters limited to two or three types, setting, milieu, manners, everyday life left undefined" are typical.[63] But the tragic paradigm allows us to grasp an absence incomprehensible from the vantage point of realism as a meaningful poetic choice. Sentimental novels, like tragedy, efface material details to concentrate all attention on the progress of the action. When Barthélemy Hadot explains the function of the light touch in her opening paragraphs to *Guillaume Penn* (1816), she makes clear that description dilutes sentimental action because it both presents material inessential to this action and delays its representation:

> I will not try to describe the pleasant dwelling of the admiral [Penn]. What does the reader care that it is reached by an avenue of more than a quarter of a mile *[lieue]*, which is covered, in summer months, by a dome of green; that the front staircase is made of twenty steps of white marble, which lead to a peristyle; of more than thirty feet, whose arch is supported by twelve columns of granite and alabaster, and which offers entrance into apartments where elegance yields only to opulence? *Anything that could be said would doubtless have no interest for sentimental souls [âmes sensibles] who want to see the famous sailor arrive in the bosom of his family.*[64]

I pick this example to underscore that sentimental writers avoid description not because they cannot do it, as denigrating twentieth-century discussions of the subgenre imply, but because they object to it on poetic grounds. Details concerning material aspect hold no interest for "sentimental" readers eager to get to the dramas of interior conflict.[65]

---

[61] B. Monborne, *Deux Originaux*, emphasis added. I am translating from Monborne's French. See also F. Barrière's review of *Mes loisirs*.

[62] Unsigned introduction to a selection from Michel Masson's *Souvenirs d'un enfant du peuple*, 7.

[63] Bardèche, *Balzac romancier*, 14.

[64] Marie-Adèle Barthélemy Hadot, *Guillaume Penn*, 1:9–10, emphasis added.

[65] Claire, too, presents description as upstaged by more urgent matters of sentiment in an opening letter to Elise. Apologizing because she has failed to describe her surroundings

When Barthélemy Hadot's contemporaries praised the sentimental novel, they confirmed her observation. In the preface to an 1820 edition of Cottin's collected novels, for example, A. Petitot associated their "truth" with their disregard for material specifics. Cottin's novels "are not less sought after today than they were when they were new. Their success is independent of time and circumstances, because no one has known how to depict with more energy and truth the differing sentiments which stir a great passion. Her novels contain few details, few manners, few portraits."[66] "There are two kinds of truths: a material truth, a truth of facts; and a moral truth, a truth of ideas and sentiments," declared a review of a sentimental novel from 1818, placing sentimentality firmly on the side of moral truth.[67]

FEW DETAILS, FEW MANNERS, FEW PORTRAITS

The erasure of "a world-situation in its entirety" informs other sentimental narrative codes besides description (A, 2:1168). This principle shapes the scope and setting of the sentimental plot, the sentimental construction of character, and sentimental narration. Sentimental plots prefer the fewest characters necessary for the action, usually from one or two families in the same social circle. Claire, Frédéric, M. d'Albe, Elise, and Adèle, a visiting acquaintance of Claire's, comprise the entire cast of Claire d'Albe. The sentimental novel reinforces such restraint in how it handles setting. Sentimentality begins at home. These intimate family groups interact in domestic spaces: the salons, bedrooms, and gardens of the residence, although occasionally characters do travel. The more private the setting and the fewer the characters, the less structural chance there is for "a variety of incidental actions and characters in a sub-plot" that dilutes the intensity of tragic concentration (A, 2:1167).

Hegel's paradigm illuminates one further way the sentimental restriction of plot scope intensifies sentimental representation: by heightening the pathos of its founding collision. For Hegel, the most effective tragic actions occur between characters sharing familial and social identities, because these identities root the protagonists mutually not only in the ethical imperative each upholds but also in the imperative each seeks to destroy. As Hegel writes, "This sort of development [tragic] is most com-

---

in detail, Claire comments, "the haven that will soon be yours . . . deserves to be described; but what would you expect? When I take up my pen, I can busy myself only with you" (693). Here, Claire's bond with her reader is the sentimental matter taking precedence over material aspect.

[66] A. Petitot, preface to Cottin, Oeuvres complètes, 1:lxxiii.

[67] A., review of Albertine de Saint-Albe, 416.

plete when the individuals who are at variance appear each of them in their concrete existence as a totality, so that in themselves they are in the power of what they are fighting, and therefore they violate what, if they were true to their own nature, they should be honouring" (*A*, 2:1217). Living "under the political authority of Creon," Antigone "is herself the daughter of a King [Oedipus] and the fiancée of Haemon [Creon's son], so that she ought to pay obedience to the royal command. But Creon too, as father and husband, should have respected the sacred tie of blood and not ordered anything against its pious observance" (*A*, 2:1217).

The sentimental preference for characters from the same familial and social circle can work similarly to heighten the protagonists' conflicts. Claire, as M. d'Albe's wife, and Frédéric, as his cousin and ward, should respect the ties of blood and community violated by their love. Claire lucidly observes, "Elise, Frédéric is the adopted son of my husband; I am the wife of his benefactor: virtue engraves these things in letters of fire on noble souls and they never forget it" (707). Meanwhile, M. d'Albe should respect Claire and Frédéric's individual happiness, since they belong to a collective that he administers where it is a founding right. As Claire tells us of her husband's benevolent rule at the novel's beginning: "How I love my husband, Elise! how I am touched by the pleasure he takes in doing good! All his ambition is to undertake praiseworthy actions, just as his happiness is to accomplish them with success. He loves Frédéric tenderly, because he views him as a man he can make happy" (697).

The sentimental novel's restricted plot scope is inseparable from its muted reference to social differences. The narrow cast of sentimental characters generally share a common rank, and sentimental novels do not mention servants. If this social homogeneity has been amply chastised by prorealist critics, it, too, works in the service of tragic concentration. Muting reference to a variegated social panorama, the sentimental novel suppresses material that might complicate or dilute the starkness of its structuring ethical collision. This strategy is poetic, but it is also ideological. In muting reference to social difference, the sentimental novel implies its underwriting collision as the inevitable outcome of ethical life rather than as a product of particular social factors.

The rank of sentimental protagonists varies depending only on when the novels take place. In novels set in the recent past or present, the characters usually belong to the minor aristocracy, as *Claire d'Albe* demonstrates. M. d'Albe's *particule* suggests him as noble, but he is not connected to the court. He inhabits his country estate in quiet comfort, pursuing his manufacturing business. Novels set in the historical past, in contrast, place their characters at the center of power, whether it is Louis XIV and his entourage in *La Duchesse de la Vallière* or Richard the Lionhearted and the Saracen king, Saladin, in *Mathilde*. These differences in social stratum are, however, more apparent than real. All sentimental protagonists are united by their ethics of sentimental virtue. This unity is striking even in those exceptional sentimental novels that foreground class differences like *La Nouvelle Héloïse*.

Sentimental protagonists are in addition united by their way of speaking. Whatever their gender, ethnicity, national and regional identification, they use similar diction, from the child of the mountains, Frédéric, to the more worldly Claire, from Malek-Adhel, the Saracen prince, to Mathilde, the Christian princess, from the Prussian aristocracy to the royal entourage at the court of Louis XIV. This diction is characterized by a restrained, neoclassical vocabulary, the repetition of simple syntactic patterns, sentences composed of numerous fragments, and the most economical reportage possible of events, which contrasts with the expansive sentimental approach to interiority. Such diction constitutes one more way the sentimental novel pares away all unnecessary distraction from its underwriting collision. It extends to all characters in the novel as well as to the authorial persona if the novel is in the third person.

Sainte-Beuve characterizes sentimental diction well when he comments that Duras's style is *"born natural* and finished, simple, rapid yet condensed, a style like Voltaire's, but in a woman."[68] Here is an example of Duras's sentimental diction, from the frame narrative of *Edouard*. "The trip ended; we landed in Baltimore. The young passenger asked me to admit him as a volunteer in my regiment; he was listed, as in the ship's register, simply under the name of Edouard."[69] When Claire describes Frédéric's arrival at her château, the spare sentimental reportage of events starts to dilate ever so slightly, registering the beginnings of interior conflict. Claire remarks: "I only kissed my husband, and glimpsed Frédéric. He looked fine, very fine. His bearing is noble, his physiognomy is open; he is shy but not awkward. I put all possible graciousness in my welcome" (697).

Sentimental novels contain only one exception to their neoclassical lingua franca in the diction used by a distinctive type of secondary character. This character embodies a variety of moral pathologies found in high

---

[68] Charles-Augustin Sainte-Beuve, "Poètes et romanciers modernes de la France, Madame de Duras," 723. Balzac is more critical of this diction when he uses Lousteau to describe early-nineteenth-century sentimental novels in *La Muse du département*: "The literature of the Empire went straight to the facts without any detail, which seems to me an attribute of primitive times. The literature of this period was somewhere between a summary of the chapters of *Télémaque* and the indictments of the District Attorney. It [*elle*] had ideas, but disdainfully did not express them, it observed, but stingily did not share its observations with anyone!" (249).

[69] Claire de Duras, *Edouard*, 1011. Subsequent page references will appear parenthetically in the text.

society including slander, envy, egotism, and materialism, although none of these pathologies appears in *Claire d'Albe*. The most common moral pathology is the hypocrite, exemplified by the courtier Lusignan scheming to marry the sister of Richard the Lion-hearted in *Mathilde* or Madame de Vernon in *Delphine*. In private and among like-minded friends, the hypocrite describes action with the worldly, witty language of the libertine novel. To the sentimental protagonist, in contrast, the hypocrite employs a parody of sentimental narration. "Matilde and Léonce's contract was thus signed today; and the day after tomorrow, at six in the evening, they will marry: I would like to see you before this moment that is so solemn for me; come, tomorrow, to Paris, and I will go to you. Farewell; I am most affected by your sorrow," laments Madame de Vernon when she tells Delphine of the marriage contract between Delphine's beloved and her daughter that she has in fact engineered.[70] To the extent that the sentimental novel includes different idioms, it grounds these idioms in moral rather than social difference.[71]

IMAGE OF THE HEART

At moments of narrative peripeteia, sentimental texts sometimes break with their suppression of material details to provide extensive descriptions of natural beauty. These exceptions to the light touch might seem a distraction from the sentimental novel's concentrated focus on the events resulting from the collision between collective welfare and individual freedom. In fact, however, such detailed material, and above all visual descriptions of nature, reinforce the surrounding events by recapitulating them in allegorical form. Aloïse de Carlowitz calls this convention the "image of the heart" when she uses it in her sentimental social novel, *Caroline, ou le Confesseur*.[72]

---

[70] Germaine de Staël, *Delphine*, 1: 174–75. Subsequent page references will appear parenthetically in the text.

[71] In muting social specifics, the sentimental novel differs not only from nineteenth-century realism but from other novelistic subgenres of the late eighteenth and the turn of the nineteenth century. It differs, notably, from the novel of worldliness so important before the Revolution concerned with the "exploration and definition of men in the social medium," as Peter Brooks observes in *The Novel of Worldliness*, 60. It also differs from comic novels like Guillaume-Charles-Antoine Pigault-Lebrun's *L'Enfant du Carnaval* (1792) and *Les Barons Felsheims* (1798) as well as Paul de Kock's *Soeur Anne* (1825), which pay substantive attention both to material details and to the lower classes of society. What greater contrast to the sentimental novel's homogeneous and interiorized universe than the opening to *L'Enfant du Carnaval*, where a priest gets a serving girl pregnant on a table overflowing with the remains of Mardi Gras dinner?

[72] Aloïse de Carlowitz, *Caroline, ou le Confesseur*, 104. Subsequent page references will appear parenthetically in the text.

Claire d'Albe's single image of the heart occurs when Claire first re-
treats with M. d'Albe to his country château. In a letter telling Elise of
her marital harmony, Claire opens by offering a lush description of the
countryside:

> Our residence is several miles from Tours, in the midst of a pleasing mixture
> of hillsides and plains, the former covered with woods and vineyards; the
> latter with golden harvests and cheerful houses. The Cher river hugs the land-
> scape with its bends and goes to throw itself into the Loire: the banks of the
> Cher, covered with groves and meadows, are cheerful and rustic; those of the
> Loire, more stately, are shaded with tall poplars, thick woods, and rich fields.
> From the height of a picturesque rock that dominates the castle, the rivers
> can be seen rolling their dazzling waters in the sunlight for a distance of seven
> to eight miles [*lieues*] to join together in murmuring at the foot of the castle.
> (693–94)

Describing the landscape as unifying opposites in beautiful equilibrium,
Claire offers an allegory of her own relationship, which the novel is in the
process of establishing. Like the landscape, her marriage brings together a
graceful, cheerful young woman with a "stately" older man. Retrospec-
tively, Claire's allegory takes on a darker cast. The landscape becomes the
picturesque figure of a harmony Claire cannot achieve in ethical practice.

SENTIMENTAL BLAZON

The sentimental blazon is one more convention that disrupts sentimentality's overwhelming concentration on the actions resulting from the founding sentimental conflict. The sentimental novel suspends the progress of
the action to detail the physical body of the protagonist when the protagonist is the object of another character's desire. Generally, a man looks at
a woman, and the man expresses her beauty, using rhetorical strategies
from the poetic tradition of the blazon. He conjures up the woman's
charms by breaking down her beauty into her discrete, physical features,
dwelling in particular on these features' visual appeal.

If Claire is initially introduced only as "beautiful and attractive," we
get a blazon of her face when Frédéric starts to fall in love with her (692).
This blazon occurs as Frédéric criticizes a portrait of Claire made by a
skillful painter. "That is not Madame d'Albe . . . you have not even suc-
ceeded in capturing one way she looks," he objects (716). The painter
asks, "What more do you want?" "What do I want? let's acknowledge
that there exists a figure that art will never capture and that its insufficiency at least be felt. These beautiful blond locks, while detailed with
skill, have neither the shine, nor the delicacy, nor the curves of hers. I do

not see this white, fine skin reflect the shading of her blood nor the delicate down which covers it. This uniform complexion will never recall hers whose colors vary like thought. That is certainly the heavenly blue of her eyes, but I only see their color: you should have captured their gaze" (716). Frédéric concludes, "No, no, lifeless features will never depict Claire; and where I see no soul, I cannot recognize her" (716).

Frédéric here formulates his desire for Claire by concentrating on her material aspect. But in doing so, he undercuts the importance of materiality in several ways. He enumerates the beauty of Claire's face as he criticizes the picture for failing to depict it, both because Claire's beauty transcends the material representations of art and because the medium of painting freezes Claire's mobility into one static moment. He also differentiates Claire's beauty from her physical appearance. Claire's beauty is in her look, not her eyes; while it shines through the features of her face, it emanates from her soul.

Frédéric's comments are typical of the sentimental blazon, which refunctions the traditional use of this topos to exalt the sensual aspect of desire. With the blazon, the sentimental novel asserts the material/moral opposition in order to subordinate the first term to the second. While the sentimental blazon might seem to disrupt sentimental action, the topos thus in fact reinforces its importance. The sentimental blazon affirms the primacy of the ethical realm at issue in the conflicts of sentimental narrative.[73]

Cottin underlines the significance of the sentimental blazon when she delineates the painter responsible for Claire's portrait. The portrait is the work of Adèle, a beautiful young woman Claire has invited as a diversion for Frédéric. Adèle's interest in painting is of a piece with her attachment to material pleasures, which Cottin censures, representing Adèle as vain and overly attached to frivolous, sensuous pursuits like parties and dancing. At first smitten with Adèle's beauty, Frédéric soon grows disillusioned: "What a mistake I made in finding her so beautiful! I believed that this woman must bear some resemblance to you, but to my misfortune, my eternal misfortune, I see all too well that you are unique," he tells Claire (717). The discrepancy between Adèle's physical appearance and her character emphasizes that material appearance is of little significance in itself and can be epistemologically misleading.

[73] In rewriting the blazon, the sentimental novel attacks the literature of its time as well as the literary tradition. The most celebrated contemporary use of the blazon is in the libertine novel, where the trope expresses libertine desire. Correcting this view of love, the sentimental blazon simultaneously corrects the libertine novel's answer to the contradictions of the social contract. The libertine novel resolves the contradictions between negative and positive freedoms by abandoning social freedom of any sort for natural freedom: the "right

Sentimental novels often offer this lesson through denigrating purely physical beauty. In Genlis's *La Duchesse de la Vallière*, for example, Louise de la Vallière is not the most dazzling woman in the novel, but she exhibits a moral superiority that "interests" and "moves": "her features were neither regular nor striking, she seemed made to move and charm the heart and not to dazzle the eyes."[74] Vallière's perfidious rival, Madame de Montespan, in contrast, "combined regular features, a perfect figure and beauty, with all the freshness of the first youth, and the most lively and fascinating face" (142–43).

When *Claire d'Albe* takes a portrait as the occasion for a sentimental blazon, it exemplifies the common sentimental use of visuality as a synecdoche for the material term of the material/moral opposition.[75] This association is most pointed in Genlis's *Alphonsine*. *Alphonsine* begins as a sentimental novel of adultery: Diana, unhappy in a socially ordained marriage, struggles with an extramarital affair. Genlis's novel mutates, however, into a pedagogical novel when Diana's husband imprisons her in an underground dungeon to punish her for adultery. Unbeknownst to her husband, Diana is pregnant, and she gives birth in the dungeon to a daughter. In the remainder of the novel, Genlis lays out Diana's praiseworthy program for educating her daughter, Alphonsine, first in the dungeon and then in society when both are released from their imprisonment after twelve years.[76]

Genlis depicts Diana's imprisonment as having one silver lining. Since Diana has only a few candles, which she saves for emergencies, Alphon-

---

to anything that tempts" and that one "can take." Rousseau, *Social Contract*, 65. Libertine desire accordingly focuses on material possession, since, as Rousseau points out, natural freedom is rooted in "physical impulse" and material satisfaction (64).

[74] Stéphanie-Félicité de Genlis, *La Duchesse de la Vallière*, 21. Subsequent page references will appear parenthetically in the text.

[75] This use of the portrait is a sentimental commonplace reaching back to *La Nouvelle Héloïse*. Julie sends Saint-Preux her portrait as a love gift, and the portrait initially delights him. As he contemplates it, however, he grows disenchanted, offering a blazon of Julie that shows how Julie escapes her material depiction. Saint-Preux comments, for example, that while the portrait has Julie's physical features, it lacks her soul: "The first fault I find in the portrait is that it is your resemblance without being you, it has your face and has no feeling. In vain, the painter thought to depict your eyes and features exactly; he has not captured the gentle feeling that gives them life, and without which, charming as they are, they would be nothing" (269). In addition, he points out the imperfections of her material depiction. The portrait fails to capture the subtleties of Julie's appearance, including her "faults" (270). It also misrepresents Julie by immobilizing her expressiveness: "[I]n order to be able to express all your charms, it would be necessary to paint you at all instants in your life" (270).

[76] In the last part of the novel, Genlis devises a maternal version of the sentimental double bind. Diana finds herself torn between her desire to be "the universe" for her daughter and her efforts to integrate her daughter into society. Genlis, *Alphonsine, ou la Tendresse maternelle*, 39.

sine spends her childhood without exercising her sense of sight. When mother and daughter are initially liberated, Alphonsine cannot tolerate any light, and Diana must instruct her in how to see. Genlis represents this instruction as an ideal opportunity for Diana to safeguard her daughter against the seductions of the material. Using nature as Alphonsine's privileged object of contemplation, Diana teaches Alphonsine to appreciate visual, and, by implication, material aspect in Platonic fashion. Material beauty becomes the gateway to intangible intellectual and emotional pleasures and through them to an appreciation of God.

"..."

In subordinating material to moral experience, the sentimental novel participates in an antimaterialism Jean Starobinski has singled as an important intellectual current of the late eighteenth century. For Starobinski, this antimaterialism represents "a thirst for intelligible Beauty . . . against the corrupting seduction of sensual pleasure. People aspired to an art that would no longer address itself to the eyes alone but instead, though through the inevitable mediation of sight, to the soul."[77] But the sentimental novel is ambiguous concerning whether it formulates its antimaterialism as a defense against seduction.

While sentimentality sometimes warns against the erotic perils of material aspect, it more often associates the soul with an enhanced form of erotic pleasure. Saint-Preux offers his first blazon of Julie as he examines her clothes while waiting for their sexual rendez-vous: "These pretty slippers that a supple foot fills with ease; such a slender corset which touches and hugs... what an enchanting waist!... in front two faint outlines... Oh spectacle of pleasure!... the whalebone has yielded to the strength of the impression" (122). In this blazon, Saint-Preux associates material, in particular, visual details with desire, but Julie's clothes eventually transport him to a pitch of excitement beyond the body. The move beyond the material negates sensual pleasure to the benefit of erotic intensification. Similarly, in *Edouard*, Duras's hero falls in love with a woman whose spiritual "seduction" exceeds any of her features. Doing away with the sentimental blazon altogether, Edouard exclaims of his beloved, Madame de Rieux, "Oh! my friend! how to paint her for you? If she was only beautiful, if she was only attractive, I would find expressions worthy of this heavenly woman. But how to describe what all together formed an irresistible seduction? I was stirred up when I saw her; I glimpsed my fate; but I will

---

[77] Jean Starobinski, *1789: The Emblems of Reason*, 145.

not tell you that I wondered one moment whether I loved her: this angel penetrated my soul entirely" (1021).

If sentimental texts show ambiguity concerning the erotic dimension to the soul, this ambiguity crystallizes in their use of suspension points to represent sex. With suspension points, some narrators elide description of physical experience to avoid seducing the reader. But the gesture can also be used to convey a more intense eroticism than can be depicted with physical details. When *Claire d'Albe* narrates the scene where Claire gives in to Frédéric, Cottin's suspension points exhibit both faces of sentimental antimaterialism. The scene is reported by Elise, who gives us the dénouement of the novel following Claire's death to honor Claire's request that her daughter, in reading her story "could, one day, save herself from the passions to which her unfortunate mother had fallen victim" (763). Elise begins by condemning passion, but then shifts from moral censure to extolling sentimental pleasure [*jouissance*]: "Love doubled the strength of Frédéric, love and illness exhausted that of Claire.... She no longer belongs to herself, she no longer belongs to virtue; Frédéric is everything, Frédéric prevails.... She tasted in all its fullness this flash of ecstasy [*délice*], which love alone can feel; she knew that unique and exquisite pleasure [*jouissance*], rare and divine like the feeling that created it" (764).

BEYOND PURELY PERSONAL LIFE

Pro-realist critics have long denigrated sentimentality for its abstract delineation of character as well as material aspect. Bardèche, for example, remarks of sentimental heroes: "It is hard to say what they are, but one can easily designate those who resemble them, those who reflect that imaginary ideal that cannot be depicted and that can best be felt. Just about the same thing could be said of the heroines."[78] As Bardèche's comments make clear, sentimental novels abstract character in the mode of idealization.[79] Claire is virtuous, "beautiful and attractive" (692); her husband spends all his time performing "praiseworthy actions" (697); and Frédéric exemplifies "these large and vigorous strokes that must have delineated man as he left his creator's hands" (699).

If idealization is anathema in the realist novel, it is essential to the workings of tragedy according to Hegel. For Hegel, tragic protagonists stand

[78] Bardèche, *Balzac romancier,* 6.

[79] When Schor characterizes Sand's idealism as a "mirror . . . that has . . . the magical properties of blocking out the ugly and the mean and magnifying the beautiful and the good," she is in fact noticing one aspect of Sand's deep engagement with sentimentality. Schor, *Sand and Idealism,* 43.

"on this height, where the mere accidents of the individual's purely personal life disappear" (A, 2:1195). In removing characters from the "purely personal," tragedy first of all erases any "accidental" details that might dilute the significance of its founding conflict. The tragic conflict appears the inevitable outcome of ethical practice rather than resulting from a character's psychological weakness or social need.

Sentimental novels use idealization similarly. When Cottin represents M. d'Albe as a respectful and decent man, she removes factors that might justify Claire's betrayal as a reaction to psychological or physical abuse. Claire's betrayal becomes all the more egregious and yet, because Claire too is a model of virtue painfully lucid concerning her situation, it becomes all the more unavoidable. In addition, both characters' idealization permits what Hegel terms "the sufferer's moral justification" to emerge in the starkest possible fashion (A, 2:1198). In making Claire so worthy and giving M. d'Albe so many "rights to . . . [her] affection," Cottin removes any distraction from the single aspect of Claire's marriage violating correct ethical life: that it is not of her own choosing (696).

Hegel's comments on tragedy illuminate one other way idealized characters heighten the power of the sentimental novel's underwriting ethical collision. For the spectator to grasp the moral import of the tragic conflict, Hegel proposes, it is essential that he or she enter into each position fully. Hegel terms this identification the spectator's relation of "true pity" with the protagonist(s). "True pity" is sympathy "with the sufferer's moral justification" and "if the tragic character . . . is to arouse tragic sympathy he must be a man of worth and goodness himself. For it is only something of intrinsic worth which strikes the heart of a man of noble feelings and shakes it to its depths" (A, 2:1198). When sentimentality paints its characters as exemplary, it, too, solicits the reader's sympathy for them in order to reinforce the gravity of their moral dilemmas. In defining the tragic effect as a sympathetic bond, moreover, Hegel shows how much he owes to the Enlightenment discourse of sympathy informing the sentimental novel. He rewrites the "pity and fear" of Aristotelian catharsis into "the pity or compassion" founding sympathetic morality.[80]

Hegel differentiates such masculinized "true pity" from "sympathy with someone else's misfortune and suffering which is felt as something finite and negative. Provincial females are always ready with compassion of this sort. For if it is only the negative aspect . . . of misfortune, that is emphasized, then the victim of misfortune is degraded" (A, 2:1198). Sentimentality's critics have belittled the subgenre for just this focus on the "negative aspect . . . of misfortune," often using a similar rhetoric of gender disparaging femininity. But in fact, as these critics simultaneously

---

[80] Aristotle, *The Poetics*, 1465. Adam Smith, *The Theory of Moral Sentiments*, 9.

reveal in objecting to sentimental idealization, the sentimental protagonist's dilemma does not stem principally from "the negative aspect of misfortune" but rather from her or his "moral justification" (*A*, 2:1198).

ALL SHOULD BE CLEAR

While sentimental heroines and heroes are idealized from their introduction, the sentimental plot subjects its protagonists' moral worth to ample trial. Setting up the conflict between individual freedom and collective welfare from its opening events, the sentimental plot accumulates situations that test the protagonist's ability to negotiate this conflict as they simultaneously test the conflict's force.

Indeed, the trials of the sentimental plot do more than test the protagonist's moral worth; they produce it. As Carolyn Dever has incisively argued, sentimental virtue is performative.[81] When sentimental protagonists react to obstacles with lucid interior struggles, they not only confirm their virtuous character, these struggles are the form their virtue takes. "Virtue is a state of war . . . to live in it, there is always some combat to be waged against oneself," remarks Julie (607), bearing witness to the truth of Dever's insight.[82] Sentimental virtue thus requires a narrative to unfold. As Constant remarks, "morality needs time."[83] The greater the struggle, the more "touching" the performance, as Genlis proposes in her preface to *Les Mères rivales, ou la Calomnie* (1800). "It is recognized that *dramatically* repentance is more interesting than innocence, that atonement is more touching than perserverance, that virtue that has strayed in an excusable manner and that then recovers with splendour has something more sublime than unshakeable virtue."[84] Genlis's comments make clear one important difference between the eighteenth-century heroine described by Alliston and the protagonist in the sentimental subgenre. In sentimentality, virtue is an active process. It does not necessarily equal all avoidance of fault or even chastity.

The sentimental plot producing virtue exhibits a logic differing substantially from the narrative logic of the realist text. For Roland Barthes, Bal-

---

[81] Dever made this argument in "The Literary Chunnel: Britain, France, and 'the Rise of the Novel,' " a class we team-taught at New York University in the spring of 1996.

[82] Hegel offers a similar observation in the *Philosophy of Right*, differentiating virtue from "simple conformity with the duties" of one's "station" (*PR*, 107). "Virtue in the strict sense of the word is in place and actually appears . . . when one obligation clashes with another" (*PR*, 108).

[83] Constant, *De l'esprit de conquête et de l'usurpation*, 19.

[84] Genlis, *Les Mères rivales, ou la Calomnie*, 1: ix–x.

zac's "classic" narrative engages the reader in a quest of discovery.[85] Isolating two codes that are crucial to this quest, Barthes distinguishes a plot's actions, which he calls the proairetic code, from the way these actions raise interpretive problems, which he calls the hermeneutic code. And as Barthes perceptively observes, hermeneutic and proairetic codes work against each other in classic narrative to maintain the reader's interest. "The dynamics of the text (since it implies a truth to be deciphered) is thus paradoxical. . . . the problem is to *maintain* the enigma in the initial void of its answer; whereas the sentences quicken the story's 'unfolding' and cannot help but move the story along, the hermeneutic code performs an opposite action: it must set up *delays* (obstacles, stoppages, deviations) in the flow of the discourse."[86] While the unfolding events carry the plot along, they must simultaneously block the reader's grasp of their full significance. The reader experiences this interference as suspense.

The sentimental truth, in contrast, emerges from the novel's opening situation, although this truth takes the form of a conflict rather than a discovery. No sentimental text gets to the point more rapidly than *La Nouvelle Héloïse*: "I must flee you, young lady, I know it all too well, I should not have waited so long; or rather, I should never have seen you. But what is to be done today? How should I proceed?" (5). From Saint-Preux's first words, Rousseau establishes the conflict that will produce his protagonists' virtue across the novel, or rather, he suggests the conflict as established even before the narrative begins. In *Claire d'Albe*, Cottin withholds this revelation slightly longer. The reader grasps the substance of the conflict from letter six of forty letters when Claire starts to describe her interactions with Frédéric, but Cottin delays her characters' recognition of the situation until letter eighteen.

In such a situation, hermeneutic and proairetic codes parallel each other. The hermeneutic code rapidly establishes its founding truth and the proairetic code tests this truth's inexorability as it displays the virtue of the novel's protagonists. This dynamic produces a weaker form of suspense than the gripping read of Barthes's classic text. Hermeneutic questions occur on the small scale of the individual episode, as the reader wonders how the protagonists are going to negotiate a particular dilemma instantiating the novel's founding conflict. Rather than suspense, what builds across the sentimental narrative is an increasingly crushing sense that the conflict between collective welfare and individual freedom is inev-

---

[85] Generating his "classic" paradigm of narrative from a Balzac novella, Barthes leaves the realist historiography of the novel unchallenged, his polemic against realism not withstanding. Equating realism with premodernist narrative, he does not allow for the existence of narrative models that fall outside the realism/modernism binary.

[86] Roland Barthes, *S/Z*, 75.

itable. Reiteration after reiteration piles up evidence for the conflict's force until the narrative collapses under the weight of a final disaster.

If some sentimental novels are extremely long, it may result from this distinctive narrative dynamic. In a situation where hermeneutic and pro-airetic codes parallel each other, there is no structural moment when the narrative comes to a close. The anguishes of the double bind can be prolonged as long as characters are willing and able. Hermeneutic and proairetic codes have the potential to run side by side into an ever-receding sunset.

Twentieth-century critics have assailed sentimental narrative structure as repetitious and tedious. Thus, Tanner's analysis of *La Nouvelle Héloïse* dismisses what is in fact the entire substance of the novel's plot: "[I]t is not to my purpose to discuss the [novel's] endless rhetorical twistings and turnings, changes and modifications, etc."[87] As if responding to Tanner's complaints, the only English translation of *La Nouvelle Héloïse* currently in print deletes numerous episodes that try Julie and Saint-Preux's virtue, giving the novel a "classic" narrative dynamic, presumably in order to make it more readable. But we also can understand sentimental narrative logic as intensifying the reader's sympathy with the trials of the protagonist and thereby heightening the power of the sentimental double bind. In making this suggestion, I follow Denis Diderot's opinion on the narrative logic best able to inspire sympathy in "De la poésie dramatique" (1758).

"All should be clear to the spectator," Diderot suggests as guiding narrative principle in his section entitled "De l'intérêt" (Diderot uses the term "interest" in the eighteenth-century sense of inspiring sympathy).[88] Equating the reader's involvement in a narrative with full knowledge rather than enigma, Diderot writes, "I will only have a moment's pity for someone who is struck down in a moment. But what happens if the blow keeps me waiting, if I see the storm brewing, and it then hangs suspended over my head or someone else's for a long time?"[89] "Far from thinking . . . that the play's dénouement should be hidden from the spectator," Diderot proposes as ideal a drama "where the dénouement would be proclaimed from the first scene."[90]

TO INTEREST, TO INSTRUCT

The sentimental novel solicits the reader's sympathy for its protagonists even prior to the events instigating the conflict between collective freedom

[87] Tony Tanner, *Adultery in the Novel*, 115.
[88] Denis Diderot, "De la poésie dramatique," 227.
[89] Ibid.
[90] Ibid, 226, 227.

and individual welfare. Whether they are narrated in the first person or the third person, sentimental novels generally are prefaced with remarks by an authorial persona who engages the reader's "interest" and "sympathy" for the story to come in tones ranging from emphatic moralizing to understatement, if not self-deprecation. The authorial persona frames this "interest" as essential to the narrative's moral significance, its ability to instruct. In doing so, she makes a sentimental version of Hegel's point that the spectator's sympathetic bond with the protagonist heightens the impact of the tragic demonstration.

Although *Claire d'Albe*'s introductory remarks are long on self-deprecation, they are uncharacteristically reticent about soliciting the reader's compassion for the characters. "I feel so keenly all that my novel lacks, that I expect neither my age nor my sex to protect me from criticism," exemplifies the sentiment Cottin reiterates throughout her prefaces. The opening paragraphs to *La Duchesse de la Vallière* by Genlis are more typical. "I wish to paint the flaws of an unhappy love and the disastrous consequences of a guilty passion on the fate of a sensitive [*sensible*] woman born for virtue: let this picture be moral if its colors are true!" (19). And: "Could I but express all she felt, all she suffered! Her historian needs only the exact truth. How could he not interest, not instruct, if he is accurate [*fidèle*]?" (20). In her preface to *Adèle de Sénange*, Souza asks the reader to sympathize with more mundane subject matter than grand passions.

> I simply wanted to show, in life, what is overlooked, and describe those ordinary movements of the heart that comprise everyday history [*l'histoire de chaque jour*]. . . . I thought it would be possible to get fairly close to nature and still inspire interest in limiting depiction to those fleeting details that occupy the space between the events of life. . . . Every moment has its occupation, and every occupation has its motivation [*ressort moral*].[91]

As Genlis and Souza's comments make clear, sentimental novels display the "interest" of struggles located within ordinary existence as well as of exceptional destinies.

ANALYSIS OF THE HEART

To solicit the reader's sympathy, sentimental novels also employ first person forms of private writing exploring interiority, which one eminent early-nineteenth-century critic termed "analyses . . . of the heart [*analyses . . . du coeur humain*]."[92] In the analysis of the heart, protagonists exam-

---

[91] Adélaïde de Souza, *Adèle de Sénange*, 567.
[92] Féletz, review of Constant's *Adolphe*, in *Mélanges de philosophie*, 6: 161.

ine the concrete ramifications of the novel's underwriting moral conflict in vivid if not excruciating detail. We have already seen one passage exemplifying this celebrated sentimental topos where Claire explores her guilt in a letter to Frédéric. Here are two more passages from that same letter: "Frédéric, I love you, I have never loved anyone but you: the image of your happiness, of this happiness you ask from me and that I could offer, distracts my senses and upsets my reason . . . but to buy your happiness with treachery! Frédéric, that you would not wish . . . Madman [*insensé*]! you want Claire to be yours, yours alone! is she then free to give herself? Does she still belong to herself?" (739).[93] And again, "The objects I hold dearest are those I shun with the greatest terror! . . . Even you, Frédéric, I find you unbearable because I adore you; your presence kills me because I no longer have the strength to resist you; and my love only seems a crime to me because I am burning to yield to it" (740).

As is common in the analysis of the heart, these passages set out Claire's feelings in terms highlighting the contradictions of her position. The passages point to the paradoxical consequences were Claire to follow her heart. If she did indeed pursue her happiness, she would also destroy this happiness, for she would break her commitment to collective welfare and thereby lose the moral superiority that makes her worthy of Frédéric's love in the first place.

The analysis of the heart promotes the reader's sympathy for the protagonist in two ways. In this topos, as Claire's comments illustrate, heroines and heroes leave no doubt that they are fully lucid concerning their actions. They thereby reinforce their idealized status claiming our interest; as Hegel writes, "no worse insult could be given [to the tragic protagonist] . . . than to say that he has acted innocently" (*A*, 2:1215). The analysis of the heart also encourages sympathy for the protagonist in its implicit attitude towards the reader. In privileging the reader with their innermost difficulties, protagonists assume the reader to be on their high moral level. The analysis thus gives the reader no choice but to be the person of "noble feelings" whom Hegel suggests as most capable of "true pity." She who reads it must accept the position or default on the sentimental narrative contract.

OH TORMENTS OF AN UNEASY CONSCIENCE!

Another sentimental code soliciting sympathy is emphatic diction. While sentimental narrators generally speak in spare and understated fashion,

---

[93] Cottin here indicates the intensity of Claire's struggle along with her love by having Claire lapse into the familiar *tu* from the formal *vous* she usually uses to address Frédéric. This shift occurs in the sentence following "Madman!": "[Y]ou [*tu*] want Claire to be yours . . ." (739).

their narration modulates at moments of high moral effort. As the protagonist experiences the two conflicting imperatives colliding with full force, the narrative diction becomes inflated and sententious, characterized by distinctive grammatical traits. Whether authorial persona or character, the narrator switches from the past tense to the present tense to convey the urgency of the situation, employing exclamations, rhetorical questions, hyperbole, direct address to the reader or a character standing in for the reader, and the repetition of complex syntactic patterns. The narrator also peppers her or his remarks with moralizing commentary as well as social and psychological maxims. Claire realizes her feelings for Frédéric, for example, in a letter to Elise that ends as follows: "How can I share with you what I suffer? Adèle left yesterday, and since that moment, my husband, worried about my health, leaves me alone as little as he can; I must swallow my tears, I tremble that he might see their trace and guess their cause. He is surprised that I will let no one come into my room. . . . Oh torments of an uneasy conscience! thus, I suspect, in the most truthful, the best of men, dissimulation of which I alone am guilty; and I see all too well that the first punishment of the wicked is to think that others resemble them" (730).

If sentimentality's emphatic narration has been criticized by twentieth-century literary history as didactic and overblown, it too makes sense from the vantage point of Hegel's tragic aesthetic. With such narration, the sentimental novel enacts the gravity of the protagonist's dilemma on the level of rhetoric. Calling attention to the magnitude of the protagonist's struggles, it underlines her or his moral merit crucial to the creation of "tragic sympathy."[94]

TABLEAU

The sentimental novel reinforces the reader's sympathy for its protagonist with the topos of the tableau. When the novel's underwriting conflict reaches such a level of intensity that it threatens to explode, the narration loses access to the protagonist's interiority, as if overcome by the tension it represents. Instead of following the movements of the soul, the narration offers a picture. It describes the protagonist staging the crisis with her or his body. It also reports dialogue, if the protagonist manages to articulate the crisis to a character who plays the role of spectator.

One tableau in *Claire d'Albe* occurs when Claire lets Frédéric know she loves him. Claire narrates this moment in a letter to Elise:

---

[94] Melodrama's use of emphatic rhetoric at moments of high moral effort owes much to the sentimental novel, which predates the theatrical form's invention. The close links be-

"If I love you, Frédéric! dare you ask it? imagine what such a passion must be if it reduces Claire to the state where you see her now; yes, I love you ardently, violently; and in the very moment, when I forget my most sacred duties to tell you this, I delight in the excess of weakness which proves to you my love. Oh, indelible memory of pleasure and of shame!"

At that instant, Frédéric's lips touched mine; I would have been lost, if virtue, in a last effort, had not rent the veil of sensual pleasure enveloping me: wrenching myself from Frédéric's arms, I fell at his feet. (735)

In a physical gesture marking the intensity of her struggle, Claire collapses, her "strength" having been tested to its limit. She then expresses her torment in dialogue where she refers to herself in the third person, as she implores Frédéric not to take advantage of her distress by seducing her: "Frédéric! Frédéric, look at her, prostrate at your feet, and deserve her eternal thanks in not turning her to the lowest of creatures" (735).

In his illuminating analysis, Jay Caplan points out that the tableau occurs at a moment of sacrifice. Sacrifice is a privileged term in the sentimental vocabulary to describe an individual's abnegation of individual freedom out of respect for collective welfare. In the scene from Claire d'Albe, Claire sacrifices happiness to preserve her sworn duty to her husband. Caplan also suggests that the tableau extends sentimental sacrifice beyond the protagonist. Performing a sacrifice, the protagonist not only solicits the beholder's sympathy but encourages the beholder to a sacrifice of her own.[95] By beholder, Caplan designates both the character witnessing the scene and the reader. After observing Claire's gesture in Claire d'Albe, Frédéric responds as if he had read Caplan's analysis. He offers Claire "the greatest sacrifice of which human strength is capable" (736). For him, this sacrifice is restraining the natural impulse to act on his love.

Caplan understands the tableau as both testimony to and consolation for some loss. The tableau "asks the beholder to be partial to the suffering of the represented characters, and thereby also to define himself as the missing part."[96] Caplan makes this generalization starting from the example of a tableau that takes shape around a corpse. If we broaden his notion of loss to insufficiency or incompleteness, Caplan's observation applies to the sentimental novel, too. When Claire falls at Frédéric's feet, she offers

---

tween the sentimental novel and melodrama are indicated by the fact that sentimental novels provide an important source for melodramatic plots, along with the Gothic novel.

[95] Caplan explains tears as playing an important role in the replication of sentimental sacrifice. Caplan comments, "The beholder's tear repeats the sacrifices that the represented characters have made and also represents the beholder's own sacrifice. In the dialogic structure of the tableau, tears perform a triple function . . . : they *relate* a sacrifice, *repeat* it, and *represent*, or *signal* it." Jay Caplan, *Framed Narratives*, 20.

[96] Ibid., 19.

a gesture that dramatizes the impossibility of reconciling the two ethical imperatives in conflict throughout *Claire d'Albe*.

Caplan has argued that the tableau turns the body into a "fetishistic snapshot in which the transitoriness of the real world is magically transformed into an ideal fixity."[97] But the stasis unleashes a kind of ethical movement that supersedes the fetishistic fixation on visual aspect. When the tableau exhibits the heroine wracked in interior torment, it uses her body to call attention to the suffering that is its cause. Displaying the material to point to the moral, the tableau treats materiality in a fashion similar to the sentimental blazon and the image of the heart.

In *Claire d'Albe*, the tableau solicits our sympathy for Claire's moral effort by means of a body that we have been told is attractive. Caplan rightly talks about the "strange eroticism" of the tableau, its use of a body "seductive in its vulnerability."[98] For Caplan, this alignment of ethics and erotics is perverse: the "tableau is ethically, and *therefore* erotically moving, a perversity that is too frequently overlooked. Once one has recognized this erotic dimension of the tableau, it becomes difficult to view the device as simply a maudlin appeal to middle-class values."[99] But middle-class ideology works through depicting the ethical as erotic, as Armstrong has argued of British domestic fiction contemporary with the sentimental novel. In the tableau, too, eroticism heightens its ideological appeal, although in France this ideology is hybrid rather than specifically middle-class. Claire at Frédéric's feet is the tragic pendant to Darcy declaring himself to Elizabeth in *Pride and Prejudice* or Wentworth and Anne Elliot reconciled in *Persuasion*. The sentimental blazon works in similar fashion when it subordinates the material to the moral via a traditional topos of desire.

A SECURE REFUGE

Explaining how the tragic dénouement vindicates rationality, Hegel hinges this restoration above all on one tragic code. The chorus reassures spectators unsettled by the excesses of the protagonists with its sympathetic, judicious, and contemplative commentary on the action. Offsetting the "fearful collisions" of the protagonists, "the chorus gives us . . . the consciousness that such a secure refuge ["the equilibrium of a stable life"] is actually present" (*A*, 2:1211). In the sentimental novel, in contrast, "statues stand under the open sky without such a background," to cite

---

[97] Ibid., 18.
[98] Ibid., 21.
[99] Ibid.

Hegel on modern as opposed to classical tragedy (*A*, 2:1211). And without the guarantee offered by the chorus, what would safeguard the sentimental novel's portrayal of extremes from completely unhinging the moral order? This risk might seem intensified by the inherently private experience of reading a novel.

But I think the sentimental novel does "give us . . . the consciousness that such a secure refuge is present" in a fashion specific to its genre. Sentimental codes, such as *idealized characters, all should be clear, to interest, to instruct*, the *analysis of the heart, emphatic narration*, and the *tableau*, do more than promote the reader's sympathetic involvement in moral conflict. In addition, they help create a community of readers that is the novelistic equivalent to Hegel's chorus and that is essential to the successful persuasions of the sentimental dénouement. Diderot offers insight into how codes soliciting sympathy help restore the moral order in his "Eloge de Richardson," which remains one of the best analyses of the sentimental aesthetic.

In this essay, Diderot is interested above all in tracing the effect of the sentimental novel on the reader. Diderot paints the reader's sympathetic response to Richardson's novels as a form of the sublime. When the reader witnesses the sufferings of virtuous protagonists, she does not experience their inner conflicts directly. Rather, the reader pities them at a pleasurable aesthetic distance: Diderot writes of Richardson's novels as inducing "a feeling of melancholy, both pleasing and enduring."[100] Elsewhere he qualifies the sentimental sublime as the "pleasure of feeling compassion [*s'attendrir*] and shedding tears."[101]

Sympathizing with the protagonists' sufferings, the reader enters into a community with them. Aestheticized misery, moreover, loves company. Diderot places the sentimental community of reader and text on a continuum with a community of all sympathetic readers. Just as we cry for the protagonists, sentimentality promises, others will cry for us, and, indeed, others are already sharing our own sweet pleasure. "Come and learn . . . how to come to terms [*vous reconcilier*] with the evils of life," Diderot declares of the response provoked by Richardson, "come, we shall weep together over the unfortunates in his stories, and we will say: 'If fate casts us down, at least honest [*honnêtes*] folk will also weep over us.' "[102] Diderot repeatedly emphasizes the power of the sentimental novel to generate a community of readers, whether one reads it in private or aloud with others: "I have observed that, among people who read Richardson to-

---

[100] Diderot, "In Praise of Richardson," 85.

[101] Diderot, "Poésie," 189.

[102] Diderot, "Richardson," 85.

gether or separately, the conversation was all the more interesting and lively."[103]

This community of sympathetic readers reassures the reader concerning the stability of the ethical order in counterpoint to the disruptive actions represented by the novel. It offers reassurance in a somewhat different fashion, however, from the "secure refuge" of Hegel's tragic chorus speaking with one voice. When Diderot writes of the "lively" conversations that result from reading Richardson, he points out that readers not only cry over Richardson's texts, they also discuss "the conduct of the characters" and "the most important questions concerning morality and taste."[104] In the process, they enter into disagreement. "I have seen how the diversity of judgements gave rise to secret grudges, hidden contempt, in fact the same divisions between united friends [*personnes unies*] as if they had been involved in some serious dispute [*l'affaire la plus sérieuse*]."[105]

In depicting the community of sympathetic readers as rife with dissension, Diderot might seem to undercut this community's ability to offset the excesses of the sentimental plot. Rather than simply crying together, readers of sentimental novels engage in conflict and specifically in a conflict whose terms resemble those at stake in the sentimental double bind. In their experience of the "divisions between united friends," sentimental readers confront the difficulty of reconciling individual judgments within a collective context and the potential of clashing judgments to destroy community. But Diderot qualifies the conflicts of sentimental readers with the crucial aesthetic "as if [*que si*]." Readers experience the collision between individual freedom and collective welfare in the aesthetic sphere, which Diderot distances from the sphere of action.

The sentimental novel thus offers specific consolations for political tension as well as general reassurance concerning the power of reason. It creates a community where readers play with the conflict between negative and positive notions of rights in the form of the conflict between freedom of judgment and collective consensus; where readers enjoy the dissension threatening the very integrity of the social order as the dissension of taste. In offering aesthetic community as a safe substitute for the conflict between negative and positive notions of rights, the sentimental novel exemplifies what Jochen Schulte-Sasse characterizes as the Enlightenment understanding of the social function of literature more generally: "to reconcile the interests of the individual with the interests of the general."[106] The conflicted nature of sentimental community, however, complicates Schulte-Sasse's description of aesthetic reconciliation as unification.

[103] Ibid., 88.
[104] Ibid.
[105] Ibid., 88–89.
[106] Jochen Schulte-Sasse, afterword to Caplan, 112.

Diderot writes, "all that Montaigne, Charron, La Rochefoucauld and Nicole expressed in maxims, Richardson has expressed in actions."[107] If we accept the distance he maintains between sentimental representation and reader, it becomes clear that sentimentality's moral lessons differ substantially from the vulgar mimesis anti-sentimental writers love to parody.[108] Rather than exhorting the reader to the heroics of its protagonists, the sentimental novel allows her to explore the contradictions that produce them. "What is virtue?" asks Diderot, to which he answers, "a sacrifice of oneself."[109] This statement resonates very differently for sentimental protagonist and sentimental reader. While a heroine like Clarissa experiences sacrifice as a painful loss, the armchair heroine recuperates sacrifice as a liberating gain. Suspending her own interests to engage Richardson's fictional world, she discovers a realm of play rather than the rigors of ethical duties.

Diderot registers the difference between the sacrifice of the protagonist and the sacrifice of the reader when he continues, "The sacrifice one makes of oneself in imagination [en idée] is a preconceived inclination to do the same in reality."[110] Diderot's choice of words is telling: experiencing sentimental sacrifice "in imagination [en idée]" creates a "preconceived inclination"; it does not produce direct imitation. Indeed, Diderot presents the sentimental text as actively discouraging its readers from translating its representations directly into their own lives. His enjoyment of Richardson interrupted "by important activities [occupations sérieuses]," Diderot comments, "I felt an overwhelming reluctance [dégoût]; I abandoned my duties [le devoir] and took up Richardson's book again."[111]

"TRAGEDY NOW IS POLITICS" (NAPOLEON, 1799)

When Peter Szondi analyzes the aesthetics of sentimentality in an article on Diderot and eighteenth-century bourgeois drama, he proposes sentimentality as the consolation of a class blocked from political power. In

---

[107] Diderot, "Richardson," 82.

[108] At the beginning of *Justine ou les malheurs de la vertu*, for example, Sade sends up sentimentality for asking readers to imitate completely unrealistic lessons of suffering virtue. He comments, "It is cruel, to be sure, to be obliged to describe a host of misfortunes overwhelming the sweet and sensitive [sensible] woman who most respects Virtue. . . . And yet if some good arises from the representation [tableau] of these adversities, can one regret having depicted them? Can one regret having stated a fact from which the wise reader will derive the profitable lesson of submission to the decrees of Providence?" Donatien Alphonse François de Sade, *Justine or the Misfortunes of Virtue*, 2.

[109] Diderot, "Richardson," 83.

[110] Ibid.

[111] Ibid, 85.

Szondi's account, sentimental texts depict a purely private form of virtue that consoles the citizen for "the intrigues and wickedness of society within the security of his four walls." This citizen is the bourgeois citizen "deprived of his rights" under absolute monarchy.[112]

My argument for the social significance of the sentimental novel has modified Szondi's analysis in important ways. First of all, I have suggested a community of sentimental readers as crucial to sentimental consolation. This community does not constitute a private refuge from public life. Rather, it exemplifies in microcosm the liberal public sphere where unity takes the form of debate and conflict; "the diversity of judgements," to use Diderot's term. The liberal public sphere is a form of social organization with substantial political power. Historians from Tocqueville to Furet have, for instance, credited the liberal public sphere with a role in catalyzing the French Revolution.

To put my differences with Szondi in terms of the social group whose values are at issue in sentimentality: the sentimental novel engages one important tension in the ideology of a hybrid class crossing traditional class distinctions that is far from completely "deprived of its rights." This hybrid class is certainly blocked from a full exercise of political power before the Revolution in ways that differ for the *noblesse de robe*, the *noblesse d'épée*, and the bourgeoisie. But it nonetheless already has substantial political, cultural, and economic importance in the second half of the eighteenth century and will emerge to hegemony with the Revolution. Indeed, if the sentimental novel takes shape while this hybrid class is still dominated, it enjoys the most critical and economic success when the class triumphs, albeit in a situation of symbolic and political disarray. We come to the question of the sentimental novel's relation to the Revolution. If sentimentality is among several significant novelistic subgenres before the Revolution, why does the form become so important in its wake?

When materialist critics explain the ascendancy of nineteenth-century realism, they propose its codes as persuasively addressing the ideological contradictions that resulted from France's transformation into a hub of nineteenth-century modernity. Similarly, we may understand the sentimental novel's boom at the turn of the nineteenth century as resulting from the power of its aesthetic problem-solving in the aftermath of the Revolution. Before the Revolution, the sentimental novel resolves a key problem confronting a powerful, emerging ideology. With the Revolution, this resolution takes on profound collective resonance, for the tensions at stake in sentimentality are both a source and synecdoche of contemporary social devastation. Across the historiographical spectrum, historians represent the Revolution's tragedies in terms that make French history resem-

---

[112] Szondi, "*Tableau* and *Coup de Théâtre*," 335.

ble a sentimental novel. They show the conflict between negative and positive rights to be both one among many reasons for the Revolution's inability to come up with a stable form of political organization and a privileged way this inability is identified in Revolutionary debate.

The tension between negative and positive notions of rights already appears in the epoch-making "Declaration of the Rights of Man and the Citizen" (1789) which is, as Etienne Balibar observes, "an intrinsically equivocal text."[113] From the words of its title, the Declaration cannot find a single term to define the new political subject created by the Revolution. This subject is both "man" and "citizen," as the Declaration splits the subject's private rights to the enjoyment of personal life from his public rights to participate in government. In an analysis of the Declaration that we have seen Furet and Ozouf extend to "the French case" in general, J. Kent Wright remarks: "[T]he French Constituent Assembly tried to synthesize two distinct conceptions of liberty: the liberal conception characterizing the Anglo-American tradition, which consists in protecting natural rights of individuals against all encroachment of power; and the conception according to which liberty exists fully only in the individual's participation in the collective."[114]

The Constituent Assembly sought to resolve the ambiguities of the Declaration through law. It initially established "two categories of citizen—the active and the passive," to cite Joan Scott: those citizens enjoying both positive and negative rights and those enjoying only negative rights. This distinction continued to inform subsequent articulations of citizenship, "even if it was no longer mentioned in official political documents."[115] In an argument suggestive for women writers' prominent role in the sentimental novel at the turn of the nineteenth century, Scott points out that women were assigned the status of passive citizens throughout the Revolution, although they had entered it demanding a place in the res publica. Scott proposes that this outcome produced a specifically female experience of the conflict between negative and positive notions of rights, which she credits with the birth of modern feminism.

But legislative compromise failed to dissipate this conflict, which came to a head in the Terror. As Simon Schama observes, "The Terror thus represented the liquidation of the initial dream of the Revolution: that liberty and patriotic power were not only reconcilable but mutually de-

[113] Balibar, "Citizen Subject," 44.

[114] Furet and Ozouf, preface to *Siècle*, 12. J. Kent Wright, "Les sources républicains de la Déclaration des droits," in Furet and Ozouf, 162. Wright bases his comments on Philippe Raynaud's "La Déclaration des droits de l'homme," in *The French Revolution and the Creation of Modern Political Culture*, edited by Colin Lucas. On the tensions between negative and positive rights in Revolutionary ideology, see also Lucien Jaume's *Echec au libéralisme*.

[115] Joan Scott, *Only Paradoxes to Offer*, 35.

pendent."[116] Claude Lefort argues that the nightmares of the Terror exhibit a fundamental revolutionary phantasm where the conflict between negative and positive notions of rights appears in demonized form. This phantasm expresses positive rights in the person of "a new man whose vocation it is to become a universal historical agent, and whose public existence merges with his private existence: the revolutionary militant." To this ideal, the Revolution opposes the individual rapaciously pursuing "the egotism of interests."[117]

The sentimental novel thus has the unhappy good fortune to diagnose one of the most spectacular tensions fissuring Revolutionary efforts to put into place a new society. For confirmation that this tension takes on particular urgency in the wake of the Revolution, we have only to look to Constant, both sentimental novelist and political theorist. In justifying his theoretical efforts to clarify the relation of negative to positive rights, Constant points to recent social catastrophe. "But if law stipulated, as it often did during the years of trouble, if it stipulated, I say, to trample on our affections and our duties, if . . . it forbade us to be faithful to our unhappy friends . . . anathema and disobedience to the drafting of injustices and crimes thus dressed up in the name of law!"[118] I cite this version of Constant's observation because it shows how intertwined sentimental rhetoric has become with the problem of accommodating negative and positive rights. To make the potential violations of individual freedom vivid, Constant imagines what could be the plot of a sentimental novel. He solicits our sympathy for a conflict between public law and private *devoirs*, using sentimentality's emphatic diction at moments of moral crisis.[119]

---

[116] Simon Schama, *Citizens*, 755.

[117] Claude Lefort, *Democracy and Political Theory*, 106, 107.

[118] Constant, *Annexes* to the *Principes*, 439. Hegel, too, cites the Terror as an impetus to define freedom in the *Philosophy of Right*. While both link the Terror's abuse of freedom to Rousseau, they split the liberal double bind in how they explain his harmful influence. Constant ascribes the Terror to an abuse of positive rights encouraged by the notion of the general will. Stressing the Romantic side of Rousseau, Hegel, in contrast, censures a way of looking at freedom "especially popular since Rousseau, according to which what is fundamental, substantive, and primary is supposed to be the will of a single person in his own private self-will . . . and mind as a particular individual, not mind as it is in its truth. . . . And the phenomena which it has produced both in men's heads and in the world are of a frightfulness parallel only to the superficiality of the thoughts on which they are based" (*PR*, 33).

[119] Constant often formulates the conflict between negative and positive notions of rights with a sentimental vocabulary of duty, sacrifice, compassion, and virtue. In the *Principes de politique*, for example, he writes: "We owe public peace [*repos public*] many sacrifices; we would be guilty in the eyes of morality if we resisted all laws that seemed to violate them by too inflexible an attachment to our rights; but no duty binds us to those laws . . . that . . . order us to actions that go against those eternal principles of justice and pity" (275).

In invoking sentimental rhetoric to describe Revolutionary turmoil, Constant echoes the rhetorical practice of revolutionaries across the political spectrum. David Denby perspicaciously observes that "the language of sentimentalism is a structuring force in some of the key debates of the Revolution."[120] As Denby's examples make clear, Revolutionary rhetoric is filled with hyperbolic displays of emotions, the solicitation of sympathy for suffering, and a vocabulary of sentimental moral abstractions including virtue, sacrifice, pity, and duty.

When Denby explains the sentimental character of Revolutionary virtue, he persuasively shows that revolutionaries make great use of a conflict pitting suffering, oppressed, and often enfeebled virtue against empowered vice. But Denby's notion of virtue is melodramatic, not sentimental, although Denby subsumes both melodrama and the sentimental novel into a cultural discourse that he calls "sentimentalism." In the sentimental novel, virtue is not one term in a Manichean opposition but rather a response to the conflict between two equally valid imperatives, collective welfare and individual freedom. And the sentimental novel's notion of virtue figures prominently in Revolutionary rhetoric along with melodramatic virtue.

Robespierre, for example, calls on sentimental virtue to justify the Terror's suspension of political opposition and personal liberty. "What is virtue?" we have seen Diderot query, to which he responds, "a sacrifice of oneself." Robespierre would agree. "What! have we made so many heroic sacrifices, including painfully harsh acts, have we made these sacrifices only to fall again under the yoke of a few plotters?" he asks, praising himself and "the French people," as he warms up to his accusation of Danton on 11 Germinal.[121] With his assertion that sacrifice drives Revolutionary action, Robespierre lays the groundwork for Danton's crimes: "Citizens, the moment has come to speak the truth. In everything that

---

[120] Denby, *Sentimental Narrative*, 154. Nowhere are the Revolution's links to sentimentality made more explicit than in England. As Nicola Watson notes, "revolutionary politics were understood crucially in terms of sentimental fiction—and in particular the plot of a single novel, *La Nouvelle Héloïse*" (*Revolution*, 4). In these responses, the Revolution becomes the consequence of a sentimental challenge to received authority; indeed, Watson cites writings that attribute the Revolution to marital disobedience encouraged by sentimental novels. Watson also shows that British writers who emplotted the Revolution sympathetically framed it in sentimental terms. In her *Letters from France*, for example, Helen Maria Williams offers tales depicting young lovers separated by ancien régime fathers.

[121] Robespierre's words are quoted in J.-B. Buchez and P.-C. Roux, *Histoire parlémentaire de la Révolution française*, 70. In defining virtue as painful sacrifice, Robespierre significantly modifies the political rhetoric of Roman antiquity, which constitutes one of his important inspirations. Cicero's speeches, for example, define virtue as "military prowess, bravery, and excellence," to cite Werner Eisenhut's *Virtus romana*, 52. These speeches also have nothing of Robespierre's emphatic diction soliciting the listener's sympathy.

has been said, I can find only ominous signs of the destruction of freedom and the decadence of principles. Who in fact are these men who sacrifice the interests of the fatherland [*patrie*] to personal connections, to fear perhaps?"[122] While Robespierre's own revolutionary sacrifice, like that of the French people, gives up personal freedom for the public good, Danton has betrayed "the interests of the country" to a degraded personal freedom taking the form of "personal connections" and "fear." In doing so, he undermines freedom along with morality and perverts revolutionary sacrifice into treason.

The sentimental notion of virtue as sacrifice crosses political affiliation. When Charlotte Corday defends her murder of Marat to the Revolutionary Tribunal, she paints herself as sacrificing her private existence to follow her collective duty. "Corday: 'I have never lacked energy.' Montané: 'What do you mean by energy?' Corday: 'Those who put their own interests to one side and know how to sacrifice themselves for the *patrie*.' "[123] In her defense, Corday not only invokes sentimental sacrifice, she gestures to an important literary source for the sentimental tradition. A direct descendant of Corneille, Corday presents herself as one of her "ancestor Corneille's tragic heroines, dying in virtue."[124]

The importance of sentimentality in Revolutionary self-representation may help explain the power of the sentimental novel in the Revolution's wake. Besides diagnosing a key tension thwarting Revolutionary efforts to invent a new society, sentimentality offers the rhetoric in which this tension is fought out. The sentimental novel, we might say, stands in the same relation to the Revolution as David's 1785 *Oath of the Horatii*, often cited as an emblem of Revolutionary hopes and failures, though the picture predates the Revolution by several years. Like the sentimental novel, David's painting diagnoses the conflict between negative and positive rights that will fissure the Revolution.[125] And revolutionaries borrow from this painting, as from the sentimental novel, to invent the Revolution's distinctive symbolic vocabulary.

In confirming the sentimental novel's social acumen, the Revolution also transforms the content of sentimental consolation. Before the Revolution, the community of sympathetic readers resolves the tensions of an

---

[122] Robespierre in Buchez and Roux, *Histoire*, 71.

[123] Cited in Schama, *Citizens*, 738.

[124] Ibid., 739. As Schama points out, Corday refers her actions to the plays of Thomas, not Pierre.

[125] Indeed, the story of the Horatii exemplifies the conflicting notions of rights at issue in French liberalism even better than *Antigone*. The Horatii's sister, Camille, loves a son of the family that her brothers and father challenge to battle in order to preserve their country. She thus resists collective welfare in the name of individual freedom and erotic love rather than in the name of the family and the cult of the dead.

ideology that has not yet been tested in the political arena. After the Revolution, it reconstitutes a collective that has been shattered by its inability to make this ideology work in practice. Following the Revolution, sentimental representation thus becomes a form of mourning. Mourning works through sympathetic identification, only the sympathetic bond is with an object that is lost rather than present.[126]

Sentimental novels register this shift in ideological work following the Revolution as a shift in tone rather than as the transformation of any poetic code. Post-Revolutionary sentimental novels frequently invent extreme situations of suffering to test their protagonists and are strewn with deathbed scenes and melancholy pathologies. This shift in tone, apparent to critics at the time, was perhaps most eloquently formulated in the 1818 article previously cited to vindicate Cottin's representation of love as individual freedom resisting the Terror. To highlight the historical specificity of Cottin's novels, the article contrasted them with the novels of the ancien régime, which it epitomized with Riccoboni.[127] Riccoboni's works express the dissatisfaction of a society whose political and juridical institutions lag behind the way people actually live: "The ancien régime, which, truth be told, was never constituted as such, was completely dissolving. The Revolution had already been effected in manners, while authority was still trying to restrain institutions and laws, which provoked society's general malaise." Placing Cottin's novels on the other side of a Revolutionary divide, the article attributed their feverish tone to recent social cataclysm. "It is easy to recognize, from her burning ardor and the catastrophes in which she evidently delights, that she wrote in unhappy times, when social upheaval, the terrible disruptions of life, and the continual danger of losing it still excited in young people the stormy passion of love . . . and the fervent novices of both sexes encouraged each other to gather the martyr's palms."[128] From malaise to martyrdom: the distinction captures the post-Revolutionary sentimental novel's heightened drama as well as the grief resonating in its affirmation of reason and community.

[126] On mourning, sympathy, and the Revolution, see my "Melancholy, Mania, and the Reproduction of the Dead Father," in *Corinne: New Critical Perspectives*, edited by Karyna Szmurlo.

[127] In fact, however, Riccoboni's novels are on the cusp of the paradigm I am describing. While they grapple with the tension between individual freedom and collective welfare, they lack the plot of double bind. In the *Lettres de Mistriss Fanni Butlerd* (1757), for example, the heroine suffers from the clash between these two imperatives, but she herself does not confront a moral dilemma. Fanni unconflictedly advocates individual freedom, along with the need to respect freely contracted obligations to others, in contrast to the negative version of collective obligation embodied in Lord Alfred's treacherous betrayal of Fanni to marry a woman who will enhance his social standing.

[128] Review of the complete works of Riccoboni and Cottin, 14.

CHAPTER II

The Novel Is a Young Man of Great Expectations:
Realism against Sentimentality

SO WOMEN WROTE UNDER THE EMPEROR?

Balzac sets his most extensive discussion of the early-nineteenth-century novel in the salon of Dinah de la Baudraye, provincial woman of letters, where the leading local luminaries have gathered for an evening's entertainment. On this night in 1836, Dinah has a treat in store for her audience: two visiting native sons who have made good in Paris, the journalist, Etienne Lousteau, and the doctor, Horace Bianchon. Bored in the wasteland of the provinces and eager to impress his hostess, Lousteau is negligently examining some proofs he has received from his Parisian newspaper. "But look at the nicest novel ever, contained on the paper wrapping your proofs," remarks Bianchon, ever the acute observer. "See, read here: *Olympia ou les Vengeances romaines.*"[1] The first thing Lousteau and Bianchon notice about these pages testifies to the importance then accorded genre: *Olympia* is a *roman noir*. Who, they next ask, was the novel's author? The question turns into a parlor game as the cultivated members of the party close-read textual fragments Balzac has reproduced literatim.

"The style is weak; maybe the writer worked as a tax collector, he composed the novel to pay his tailor," Lousteau speculates (241). But as Lousteau looks more closely at the book, its engravings raise his estimation of its author's influence. "To have had vignettes that were woodcuts, the author must have been a member of the Council of State or Madame Barthélemy-Hadot, the late Desforges or Sewrin" (244). Lousteau drops Desforges and Sewrin as possibilities without comment for reasons evident to anyone conversant in the literature of the time: both write *romans gais*, and the pages in question belong to a *roman noir*. Noticing the typos, he further narrows his speculations. "Obviously, neither Maradan, the Treutels and Wurtz, nor Doguereau printed that novel . . . because they had proofreaders working for them who would send back the proofs. . . . It must have been some low-rent printer on the Seine" (246). "In any case, it was no member of the Council of State," Bianchon follows up. "Maybe

---

[1] Balzac, *La Muse du département*, 239. Subsequent page references will appear parenthetically in the text.

it is Madame Hadot," proffers Lousteau (246). Barthélemy Hadot's name is not familiar to the provincials watching the display of critical acumen. "Why are they getting Madame Hadot de la Charité involved in this?" asks one of them, referring to a local lady. "This Madame Hadot," answers the woman of letters, "was a woman writer who lived during the Consulate...—So women were writing under the Emperor?" another provincial asks. "And Madame de Genlis, and Madame de Staël?" says one of the hostess's admirers, who is "nettled on Dinah's behalf by this observation," as the narrator remarks (246).

Twentieth-century literary historians resemble Balzac's clueless provincials in part because of the realist position-taking against sentimentality exemplified by this scene. In the exchanges around *Olympia*, Balzac illustrates an important rhetorical strategy in the realist polemic against the sentimental form: the gesture of simultaneous erasure and denigration. "The literature of the Empire" at issue in *La Muse du département* is, after all, that of the years when sentimental works took the novel by storm (249). Balzac both obliquely refers to these works and skirts them when he names their authors, but epitomizes the literature produced during these years with a *roman noir*. Sentimental authors/literature of the Empire/*roman noir*: with this slippage, Balzac first of all suggests the antiquated character of early-nineteenth-century novels. As the literary critics of *La Muse du département* point out, the *roman noir* belongs to bygone times: "The novel is from the good old days of Anne Radcliffe," is the title to one of *La Muse du département*'s chapters on *Olympia*. But while the *roman noir* peaked in popularity in the 1790s to 1810s, the dominant sentimental novels of the post-Revolutionary decades remained widely read throughout the first half of the nineteenth century.[2] Balzac reinforces his suggestion that novels written in the post-Revolutionary decades belong to the past by periodizing the early-nineteenth-century novel in political terms. Politics and the novel are, however, in a relation of unequal development in the years 1790–1830, and the dominant subgenre of the Empire has not yet been exiled from the balance of European novelistic power.

Balzac's slippage also implies the low literary merit of all early-nineteenth-century novels, including his unnamed competition. The *roman noir* enjoyed economic success, but received little critical respect even at the height of its appeal. As we have seen, this was not the case of the prominent sentimental novels of the post-Revolutionary years, which remained appreciated until the middle of the century. Sainte-Beuve's article on Souza in *La Revue des Deux Mondes* (1834) states an opinion com-

---

[2] Lyons places Staël's *Corinne* and Cottin's *Elisabeth* on his list of the top best-sellers of 1836–40, but makes no mention of any Gothic novels. No novels by Balzac make it onto the best-seller list during this time.

mon in criticism of the 1830s and 1840s: "Among novelistic inventions that have achieved the reality of life, Adèle de Sénange [Souza] is definitely the sister of Valérie [Krüdener], just as she is also the sister of Virginie [Saint-Pierre], Mademoiselle de Clermont [Genlis], and the Princess of Clèves [Lafayette], and as Eugène de Rothelin [Souza] is a worthy brother of Adolphe [Constant], Edouard [Duras]. . . . he [sic] who will give birth to a being worthy of their company is fortunate indeed."[3]

La Muse du département reinforces Balzac's insinuation that his novelistic predecessors lacked literary merit through the specific author he associates with Olympia, Madame Barthélemy Hadot, known both for her romans noirs and her sentimental novels set in the historical past. Barthélemy Hadot's popular appeal can be gauged from the fact that her portrait graced the frontispiece to Antoine Marc's 1819 Dictionnaire des romans counseling booksellers on the novels that would draw the largest audience. When it came to literary value, however, Barthélemy Hadot was ranked in the second tier. "Her novels do not shine for their style, but they are the fruit of dazzling imagination and of feeling. The success of her novels can be judged by the speed with which they disappear," was Pigoreau's estimation of Barthélemy Hadot in his Petite Bibliographie biographico-romancière (1821).[4]

Is Barthélemy Hadot in fact the author of Olympia ou les Vengeances romaines? "In the end, it must be admitted that this text is quite simply by Balzac," Bernard Guyon comments in his introduction to La Muse du département, after "a scholarly hunt" for sources (120). When the roman noir depicts persecuted virtue, the persecutor is usually an empowered, sexualized man and the victim a passive, attractive young woman.[5] Bal-

---

[3] Sainte-Beuve, "Madame de Souza," 699. This opinion persisted throughout the 1830s and 1840s. "Calixte [sic] is one of those novels that are not written much today, where the heart prevails over imagination . . . where the author prefers to paint true sentiments simply rather than to stage bizarre adventures with an emphatic style," declared an unsigned review of Charrière's sentimental novel Caliste (286). When an 1837 review awards "the prize for the novel of private life [roman intime] to women," it illustrates the accepted contemporary ranking of the sentimental novel over the Gothic that was the unspoken context framing Balzac's polemic. Naming Radcliffe as preeminent along with Staël, Cottin, and Sand, the review praised Radcliffe by grouping her with noted authors in the sentimental lineage, in contrast to La Muse du département's use of the roman noir to erase sentimentality. Review signed L.D. of Régina, 8.

[4] Pigoreau, Petite Bibliographie (1821), 214.

[5] I owe this insight to April Alliston. Alliston observes two variations on this scenario: The sexualized persecuting man sometimes locks up a man of sensibility, and the persecutor of the young woman may be a vain, older woman seeking to upstage the young woman with her own sex appeal even though the young woman is infinitely more desirable. See Alliston's chapter on The Recess in Virtue's Faults for an illuminating discussion of the gender politics of Gothic persecution as well as the links between the Gothic and eighteenth-century novels of sensibility.

Madame Barthélemy Hadot, frontispiece to *Dictionnaire des romans anciens et modernes* by Antoine Marc, 1819.

zac's pastiche, however, reverses the typical gendering of the Gothic scenario of persecution. In *Olympia ou les Vengeances romaines*, the female protagonist is, as Dinah recognizes, "*An older woman* [*Une femme de trente ans*]!" Or rather, Olympia, the Duchess of Bracciano, pushes her effrontery farther than any adulterous woman in Balzac's novels set in post-Revolutionary France. Not only has the Duchess imprisoned her husband in a cage, the better to enjoy the embraces of her young French lover named Adolphe, appropriately for a novel taking a position against sentimentality, she also spices her freedom with libertine cruelty. As the Duke explains to a man who rescues him, "In the evenings, I crossed the floorboards, hoisted by a cleverly arranged counterweight, and saw the Duchess in the arms of her lover; she threw me a piece of bread, my nightly pittance. This has been my life for thirty months!" (251). If Balzac's fantasy of menacing and empowered femininity locking up the rightful male ruler is nowhere in the *roman noir*, might it be a response to the prominent women who were his literary competition when he started writing? The Gothic trope of the imprisoned, persecuted wife originates, to my knowledge, with the celebrated *Adèle et Théodore* (1782) by Genlis.[6]

Balzac pursues his simultaneous erasure and denigration of the dominant post-Revolutionary novels in his few explicit comments on the sentimental form. Speaking favorably of sentimentality, Balzac writes, "The true novel distills to two hundred pages in which there are two hundred events. Nothing betrays the impotence of the author more than heaping up facts. Without establishing this observation as a system, I would point out how few facts there are in the works of the skillful novelists (*Werther, Clarissa, Adolphe, Paul et Virginie*). Talent shines forth in painting the causes that beget facts, in the mysteries of the human heart, whose movements are neglected by historians."[7] Goethe, Richardson, Constant, Saint-Pierre: the category of masculinity offers Balzac a way to elide his major generic competition even as he authorizes his own claims to inherit the sentimental mantle. Balzac must, however, engage in dubious literary criticism to masculinize the sentimental lineage entirely. While *Clarissa* does inaugurate the sentimental double bind between collective welfare and individual freedom, it hardly exemplifies the restrained narration that Balzac admires in sentimentality. *La Princesse de Clèves* offers a better early example of Balzac's formula for sentimental classicism: "two hundred pages . . . two hundred events," and it was commonly placed at the inception of the sentimental genealogy by Balzac's contemporaries.

Balzac's substitution of *Clarissa* for *La Princesse de Clèves* is only one way his genealogy runs counter to the critical commonplaces of his time. As previously cited reviews indicate, critics throughout the first half of the nineteenth century accorded female writers expertise over all areas of

---

[6] The novel contains a framed narrative where a virtuous Duchess describes how her jealous, proud husband imprisoned her in a basement underneath his chateau for a betrayal she did not commit. Genlis was an important source for Anne Radcliffe. For an overview of French-British literary exchange in the history of the Gothic, see Alice M. Killen's *Le Roman terrifiant*. The Gothic does contain women who flaunt their sexuality, but, as Alliston observes in *Virtue's Faults*, these women are generally widows in competition with a younger woman, who is often a blood relation.

[7] Balzac, "Lettres sur la littérature, le théâtre, et les arts," no. 1, 278.

private life. To recall this view, I choose an example that makes clear the overlap between sentimental concerns and Balzac's ambitions in *La Comédie humaine*. In the *Avant-Propos*, Balzac extolls himself for depicting "the history forgotten by so many historians, the history of manners."[8] With this statement, he appropriates standard critical praise for sentimentality:

> It has been said that love, merely an episode in the existence of men, is the entire existence of women. The novel should then be for them what history is for us. . . . This branch of literature belongs to them; it exists only through them and for them. . . . if history keeps a faithful record of all the events of public life, if its task is to depict the passions of the senate and the forum, private life [*la vie intérieure*] fell to the novel; the domestic hearth is its domain, the novel observes and reproduces its storms and paints all its torments as well as the joys of the heart, and even though these narratives are called fables, their truth assures their success.[9]

If Balzac is so concerned to denigrate sentimentality, as we will see, it is not simply because the subgenre dominates the novel when he starts writing but because he lays claim to important features of its project.

One would certainly never know that any serious history was at stake in sentimentality from the scant instances where Balzac mentions important early-nineteenth-century sentimental novels by name. In these moments, Balzac uses a rhetoric of femininity to trivialize sentimental novels as appealing to sexually frustrated women's overheated imaginations. *Corinne* inspires pretentious aging blue-stockings like Madame de Bargeton who seduces Lucien by "counterfeiting the improvisations that disfigure the novel" (64). Meanwhile, Genlis's *La Duchesse de La Vallière* appeals to naive adolescents like Louise de Chaulieu at the beginning of the *Mémoires des deux jeunes mariées*, compensating for the boredom of convent education: "To be alone in the convent of the Carmelites at Blois, beset by fears about becoming a nun there, without the preface of Mademoiselle de La Vallière and without my Renée! what an illness, a fatal illness."[10]

NOVELS FOR CHAMBERMAIDS AND SALON NOVELS

The early-nineteenth-century sentimental novel along with its prominent female practitioners do not fare much better at the hands of Stendhal. As Waller observes, "While Stendhal gave explicit and implicit homage . . .

---

[8] Balzac, *Avant-propos*, 11.

[9] Review of *Vanina d'Ornano*, 3–4.

[10] Balzac, *Mémoires de deux jeunes mariées*, 196. Subsequent page references will appear parenthetically in the text

to women writers long gone, his attitude toward the female authors who were his contemporaries and rivals was problematic at best."[11] Stendhal offers an exemplary display of this attitude in his 1832 "Appendice" to *Le Rouge et le noir*, where he exalts his work by comparing it to the state of the French novel before he appeared.

In the "Appendice," Stendhal characterizes the novels of the first decades of the nineteenth century by focusing on their readership rather than their construction, as Balzac does in *La Muse du département*. For Stendhal, these novels are principally distinguished by their readers' gender. "The great occupation of provincial women in France is reading novels," his "Appendice" begins.[12] It goes on to trivialize novels for women's ignorance, vulgarity, pretension etc.

Denigrating the novels before *Le Rouge et le noir* for their feminine readership, Stendhal employs a long-standing strategy for taking aim at the form. Given critics' tendency to take the "Appendice" at face value, it should be stressed that Stendhal's assertions are polemical. If writing is evidence for reading, women's importance in the early-nineteenth-century novel makes clear that women were not the stupid readers Stendhal depicts, not that this point needs any argument. The commonplaces circulating in contemporary criticism, moreover, challenge Stendhal's perception that novels appeal only to women, leaving aside the difficulties of isolating the actual reading practices of a historical moment. This perception was one of two ways critics characterized the novel's principal audience in the first half of the nineteenth century. The other view was that novels appealed to a readership of both sexes with *leisure*.[13] Balzac follows the

---

[11] Waller, *Male Malady*, 115–16.

[12] Stendhal, "Appendice sur le Rouge et noir [*sic*]," 509.

[13] Féletz, for example, began his review of Souza's *Eugène de Rothelin*: "If, according to the definition of a scholarly and renowned prelate, novels should be considered *pleasant entertainment for lazy gentlefolk* [*honnêtes paresseux*], it must be admitted that *lazy gentlefolk* have never been happier nor more entertained: they have above all boundless obligations to a number of our ladies, who, endowed with a lively and fertile imagination, with a rare talent for writing, for observing manners and society, for painting feelings and passions, for seizing their subtle and fleeting nuances and their exquisite delicacy, tirelessly and zealously use these gifts of nature so happily suited to the genre of the novel, to provide them with enjoyable diversions that follow one another without interruption, or even that vie with one another for the honor of entertaining them." Féletz, *Mélanges* 6: 138–39. Similarly, we saw Dupaty praise the "enjoyable hours we have passed with the superior works" of Staël, Genlis, Cottin and Souza in the 1821 review of *Les Séductions*, 547. Parent-Lardeur finds the commonplace equating novel reading with leisure in advertisements for the *cabinets de lecture* in the Restoration and the July Monarchy, which propose novels as appealing to "the lawyer without a client, the actress without a role, the bachelor without a job, the courtier out of favor, the gentle [*honnête*] and sentimental [*sensible*] wife, the lewd and shameless courtesan, the independently wealthy person on his deathbed, the hypocritical pious lady in secret, the shopkeeper isolated in his store, the farmer's wife on the outskirts

latter view when, in *Le Contrat du mariage*, he depicts Paul de Manerville as ruined by a frivolous ancien régime education that consists largely of reading too many novels, or when he draws an ungendered portrait of his reader at the beginning of *Le Père Goriot*: "You will do likewise, you who hold this book in your white hand, you who sink into your comfortable armchair, saying, 'Perhaps this will entertain me.' "[14]

Stendhal's feminization of the novel serves a polemical function beyond simply denigrating the form. Stendhal makes use of the slippage between femininity and sensibility common in the nineteenth century to challenge the power of sentimental sympathy. In the "Appendice" to *Le Rouge et le noir*, the tears of Diderot's man of feeling no longer mark sublime sacrifice but rather feminine frivolity. "Provincial petty bourgeoises ask the author only for extraordinary scenes that put them all in tears," Stendhal writes, adding to femininity the insults of region (the provinces) and class (not just the bourgeoisie but the *petty* bourgeoisie).[15]

Indeed, the association of novels and women provides Stendhal with a wealth of strategies for challenging the authority of sentimentality. Sliding between readers and texts, Stendhal offers his own breakdown of the subgenres of the novel in the first decades of the nineteenth century. "All women in France read novels," Stendhal emphasizes, "but all do not have the same degree of education, from this, the distinction which has been drawn between novels for *chambermaids* (forgive me for the crudeness of this word invented, I believe, by booksellers) and the *salon* novel."[16] According to Stendhal, novels for "chambermaids" are characterized by this "hero who is always perfect," "unhappy, innocent, and persecuted women" and "extraordinary scenes that completely dissolve them in tears."[17] The salon novel differs primarily in its ambitions to high literary

---

of town when her husband is in the fields." Parent-Lardeur, *Cabinets*, 125–26. Girault, too, characterizes novel readers as idle rather than specifically feminized in the preface to his *Revues des romans* (1839) which addresses itself "to the mother, the young husband, the serious woman, to whomever in their hours alone, through a long night awake, seeks in the novel emotions, an imaginary world, in short, losing oneself [*l'oubli de soi-même*]." Pierre-Eusèbe Girault de Saint-Fargeau, *Revue des romans*, 1:vii. When Junot d'Abrantès depicts the occupations of the frivolous Count André de Mesnevalles in her sentimental social novel, *La Duchesse de Valombray* (1838), she confirms Giraud's observations: "The Count of Mesnevalles . . . read a novel while awaiting the hour to go make some visits. It was one of those days of idleness and boredom where everything new seemed attractive to him." Junot d'Abrantès, *La Duchesse de Valombray*, 1:269.

[14] Balzac, *Le Père Goriot*, 50. Subsequent page references will appear parenthetically in the text.

[15] Stendhal, "Appendice," 513.

[16] Ibid., 511.

[17] Ibid., 512.

value and its insistence on plausibility: "Parisian ladies . . . are devilishly hard on *extraordinary* events."[18]

While Stendhal's distinction has gone on to subsequent literary fame, to what does it in fact refer? Is the salon novel the sentimental novel? If so, what are "novels for chambermaids"?[19] The "extraordinary events" of the "novels for chambermaids" are the province of the Gothic novel (*roman noir*) during the first decades of the nineteenth century, but this subgenre is known for producing a pleasurable frisson in its readers rather than sentimental tears.[20] Stendhal further confuses the matter by his choice of the authors who put the "provincial petty bourgeoises . . . in tears." The Baron de LaMothe-Lagnon, Paul de Kock, and Victor Ducange are in fact known for their comic novels; Lamothe-Lagnon also wrote Gothic novels.

In confusing the recognized generic categories of the early nineteenth-century with his misogynistic classifications, Stendhal creates a distraction from the subgenre which has dominated the novel with such authority.[21] The polemic in this distraction emerges vividly when the "Appendice" designates specific authors to represent narrative practices for depicting society prior to *Le Rouge et le noir.* "Before analyzing this work," Stendhal declares, "we should indicate another result of the moral habits of France, of its *manners* as they have taken shape betwen 1806 and 1832; it can be said that they are entirely unknown to the foreigner who is still

[18] Ibid., 513.

[19] Does the category "novels for chambermaids" even belong to the terminology of booksellers of the Restoration, as Stendhal claims? Parent-Lardeur asserts that it does, although she gives no examples (134). It is certainly striking that if, as Stendhal proposes, "the novel for *chambermaids* is in general printed in-12 by Monsieur Pigoreau," Pigoreau makes no mention of such a distinction in his *Petite Bibliographie* (511). Would Stendhal be giving a characteristic wink to his readers, tipping them off to his games in the way he establishes the generic categorization literary historians have swallowed *tel quel*: "Please forgive me for the crudeness of the word invented, *I believe*, by booksellers" (511, emphasis added).

[20] Stendhal gives his own evidence that there may not be such a difference between these two different forms of novels when, as Waller observes, he suggests that there may not be such a difference between their readers. In a letter on *Armance*, he writes: "The principal fear I had in writing this novel was being read by chambermaids *and the marquises who resemble them.*" Cited in Waller, 134, Waller's emphasis.

[21] A review signed "J. J." eloquently testifies to the power of sentimentality at the time *Le Rouge et le noir* first appears when it reads Stendhal's novel as a variation on the paradigmatic sentimental plot of conflict. Framing Julien as caught between two imperatives in a struggle to the death, the review conceptualizes these imperatives as political rather than ethical. "These two men represent two principles," writes J. J. "Monsieur de Rênal is a man of the Cabinet. . . . Monsieur Valenod is the Jesuit in a short robe. The author will pursue this fertile idea in his book. He links it to the life of a young man who grows up, bounced between the two principles; sometimes liberal, sometimes Jesuit, equally uncomfortable here and there, and who ends by dying on the scaffold to escape the horrible choice of being either a great lord or a bourgeois. . . . The position is excruciating and true in certain ways: but what efforts to figure it out!" (3).

looking for images of French society in the tales of Marmontel or in the novels of Madame de Genlis."[22] Genlis and Marmontel: Stendhal's choice of representative authors implies the antiquated state of the novel before him in a gesture similar to Balzac collapsing the novel of the Empire into the *roman noir*.[23] If Genlis certainly exemplifies the sentimental strategies for depicting society that were celebrated in the decades before realism, the same cannot be said of Marmontel, who became famous with his *contes moraux* first published in the *Mercure* between 1755 and 1759.[24] Stendhal's identification of Genlis and Marmontel as exemplary authors also diminishes the importance of Genlis's novels and, by implication, other works like her own. Although they were successful in their time as well as in the post-Revolutionary decades, the *contes moraux* enjoyed nothing like either the popularity or reputation of novels by Genlis, Staël, Cottin, Souza, Krüdener, and Montolieu.

Stendhal is making a further polemical point in yoking together Genlis and Marmontel for how they paint society, in particular. Marmontel understands his tales as the illustration of moral precepts: "The worthiest object of literature, indeed, the only one that dignifies and honors it, is its moral usefulness."[25] The sentimental novel, too, has moral aspirations, but morality is only one focus of sentimental representation, inseparable from sentimentality's claims to social accuracy. "Her historian needs only the exact truth," we remember Genlis writing of the Duchess de la Val-

---

[22] Stendhal, "Appendice," 510. Stendhal allows only two exceptions to his general condemnation of the state of the novel and they are both foreign: "Walter Scott and M. Manzoni . . . these great poets" (512). The realist interest in Scott and Manzoni as "great poets" fits well with Bourdieu's theory that writers' antagonistic relation derives from competition for the same capital. In nineteenth-century France, cultural capital is primarily distributed through institutions on the level of the national literary field. As foreigners, Scott and Manzoni do not compete directly with French writers for their shares of cultural capital, although they certainly compete for economic capital.

[23] Victor Hugo, too, uses similar rhetorical strategies to settle realist accounts with sentimentality as late as *Les Misérables*, composed during the July Monarchy and the Second Empire (1845–48; 1860–62), and published in 1862. Hugo simultaneously skirts the sentimental subgenre then dominating the novel, alludes to it, treats it as an outmoded form, and denigrates its literary importance, when he portrays the reading that completes the debasement of the brutal tavern keeper's wife, Madame Thénardier, in his chapter on 1817. Like Balzac, Hugo uses Barthélemy Hadot to epitomize the sorry state of the novel in those bygone days. He writes, "During this period, the antique classical novel . . . still aristocratic but ever more vulgar and fallen from Mademoiselle de Scudéri to Madame Barthélemy-Hadot and from Madame de Lafayette to Madame Bournon-Mallarmé, ignited the loving souls of Parisian concierges [*portières*] and even made a few inroads in the suburbs. Madame Thénardier was just smart enough to read these kinds of books. She lived on them. In them, she drowned what was left of her brain." Hugo, *Les Misérables* 1:195.

[24] Marmontel died in 1799. *Dix-sept Nouveaux Contes moraux* were published posthumously in 1801.

[25] Jean-François Marmontel, *Essai sur les romans considérés du côté moral*, 287.

lière. "How could he not interest, not instruct, if he is accurate [*fidèle*]?" Critics throughout the first half of the nineteenth century testify that sentimental novelists, Genlis among them, lived up to their ambitions. "No author is better at depicting the manners of her time," declared the Countess de Bradi of Genlis several years after realism had exploded onto the literary scene.[26] Drawing attention to Genlis's kinship with Marmontel, Stendhal downplays this aspect of sentimentality and thereby obscures the affinity between his own ambition to paint contemporary manners and the sentimental project: "No one before M. de Stendhal had dared to paint the portrait of these unappealing [post-Revolutionary] manners," the "Appendice" proclaims.[27] If Stendhal uses Genlis, specifically, to obscure his continuity with the sentimental project, it may be because her works lay the most emphasis of all the prominent early-nineteenth-century novelists on "moral usefulness." Stendhal may also wage his polemic via Genlis because her literary merit was more disputed than that of Staël, Cottin, or Souza throughout the years when she enjoyed great fame.[28]

But perhaps the best evidence for the polemic in Balzac and Stendhal's dismissal of sentimentality is their own novelistic practice. From their literary beginnings, these writers forge key realist codes through appropriating and transforming fundamental tenets of sentimental poetics, as the remainder of this chapter shows.

WOE TO THOSE WHO ACCEPT THE SOCIAL CONTRACT

Balzac's first novel is neither a Gothic tale of haunted castles nor a historical resurrection of colorful times gone by. Rather, the unfinished *Sténie*

---

[26] Countess de Bradi, in the *Biographie des femmes auteurs contemporaines françaises*, 165. Similarly the *Galerie des dames françaises distinguées dans les lettres et les arts*: "Madame de Genlis has since published twenty works, many of which have remained . . . as models for the truth of their observations." *Galerie des dames françaises distinguées dans les lettres et les arts*, plate 31. While the work has no date, it was most likely published in the early 1840s for it refers to the death of the Duchess d'Abrantès (1838) as taking place several years ago.

[27] Stendhal's "Appendice," 511. Stendhal's Garnier editor, Henri Martineau, completely misses Stendhal's polemic when he writes, "On each page of his work, Stendhal cites Marmontel and Madame de Genlis as painters of French society. Marmontel . . . is the type of the mediocre author who is cold and flat. . . . One should always be on one's guard with Madame de Genlis, she has seen much, remembered much, but her lies are flagrant throughout and Stendhal loathes them. She herself is a figure of the utmost ridicule" (Martineau, *Rouge*, 598).

[28] Pigoreau observes that Genlis is known for "[t]he fertility of her imagination, the richness of her style, the beauty of the feelings she presents. . . . She has nonetheless encountered censors and judges who are a bit harsh; but has she not herself judged others a bit harshly!" Pigoreau, *Petite Bibliographie*, 204.

(1818–20) is an epistolary novel of adultery where lovers struggle, paralyzed in the tragic double bind pitting individual freedom against collective obligation.[29] "What law forbids my love? Am I a criminal? . . . Oh Job, I belong to you, I follow your laws, only God can part us," the married heroine, Sténie, declares in private, giving primacy to the law of the heart.[30] Listening to her lover Job's "burning prayers" face to face, she emphasizes the weight of collective bonds: "You forget that I no longer belong to myself; you know how much I love you, and you have the refined cruelty to increase the weight of my unhappiness?" (129). Job, however, does not deserve these reproaches for he, too, is keenly aware of the contradictions of his situation. While he longs to consummate his love, he also recognizes that his act would force Sténie to violate her obligation to collective welfare and thereby undermine her moral worth, which is essential to her appeal: "Oh my sweet friend, care for your own reputation, which I guard jealously, demands that I do not see you according to my desires" (156).

Balzac reiterates the collision between collective welfare and individual freedom in ever-escalating tension across *Sténie*, using a light touch, the sentimental blazon, the image of the heart, the analysis of the heart, and neoclassical diction that mutates into emphatic rhetoric at moments of high moral effort. But the novel simultaneously makes Balzac's fundamental dispute with sentimentality evident in the way it drafts a standard sentimental character, the confidant. In sentimentality, the confidant teases out and validates the protagonist's torment, but this is hardly the function of Job's friend, Vanehrs. "It is thus indisputable that possessing Sténie is the only way to save yourself," Vanehrs scandalously declares, urging Job just to get it over with and have the affair. "I do not care about the voice which cries prejudices, laws, virtue," Vanehrs continues, "because it is about you, about a man's life" (133).

Justifying his counsel, Vanehrs makes clear that Balzac grasps sentimentality as an ideology as well as a poetics and that the content of this ideology underpins his hostility to the form. "Yes, I am not afraid to say it," Vanehrs explains, "the very presence of a social condition is a great and magnificent crime against humanity. . . . Woe to those who accept the social contract, woe to you, woe to me; at that moment man no longer exists. His will dies away, he loses his rights, and society only gives them back to him broken down, like light passing through a prism is embellished by unknown colors, but these bizarrely ordered degrading colors

---

[29] Describing Balzac's initial difficulty in coming into his own, Philarète Chasles mentions Balzac's early writing in the style of the sentimental novelist Isabelle de Montolieu. See "Romans de M. de Balzac, Troisième article."

[30] Balzac, *Sténie*, 121. Subsequent page references will appear parenthetically in the text.

do not equal noble freedom, the strength of the original [*primitif*] ray, which in any case contains them" (134). Dismissing the social contract as a fiction of domination, Vanehrs rewrites the terms of sentimental conflict to reflect his view of social relations as the play of power. Job can either accept the repressive existence offered by "the social pact of France. Obey, grovel, and die, it [your presence] will never, can never, and should never be free according to nature" (138). Or he can stop trying hopelessly to respect collective welfare as well as individual freedom and simply pursue his private interests and natural desires, even if their fulfillment breaks the law. As Barbéris comments of Balzac's mature work, "everything relating to the liberal tradition leading, according to him, only to '*an impotent freedom*' . . . his freedom is and claims to be power."[31]

In *Sténie*, Balzac has not yet invented a poetics expressing his attack on liberalism; he simply states it as a gloss on a sentimental novel of his own. The invention of this poetics will be the great adventure of Balzac's subsequent career. From *Sténie*'s opening, however, Balzac is already experimenting with alternatives to sentimental codes of representation. And from this opening, he associates his experiments with the novel's defeminization.

"As for women," the fictional editor of *Sténie*'s correspondence declares, these letters "are no concern of theirs" (3). To ensure that women will leave *Sténie* alone, the editor continues, he has decided to open the work with "two insipid letters," which he offers as "a kind of antidote. Out of one hundred who will open the book, s[ome] will take another look at it after this nauseating and soporific opening. If the hundredth reads the whole work . . . I will never congratulate her on it, and I will blame her still less" (3). The nauseating and narcotic antidote is two philosophical letters pitting Vanehrs's materialism against a Romantic spiritualism articulated by Job. Both characters' meandering and abstract reflections contrast markedly with sentimental narration, which cuts straight to the double bind. The two letters also contain a lengthy description conveying objective knowledge about the landscape, which contrasts with the two ways sentimentality treats setting: the light touch and the image of the heart, where exterior decor serves as a figure for interiority.[32]

By the novel's third letter, such transgressions of sentimental poetics have disappeared. As Job puts it once he has encountered Sténie: "My whole being is sentiment" (45). These opening letters nonetheless hit upon

---

[31] Pierre Barbéris, *Mythes balzaciennes*, 129.

[32] "Between the Loire and the Cher is a large plain, lush rather than dry and arid, and continuously watered by a kind of underground friendship, which the waves of the river have contracted [*contractée*] with the waters of the stream," runs the beginning of this description that goes on for pages, delineating precisely the same landscape found in *Claire*

one of Balzac's most powerful strategies for displacing the sentimental form, despite his inability to sustain this strategy at the time. Both philosophical discussion and objective description import high cultural discourses of knowledge then considered masculine into the novel's feminized concern for "private life [*la vie intérieure*] . . . the domestic hearth."[33] We will see Balzac pursue this strategy with great success in *La Comédie humaine*.

AN OBSTACLE, A MOTIVE, A DUTY...

Stendhal, too makes his fraught engagement with sentimentality visible from his first novel, framing *Armance* as the true inheritor of Tencin and Lafayette's legacy and vastly superior to the renowned sentimental novels of his time.[34] Stendhal contrasts *Armance* with one renowned recent sentimental novel in particular. "Madame Duras painted the most touching pictures of love struggling with difficulties and misfortunes," Stendhal declared when he wrote Duras's obituary. "The last work of this renowned author was a novel entitled *Olivier*; she read it aloud to some friends, but it will never be published. The nature of the subject led the author onto dangerous ground. Monsieur de Stendhal has nonetheless set out to defy this danger, and a second edition of *Armance* is now forthcoming."[35] Waller rightly suggests that Stendhal begins his novelistic career against Duras by capitalizing on her literary and cultural celebrity. Reconstructing Duras's relation to the forgotten horizon of early-nineteenth-century sentimentality, we can grasp how Stendhal's gesture has specifically generic stakes.

Duras's *Olivier* exhibits crucial hallmarks of the sentimental text. Using neoclassical diction, the light touch, the image of the heart, and the analysis of the heart, *Olivier* narrates the story of two childhood sweethearts, Olivier and Louise, who renew their love after the death of Louise's first husband. Olivier and Louise cannot, however, marry, because Olivier, like Malek-Adhel or Mathilde in *Mathilde*, like Oswald in *Corinne*, like Eugène de Rothelin in the novel of the same name, owes allegiance to a duty which forbids it. As Olivier tells Louise, " 'without you, life is nothing, but an obstacle, a motive, a duty...' He was unable to continue, his face

---

d'*Albe*'s opening description that I have used to exemplify the sentimental descriptive code "image of the heart" (10). The kinds of knowledge conveyed about this landscape in *Sténie* include history, architecture, geography, literature, philosophy, and ethnography.

[33] Review of *Vanina d'Ornano*, 3–4.

[34] On Stendhal's use of the *mal du siècle* gesture to express his ambivalent relationship to the sentimental lineage, see Waller's *Male Malady*.

[35] Stendhal, Paris, April 20, 1828, *Courrier anglais*, 364–65.

became deadly pale and completely distorted."[36] But Olivier's duty differs from the duty of these other sentimental protagonists in one crucial way: the reader does not know what it is. Throughout *Olivier*, this duty remains a mysterious, unnamed secret.

In turning Olivier's duty into a secret, Duras transforms the conflict at the core of the sentimental plot. The challenge to individual happiness comes now from some reservation known only to the protagonist. Is it a private "obstacle" or "motive"? Is it "duty," the term used by sentimental protagonists to designate collective welfare? The problem is never resolved. Olivier's duty, that is to say, displaces sentimental ethics towards personal concerns, and Duras encouraged this displacement in intimating to the select society who heard her read her novel aloud that Olivier's secret was impotence, although no detail in *Olivier* makes this content explicit. As the novel's rewritings by Latouche and Stendhal illustrate, the perception that Olivier's obstacle was impotence extended to the literary public of the time.[37] Denise Virieux comments, however, that details in the novel recall the life of Astolphe de Custine, whom Duras knew well, as Duras implies that the secret could also be homosexuality.[38]

When Duras substitutes a personal secret for sentimentality's collective welfare, she profoundly alters the ideological tension at stake in the sentimental double bind. Rather than playing out one of liberalism's underwriting contradictions, *Olivier* draws attention to a great unthought problem in the liberal opposition between individual freedom and collective welfare splintering the Revolution. This is the existence of "social groups and their effects: the existence of orders, of social classes," as Althusser describes the blindspot responsible for the numerous contradictions of Rousseau's *The Social Contract* at the basis of the French liberal lineage.[39] French liberalism remains stuck in the conflict between negative and positive rights because it is unwilling to ask "whose rights"; reluctant to recognize that how subjects exercise either negative or positive rights depends on the way their collective identities position them in the social formation. Instead, it treats all individuals as formally equal, material differences among them not withstanding.

In sentimentality, too, all protagonists are equal before the tragic conflict of rights. But this is not the case in Duras's works, which take shape around "an idea of inequality, either of nature or of social position,"

---

[36] Claire de Duras, *Olivier, ou le Secret*, 171.

[37] See Waller and Denise Virieux's introduction to *Olivier* for an account of the novel's reception.

[38] James Creech notes this resonance when he suggests that *Armance* takes shape around a silence on homosexuality in *Closet Writing, Gay Reading*.

[39] Althusser, *Montesquieu*, 155.

to cite Sainte-Beuve's retrospective appreciation of Duras's importance.[40] In *Ourika* and *Edouard*, the difference fracturing abstract liberal equality is socially defined: race in *Ourika* and class in *Edouard*. In *Olivier*, in contrast, the inequality is personal, if not natural. Olivier's secret makes him different from other individuals, his social equality with them notwithstanding, and he experiences this difference as suffering culminating in death.

Olivier's displacement of collective welfare transforms the sentimental construction of character as well as sentimental ideology. In the sentimental novel, the protagonist exhibits subjectivity in the transparent moral and emotional struggles to solve the impossible liberal double bind. When Duras casts Olivier's behavior as shaped by an ambiguous personal secret instead, she displaces sentiment towards psychology. Like a sentimental text, *Olivier* engenders the protagonist in self-conflict and represents character as the movements of feeling, which it presents in nuanced detail. In *Olivier*, however, the protagonist's dilemma is no longer a clear expression of founding ethical principles common to all members of society, it is tinged with pathology rather than constituting the highest display of moral worth, and one of its terms is hidden rather than displayed.[41]

The effect of *Olivier*'s secret on sentimental character is inseparable from its transformation of sentimental narrative dynamics. While the novel's plot plays out the conflict between duty and happiness with ever-increasing force, the conflict violates the sentimental imperative, "all should be clear." Since Olivier's obstacle is hidden, the reader is not in control of its morality, but what the novel loses in moral significance, it gains in suspense. Duras foregrounds the importance of enigma in her novel starting from its title, *Olivier, ou le Secret*. Like Genlis's *Les Mères rivales, ou la Calomnie* and *Alphonsine, ou la Tendresse maternelle*, sentimental titles often use an "or" to link the novel's protagonist(s) with a moral abstraction explored in the narrative. In *Olivier*, Duras transforms this abstraction from morality to mystery.

Olivier's displacement of sentiment towards psychology is one more way the novel challenges the ideology of the sentimental text. The consolations of sentimentality lie in the restoration of sympathetic community, whose prototype is the sympathetic relation between protagonist and reader. But when the novel calls upon the reader to decipher Olivier's resistant personality, it disrupts sentimental sympathy with hermeneutic concerns. Or rather, *Olivier*'s displacement of sentiment with psychology is one *other* way the novel challenges the ideology of the sentimental text,

---

[40] Charles Augustin Sainte-Beuve, "Madame de Duras," 719.

[41] As Waller's analysis shows, Duras takes her pathological view of the psyche from the Romantic *mal du siècle*.

for it works at cross purposes to the novel's thematic attention to the consequences of inequality. When the novel represents Olivier suffering because of his difference from others, after all, its demonstration depends on the reader's sympathy for its protagonist. Too bad Olivier is less of a sentimental ideal than a psychological case.

Despite this transformation of sympathy, however, *Olivier* neither abandons the sentimental repetition of transparent conflict nor forges the realist progression from mystery to revelation. The mystery is the origin of narrative rather than its goal; it is transparently displayed as one term in the double bind even while its content is obscure. As Virieux accurately observes, "The drama in *Olivier* is not, as in *Sarrasine*, in plotting that delays unveiling the enigma . . . it is from the enigma that Madame de Duras draws out the misunderstandings among her characters that provoke the drama."[42] Indicative of *Olivier*'s intermediary dynamics between revelation and repetition is the fact that Duras refuses to name the answer to her novel's riddle at its end. Instead, *Olivier* concludes with tragic impasse: unable to resolve the tension between duty and happiness, Olivier commits suicide and Louise goes mad.

A MINOR DUTY! A DUTY OF LITTLE IMPORTANCE!

"Tall, a great deal of wit, noble manners, the handsomest big black eyes in the world": Stendhal introduces *Armance*'s hero, endowing him with all requisite sentimental attractions and using the sentimental light touch.[43] Most importantly, *Armance*'s Octave exhibits an exquisite sense of duty, like Malek-Adhel, Eugène de Rothelin, or Oswald. " 'I cannot understand you; you are duty *incarnate*,' " declares Octave's uncle, the Commandeur de Soubirane, who is also a stock figure from a sentimental novel: the secondary character embodying the moral pathologies of high society. " 'Would that I could never betray duty!' said Octave, 'that I could give my soul back to the Creator as pure as when I received it!' " (6).

Stendhal would seem to be setting up a *mal-du-siècle* variation on the sentimental plot in his presentation of Octave's initial conflict. Suffering from melancholy, Octave takes individual freedom to the limit case of suicide. "Why not end it all? . . . However much I draw up courses of behavior that appear as reasonable as possible," Octave laments in his opening analysis of the heart, "my life is only a succession of misfortunes

---

[42] Virieux, introduction to *Olivier*, 53.

[43] Stendhal, *Armance ou quelques scènes d'un salon de Paris en 1827*, 5. Subsequent page references will appear parenthetically in the text.

and bitter feelings" (24–25). To this extreme example of individual freedom, Octave opposes collective welfare, which, in best sentimental fashion, he associates with his family. Not with his mother, who is "dying from consumption" (25) but rather with "the Commander, my father himself!" (25). But, Octave goes on to comment, "they do not love me; they love my name . . . only a minor duty binds me to them'... this word *duty* was like a lightning bolt for Octave. A *minor duty*! . . . a duty of little importance!" (25). Octave's statement is a lightning bolt for the reader with sentimental expectations as well. While Octave speaks sentimentality's emphatic rhetoric at moments of high moral efforts, the substance of his reflections is unthinkable in sentimental terms. Qualifying duty with comparative adjectives, Octave raises the possibility that collective welfare may be relative and thereby unsettles one of the founding absolutes in the sentimental universe.

If Stendhal aims his first novel against Duras, that is to say, it is because his project resembles rather than diverges from hers. Like *Olivier*, *Armance* chips away at sentimentality from within: by dismantling the duty to the collective underpinning sentimental morality. Indeed, *Armance* carries this gesture even further than *Olivier*. In *Olivier*, collective welfare loses its authority, but the notion of duty remains, recast from a collective to an ambiguous personal imperative. In *Armance*, Octave's doubts inaugurate the evacuation of all authority from the term.

While no word is more frequently in the mouth of Stendhal's hero than "duty," the concept becomes a moving target in the course of the novel. Octave first bares his soul to the reader in an analysis of the heart where he shows himself torn between freedom conceptualized as suicide and duty conceptualized as collective welfare. But from this standard sentimental usage, duty expands to designate Octave's allegiance to a horrible secret and Octave's obligation to Armance, as well as any of Octave's everyday efforts at self-mastery or even social grace. When Octave sees a theater poster with the word *Otello* on it, for example, the poster reminds him of a woman he once flirted with. "Perhaps she has come to Paris for *Otello*; in this case, my duty is to go speak to her one more time" (155). By the novel's end, all that remains of duty is self-imposed obligation devoid of moral authority. In keeping with this transformation of sentimental duty, Stendhal also transforms the imperative against which sentimental duty is defined. For Octave, freedom becomes unchecked impulse, the absence of self-control, rather than a fundamental ethical right.

Octave's partner in sentimental conflict, Armance, participates in the novel's evacuation of duty as well. A poor relation in love with her wealthy and socially prominent cousin, Armance would seem a paradigmatic sentimental protagonist who confronts a dilemma recalling the sufferings of Duras's Edouard. While Armance longs for personal happiness, she recognizes that her marriage to Octave would diminish his social standing. Resolving to sacrifice Octave's hand, Armance concludes, "How sweet it is ... to do one's duty! If I were the wife of Octave, me, a poor girl with no family connections, would I be as happy?" (108). Laudable sentiments; only they are not an accurate depiction of Armance's situation. Armance's marriage is in fact progressing towards its conclusion, much to Armance's delight. Indeed, Armance only allows herself the appeal to duty when Octave gives strong signs that her lack of fortune makes no difference to him: "Armance was so happy that she deprived herself of examining no objection," the narrator comments before her previously quoted analysis (105). Casting herself as caught between duty and happiness, Armance is not expressing the difficulties of her situation with painful lucidity, she is instead avoiding them. She uses the sentimental conflict to skirt the more frightening matters of Octave's melancholy and her own desires.

In the case of Armance, as in the case of Octave, then, the attack on sentimental duty spearheads the dissolution of sentimental conflict altogether. This conflict turns to the conflict between self-control and impulse for Octave and is exposed as repression in the case of Armance. The significance of Stendhal's gesture is ideological as well as poetic and it resembles Duras's critique of liberalism rather than Balzac's in *Sténie*. Throughout *Armance*, Stendhal takes his distance from liberal ideology by drawing attention to the suffering inflicted by inequality in Restoration society. As Armance's self-deluding double bind based on rank illustrates, however, Stendhal does not integrate the problem of inequality into the core of the novel's plot but rather addresses it in passing. Thus, the novel exposes the social prejudices of Octave's uncle and represents Octave's discomfort at being distinguished for his title and wealth: "But in this salon, I have the misfortune of not being exactly like others. Please God I could find there the *equality* over which these gentlemen make such a fuss" (111).

At the same time, however, *Armance* resembles *Olivier* in accompanying its thematic condemnations of inequality with a disruption of the reader's sympathy that undermines these condemnations' force. For like *Olivier*, *Armance* displaces sentiment towards psychology. Or rather, in the case of *Armance*, it is more appropriate to speak of transformation than displacement. In Duras's novel, we do not know whether Olivier's difficulty is "an obstacle," "a motive," or "a duty," and Olivier's lover, Louise, is an unreconstructed sentimental protagonist. In *Armance*, in contrast, both protagonists are clearly motivated by irrational impulses, fears, and desires, rather than principles, and their psyches are structured on a model of repression and depth.[44] Stendhal's transformation of senti-

---

[44] Comparing the two novels, Michel Pierssens observes that, "Where the characters of Mme de Duras confide in each other ... those of Stendhal put all their energy into never

ment into psychology also intensifies Duras's displacement of the sentimental relation between reader and text. The more opaque the characters
are to each other and to themselves, the more the reader seeks to figure
out their motives rather than sympathizing with their moral conflicts.[45]

The mysteries of character and plot are fundamental to realist poetics
throughout the nineteenth century. The trajectory from *Olivier* to *Armance* shows these key realist codes emerging in a psychological displacement of the sentimental construction of subjectivity through the double
bind. Balzac epitomizes this displacement in his positive comments on
sentimentality where he constructs it as the province of men: "Talent
shines forth in painting the causes that beget facts, in the mysteries of the
human heart whose movements are neglected by historians."[46] Crediting
sentimental authors with their powerful representations of interiority,
Balzac simultaneously frames the heart in realist rather than sentimental
terms: as mysteries and causes to be uncovered.

In *Armance*, Stendhal sets up a paradigmatically realist relation between reader and protagonist to characterize the heroine. Deprived of
authority over her interior life, Armance becomes an object of study, and
the reader analyzes her motives in collaboration with the narrator. Armance's own statements about her behavior illustrate a common way realist
texts retain the sentimental rhetoric of self-representation, which becomes
just that, rhetoric. Sentimentality's high moral vocabulary and its analysis
of the heart turn to the delusions of a "romantic [*romanesque*]" protagonist who is usually, although not exclusively, feminine, like Madame Bo-
vary.[47]

Stendhal's delineation of Octave, in contrast, bears witness to the con-
tinuing authority of sentimental poetics. Stendhal shapes Octave's character around a mystery that teases the reader and makes his behavior (like
throwing a servant out the window) sufficiently erratic as to disqualify
his judgments as reliable.[48] The novel, however, never completely cedes
authority to the narrator and reader, for Octave fails to hand over his
secret by its end. Rather, *Armance*, like *Olivier*, concludes with a tragic

---

talking," or rather, into talking of other things than what they are doing. Pierssens, "*Armance*: entre savoir et non-savoir," 24. Pierssens also remarks that Stendhal's characters are
made of "passions," rather than "sentiment" (24).

[45] As Gide commented of the novel, "The plot not only plays out between characters, but
above all between author and reader." See André Gide's preface to *Armance*, iii.

[46] Balzac, "Lettres," no. 1, 278.

[47] These protagonists excel at constructing imaginary plots that trivialize sentimental
moral struggle. "I must raise an eternal barrier between Octave and myself," muses Armance. "I must become a nun, I will choose the order that leaves me the greatest solitude,
a convent situated in the middle of high mountains, with a picturesque view" (67).

[48] Contemporary critics viewed the novel as taking its characters from the Charenton
madhouse, as Martineau observes in his introduction to *Armance*, xxviii–xxix.

sentimental resolution. As a result of a misunderstanding engineered by the malicious Commandeur de Soubirane, Octave comes to believe that Armance is only marrying him from duty and not from love. He thus perceives his final duty as giving Armance her freedom without compromising her, which he opposes to his happiness in her presence. Caught in a version of the sentimental double bind even while this structure has completely lost its authority, Octave marries Armance, then exits with suicide. That Octave's mystery was known as impotence to the contemporary literary public in no way diminishes the novel's recourse to sentimentality in its resolution. For the key to the mystery then depends on knowledge shared by a community of readers, which is to say on precisely the social organization underwriting sentimental sympathy.

THE WAY OF THE WORLD[49]

The narration is in the first person, by a man describing the sufferings of his youth. The scene is an aristocratic chateau and the surrounding grounds. The players are members of the noble nuclear family: older husband, beautiful young wife, their children, with one intruder, the narrator, on the threshold of adulthood. The result is an adulterous triangle where characters agonize, torn between collective welfare and individual freedom. Sacrificing love to collective welfare, the young wife, aided by the virtuous young man, goes so far as to nurse the older husband back to health when he is struck down with an illness that has every chance of killing him. In this effort, the wife paradoxically finds herself united with her lover in a way that allows her briefly to reconcile the two conflicting ethical imperatives tearing her apart. But the reconciliation lasts only the space of the husband's illness. When he recovers, the conflict returns with all its force and will end only with the young wife's death.

This plot has all the hallmarks of the sentimental novel. It is, of course, the first two sections of Balzac's *Le Lys dans la vallée*. When traditional literary historians dispute the sources of *Le Lys*, the range is seemingly wide. As Anne-Marie Meininger observes, "As to 'resemblances,' criticism has hunted them down and amassed them. To excess": *La Nouvelle Héloïse*, Cottin's *Claire d'Albe*, Saint-Beuve's *Volupté*, Stendhal's *Le Rouge et le noir*.[50] The high stakes of genre in writers' struggles to domi-

---

[49] "This phrase is, of course, the title Moretti uses for his study of the nineteenth-century realist novel. Moretti's account of realism as founded on compromise underwrites my view of the realist agon with sentimentality.

[50] Meininger, afterword to *Le Lys dans la vallée*, 336. On Balzac's specific allusions to *Claire d'Albe* in *Le Lys dans la vallée*, see Moïse Le Yaouanc, "En relisant 'Le Lys dans la vallée,' " 248–49.

nate the novel during the July Monarchy solves the riddle of such proliferation. All texts cited as sources by traditional literary history take shape
in relation to sentimentality. They either belong to the sentimental lineage
or they take a position against it, like *Le Rouge et le noir* and, moreover,
like *Le Lys dans la vallée*.

Le Rouge et le noir (1830) is the first modern realist novel and it certainly makes explicit the sentimental contribution to realist poetics in fully
developed form.[51] I show this contribution with a novel by Balzac instead
because Balzac plays a more influential role in July Monarchy struggles
over how the novel should intervene in public life. Significantly more
widely read and discussed than Stendhal at the time, Balzac was the author most frequently credited by writers and reviewers alike with inventing the realist model for representing social relations.[52] Whatever the
work analyzed, my goal would, in any case, be the same. My concern is
how a dialogue with sentimentality shapes codes crucial to the realist
paradigm throughout the nineteenth century rather than the practices of
a single author. For the current discussion, it is thus not imperative to
detail the differences between Balzac and Stendhal's versions of this paradigm. Nor is it imperative to detail the variants of the realist paradigm
practiced by other novelists of the July Monarchy like Félix Davin and
Charles de Bernard, who were significantly influenced by Balzac.[53]

In *Le Lys*, Balzac starts with the double bind founding sentimental tragedy. But this gesture indicates precisely the novel's difference (and attack)
on the sentimental plot: he *starts* with it. For the story of the unconsummated relation to Madame de Mortsauf is not all Félix de Vandenesse has
to confess. In the third and final section of the novel, Félix describes his
subsequent ascension in the world, makes clear that he betrayed Madame
de Mortsauf with the passionate, egotistical English Lady Dudley, and
that Madame de Mortsauf died from a broken heart.

In *Claire d'Albe*, Claire's husband misleads her into believing that Frédéric betrayed her. In *Le Lys*, by contrast, the betrayal is real. Even worse
than the betrayal, however, is Félix's attitude towards it. When Madame
de Mortsauf reproaches Félix for his relation to Lady Dudley, she speaks
the sentimental language of moral principles: "Virtue, Félix, the sanctity
of life, maternal love, are not then errors. . . . Bless me with one look,
with one sacred word, I will pardon you the pain I have suffered in the

---

[51] Balzac's *Scènes de la vie privée* from 1830 are novellas.

[52] Weinberg contrasts Balzac's prominence with Stendhal's relative obscurity during the
July Monarchy in *French Realism: The Critical Reaction 1830–1870*.

[53] Bernard, for example, was perceived as "the literary younger brother of Monsieur de
Balzac." Review of *Les Ailes d'Icare*.

past two months."[54] But rather than taking up this opening, Félix muddies the clarity of the tragic conflict, turns collision to compromise: "[M]y soul did not waver, but I was not master of my senses" (245). "How he reasons, and what subtle distinctions," responds Madame de Mortsauf (245).[55] As Moretti observes, "Balzacian 'realism' is founded on the rejection of sharp contrasts. . . . In structural terms: to be realistic means to deny the existence of stable and clearly opposed paradigms."[56]

Where has Félix learned his realism? When his story begins, he would seem to be an exemplary sentimental protagonist. "At my age, no interest distracted my heart, no ambition crossed . . . my feelings," Félix comments, remarking also, "To thoroughly understand my narrative, take yourself back to that fine age . . . when the mind does not bend to worldly jesuitism" (111, 29). But in associating sentimental virtue with an "age"—youth—Félix indicates the narrative of development that Balzac uses to demolish the authority of the sentimental conflict. In realism, sentimental conflict goes from the essence of ethical life to a stage in the protagonist's *Bildung*. If you're not a marxist at twenty, you have no heart; if you are a marxist at thirty, you have no brains: *mutatis mutandis*, this conservative adage captures the realist stance towards sentimental liberalism.[57]

In his experience of sentimental adultery, Félix comes to recognize the truth of the sentimental novel's vision of social life as conflict: for Félix, as for a sentimental protagonist, individual freedom and collective welfare are implacably at war. At the same time, however, he discovers the error of framing this conflict in ethical terms. Delineating Félix's time in the Mortsauf household, Balzac draws attention to the tyranny lurking in the sentimental representation of the family. In Balzac's rendition, the sentimental novel's social microcosm becomes "that horrible concert of misfortunes" (143) rather than a unit devoted to "the happiness of all." It is a structure ruled by repressive authority in the form of a self-centered, ungrateful tyrant who asserts his sickly power out of self-interest.

Félix qualifies this realization as his "first step in social life" that is "an immense measure compared to which the other scenes added on could only be small" (143). It is a giant step because it allows Félix to approach "social life" purely as a medium of self-fulfillment. With collective welfare

---

[54] Balzac, *Le Lys dans la vallée*, 244. Subsequent page references will appear parenthetically in the text.

[55] When Vautrin opens Rastignac's eyes to the way of the world, he observes, "virtue . . . cannot be parsed; it exists or it does not" (*Goriot*, 145).

[56] Moretti, *Way*, 153.

[57] Félix Davin made a similar observation in his preface to the 1835 publication of Balzac's *Etudes de moeurs au XIXe siècle*. "At twenty years of age, feelings are generous; at thirty, everything already begins to be calculated; man becomes selfish." Davin, "Introduction," 1146.

a matter of power rather than right, individual freedom encounters no other check than the strength of the ruling authority, and, moreover, loses its own ethical ground. In the French liberal lineage, the negative rights to life, liberty, and happiness can only be granted by the collective, conceived as an ethical force: "[T]he social order is a sacred right which serves as basis for all other rights," to cite Rousseau.[58] The collapse of positive rights evacuates negative rights as well, returning social liberty to natural liberty: the "right to anything that tempts" and that one "can take."[59]

Natural liberty is the reign of instinct, abusive power, and greed, according to Rousseau. For Vanehrs in *Sténie*, it is "noble freedom, the strength of the original ray" (134). For Félix, too, the collapse of the social contract results in a positive release that is, however, not precisely natural freedom but rather a kind of natural freedom adapted to second nature. "Then, suddenly, I met the woman who was continually to prod my *ambitious desires*," Félix observes when he assesses the significance of his time with Madame de Mortsauf from his postsentimental standpoint, qualifying his desires as directed towards social goals, not simply natural gratification (33, emphasis added).

In his experience of sentimental adultery, then, Félix works a displacement of the sentimental conflict that is not its complete dissolution. He remains caught in the opposition between individual and collective, but the opposition mutates from individual freedom against collective welfare to individuals seeking self-gratification against repressive authority and each other; from a struggle between opposing principles to a struggle for power. In realist terms, this struggle is the "real" or "material" struggle orienting social relations in contrast to sentimental conflict, which realist novels dismiss as ideal.[60] The struggle for power does away with the unnegotiable absolutes of tragedy; what matters now is not principles but how well one plays the game. As Rastignac remarks when he discovers "worldly jesuitism [*le jésuitisme du monde*]": "To be faithful to virtue, what a sublime martyrdom! Bah! Everyone believes in virtue; but who is virtuous? Peoples take freedom as their idol; but where on earth is there a free people?" (*Goriot*, 146).

How Balzac can be both a royalist and a materialist is a problem that has troubled marxist critics across the twentieth century.[61] From the per-

---

[58] Rousseau, *Social Contract*, 50.

[59] Rousseau, *Social Contract*, 65.

[60] Critics objecting to Balzac's work in the 1830s and 1840s described his narratives of power and compromise as antisentimental, often using the term "sentiment" in a psychological rather than a specifically literary sense. "Monsieur de Balzac's analysis corrupts and degrades all the feelings which it attacks" remarked Paul Gaschon de Molènes in the "Revue littéraire," 984.

[61] The response remains constant from Lukács to Barbéris and Jameson: the man had prejudices the brilliant novelist overcame.

spective of sentimental liberalism, royalism and materialism share one important axiom common to realism as well. Both paradigms found social life on relations of power rather than relations of right.[62]

Félix's transformation of sentimental tragedy can also be put in narratological terms. Exposing collective welfare in conflict with individual freedom as desire struggling against repressive authority, *Le Lys* thematizes the antisentimental genesis of the psychosocial conflict structuring all realist narrative, according to the most recent influential analyses of the form.[63] As these analyses have shown, the realist conflict between desire and the law offers a profoundly unsentimental narrative structure in addition to a profoundly unsentimental ideology. In realist narrative, the protagonist is released from the conflict between static absolutes into a conflict that has a direction: the struggles of desire pursuing satisfaction.

No scene better exemplifies the realist rewriting of sentimental conflict than Félix's version of sentimental sacrifice. A classic example of sentimental sacrifice is Frédéric restraining his love for Claire to preserve collective welfare in *Claire d'Albe*. When Claire asks Frédéric not to overwhelm her conflicted position and push their relationship to erotic gratification, he responds, "Do not forget that you have obtained from me the greatest sacrifice that human strength can perform" (736). When Madame de Mortsauf appeals to Félix for similar restraint, his response, superficially similar, is self-interest by other means. Félix assesses Madame de Mortsauf's morality as a challenge to be overcome, not by brute force but by strategic manipulation: "I had to calm her down, promise never to cause her pain, and love her at twenty like old men love their last child" (116).[64]

Félix's strategy never completely succeeds. It does, however, have, an unexpected worldly return. In Balzac's rendition, sentimental self-denial is depreciated to a useful *dispositif* of self-construction, testing Félix's determination and honing his interpersonal skills. From the apprenticeship in sentimental sacrifice, Félix perfects deferring desire; seducing and

---

[62] "Today, Machiavelli would not have entitled his book: *The Prince* but rather *Power*. POWER, moral being, creature of reason, obligated to remain one and strong, is something greater than THE PRINCE studied by the celebrated Florentine. There is progress," writes Balzac in "Du Gouvernement moderne," 550.

[63] On this conflict, see, notably, Leo Bersani, *A Future for Astyanax*; Barthes, *S/Z*; Prendergast, *The Order of Mimesis*; Brooks, *Reading for the Plot*; Jameson, *The Political Unconscious*; and Schor, *Breaking the Chain*.

[64] Prendergast observes, "[T]he road of virtue [in Balzac] is a matter of 'investment', profit and prices." Prendergast, *The Order of Mimesis*, 108. It is also a matter of power. For Stendhal, too, virtue is a "calculation of the most personal and prosaic self-interest," as he writes in *De l'amour*, the text where he first attacks the sentimental paradigm. Stendhal, *De l'amour*, 220. In *De l'amour*'s rewriting of sentimentality, Rousseau's *Julie* remains faithful "solely to avoid being burned in the other world in a great cauldron of boiling oil" (221).

manipulating people into furthering his ends; and reading interactions for the self-interest structuring them, rather than for their surface content. Félix tells us only cursorily about the social triumphs that transformed him into a successful young man "at the pinnacle of public affairs" in this narrative of his beginnings, but we need no convincing, because we already know his skill on the level of domestic politics; his calculating ability, for example, to play up to Monsieur de Mortsauf by manipulating the old man's fondness for backgammon (185). Félix comments, "Later, when the curtain of the social stage lifted for me, how many Mortsaufs did I see" (146).

From sentimental tragedy to sentimental education. Twentieth-century materialist accounts of "modern tragic realism" have understood the insolubly fractured relation between individual and collective launching the protagonist into the wide world as Balzac and Stendhal's brilliant responses to the French Revolution, which dismantled a society of status but left no stable social or political organization in its wake.[65] "For the first time, the social world around him became a problem," Auerbach declares of Stendhal, and subsequent critics have extended Auerbach's observation to realism's plots and characters.[66] An archaeology of the early-nineteenth-century novel makes clear, in contrast, that realism appropriates this fractured relation from the sentimental novel rather than from the Revolution directly, transforming it from ethical dilemma to a psychosocial fact and from tragedy to enriching if brutal opportunity.[67] As we have seen, moreover, literary and political chronologies do not line up as neatly as in prevailing critical accounts. The sentimental fracture between individual and collective first emerged with the Enlightenment liberalism that itself shaped the Revolution, even while the Revolution gave this fracture profound new social resonance.

The realist debt to sentimental conflict not only complicates the reigning critical narrative that realism springs full-grown from the head of the Revolution; it complicates critical validations of realism as the Revolu-

[65] The quoted term is Erich Auerbach's in *Mimesis*, 458.

[66] Auerbach, *Mimesis*, 461.

[67] Brooks testifies to the importance of sentimental conflict in shaping realism when he compares the realist plot of *Bildung* to education in the novel of worldliness before the Revolution. For Brooks, the principal effect of the Revolution is to transform the world into a zone of contradiction. He writes, "[r]equired now is an intelligent perception of what Marx would soon call the contradictions of society. . . . Such contradictions did not exist within *le monde*; or rather, the system of *le monde* had relegated them to unconsciousness—until they violently asserted their reality in Revolution." Brooks, *Worldliness*, 280. Like all twentieth-century literary historians, Brooks credits Balzac and Stendhal with the literary inscription of Revolutionary contradictions, writing a genealogy of worldliness that skips from Laclos to realism as if no significant novels about society had emerged in the intervening forty years.

tion's direct literary heir. If realism responds to an " 'open' society, where everything is relative and changing," this situation is post-Revolutionary in the sense of *after* the Revolution.[68] The realist conflict between desire and the law grapples with the Revolution's consequences rather than its aims, and it does so by betraying the Revolutionary ideals negotiated intact in sentimental tragedy.

Once we uncouple realism from the Revolution, we can identify how realist poetics are responding to the July Monarchy social formation specifically. In his struggle to succeed, Félix experiences the social order in radically different fashion from the sentimental protagonist. In sentimentality, I have argued, the protagonist's social position is usually taken for granted; what matters is how s/he upholds society's moral foundations. For Félix, in contrast, social position is all; his trajectory in the novel is his metamorphosis from a "poor man, with no other future than my courage and my abilities," to one of the intimates of Louis XVIII (100). With this transformation of ethical heroism into social climbing, Balzac draws the reader's attention to the same liberal blindspot we have seen at issue in *Olivier* and *Armance*: the consequences of unequal social division.

In nineteenth-century politics, the blindspot does not remain unperceived for long. The problem of social division emerged onto the political stage with the liberal opposition to the Restoration. In these years, it was primarily configured as "the struggle of the people against the oppressive interests of the aristocrats," and it was thus mitigated by the promise of a solution: for France to return to the project of 1789.[69] With the advent of Louis-Philippe, in contrast, unequal social division started to vex political and social debate as an undeniable yet insoluble question. The question is, after all, another name for one of the central contradictions of the July Monarchy that erupted in numerous revolts and eventually brought down the regime with the Revolution of 1848: the flagrant discrepancy between the July Monarchy's symbolic legitimation in the ideals of the Revolution and its political structures, which institutionalized government by the privileged classes.[70] This contradiction was exacerbated

---

[68] Moretti, *Way*, 131.

[69] Furet, *Révolution*, 84.

[70] Furet writes, "Far from being a 'glorious revolution' . . . July 1830 revives and deepens all the conflicts born of 1789 . . . it exacerbates the Revolutionary character of French political culture" through "joining the recovery of freedom with the confiscation of political rights by the richest" (146). In Furet's neoliberal view, this contradiction is fatal to the French democratic tradition, encouraging "its least liberal aspect: a mixture of Jacobinism and Bonapartism" in response to the "spectacle of social inequality" (146). Furet distinguishes the democratic critique of social division from "[a]nother passion that plays a central role at this time in the civil struggles of the country and that entrenches its features yet further: this passion nourishes itself . . . on the idea of social class" (146). But in terming

by the rapid expansion of modern industrial capitalism during the 1830s and 1840s, accompanied by the spectacle of entrepreneurial exploitation and worker uprisings, which brought to national attention the conflict between Revolutionary ideals and social practice in the domain of economic production.[71]

For the young man of great expectations, however, the contradiction between Revolutionary aspirations and a regime of privilege can be unproblematically, if strenuously, resolved. While Félix is born to impoverished obscurity, his consummate abilities open to him a brilliant future. The realist plot of *Bildung*, in other words, responds to the problem of social division by discarding the principle of equality assumed by liberalism and posed as the goal of progressive July Monarchy politics when the inequalities masked by liberal ideology are revealed. In society conceived as "the war of interests," the strong dominate the weak, careers are open to talents, and freedom is seized rather than accorded as a founding human right (163).

JUST WANT IT!

The phrase "the war of interests" comes from Madame de Mortsauf, an unlikely spokesperson for the realist way of the world. But while this heroine seems the unadulterated residue of a sentimental novel in her view of adulterous love, her approach to worldly matters tells another tale.[72] When Félix first offers to stay with Madame de Mortsauf as tutor to her children, Madame de Mortsauf puts him on guard against his sentimental

---

the modern socialism invented during these years "another passion," Furet obscures its profound links to the period's versions of democracy. Both democratic and socialist discourses of the July Monarchy are in fact responding to the same spectacular contradiction between the symbolic foundations of the regime and its political and economic organization. The most influential account of social class to emerge marked by the political conflicts of these years is, of course, Marx's theory of history as class struggle, which owes so much to the tragedies of French politics since 1789 and specifically to the political climate of "Paris . . . the old high school of philosophy . . . and the new capital of the new world" during the 1830s and 1840s, to cite an 1843 letter by Marx, written as he prepared to journey to France, "because the air here makes me a serf and I see no room at all for free activity in Germany." Karl Marx, letter to Arnold Ruge, Kreuznach, September 1843, 211, 211–12.

[71] According to Pierre Rosenvallon, "The central problem of the first years of the July Monarchy is indeed that of social separation. The beginnings of industrialization frayed the torn social fabric yet further even as political tensions were heightened by the disappointment of hopes awakened during the Revolution of July." "La République du suffrage universel," 371. This problem only intensified across the 1830s and 1840s.

[72] What could be more paradigmatically sentimental, for example, than Madame de Mortsauf's definition of virtue: "If virtue does not consist in sacrificing oneself for one's children and husband, what, then, is virtue?" (249).

impulse. "Your heart will do you harm," she tells Félix. "I claim, from this moment, the right to teach you certain things" (132). Madame de Mortsauf distills these "things" in a letter she writes as Félix sets off to make his fortune in Paris, which Félix credits with his wordly success.

This letter opens in sentimental fashion, by refusing the theory that society serves individual gratification: "To explain society according to the theory of individual happiness skilfully enjoyed at the expense of all is a fatal doctrine" (154). Above this imperative, Madame de Mortsauf ranks duty to others: "In your eyes, society will thus only be explained . . . by the theory of duties" (155). By the end of her letter, however, Madame de Mortsauf is justifying adherence to duty as the best path to the top of contemporary (Restoration) society. Displacing the liberal opposition "individual happiness" and "duty" with the eminently realist watchword, success, she advises, "*just want it!* Your future is now in this motto alone, the motto of great men" (168). Vautrin could not have put it better. Nor would he quarrel with the figure of Napoleon that the royalist countess somewhat surprisingly offers as a model for how to dominate society.[73]

How are we to make sense of the contradictions in Madame de Mortsauf's view of public life, which are reinforced by her private allegiance to sentimental ethics? Unless Madame de Mortsauf is not as sentimental as she seems. The sentimental heroine regards the two imperatives tearing her apart as positively constituted ethical duties. Thus, Claire d'Albe will not betray her children, because they belong to her "sacred duties" (735). Madame de Mortsauf, in contrast, depicts her maternal bond as an intoxicating passion: "[I]t is as if my heart is drunk with motherhood," she tells Félix (93). Similarly, she does not depict her duty to her husband in positive terms, representing it as suffering and saintly martyrdom.

Madame de Mortsauf also does not cast her motivations as positively constituted ethical duties when it comes to her own happiness. Claire d'Albe frankly owns her love even while she insists on the impossibility of its consummation. Madame de Mortsauf, in contrast, sublimates its erotic character, which she will only act out somatically in her death from jealousy. Her manner of death reinforces her difference from a sentimental heroine. She dies from a negation of the imperatives tormenting her, from anorexic refusal, rather than from the shock when the two conflicting imperatives collide with all their force, like Claire.

What then motivates Madame de Mortsauf if not the sentimental "conflicting duties"? On her deathbed, stripped of "all social disguises," her wasted face expresses "the aggressive daring of desire and repressed

---

[73] "You know how much Monsieur de Mortsauf hated Napoleon . . . well! he admired him as the boldest of captains, he often explained his tactics to me. Couldn't this strategy be applied to the war of interests?" (163).

threats," according to Félix (295, 293). Félix is yet more explicitly in the utopian moment when he helps Madame de Mortsauf nurse her ailing husband back to health. Madame de Mortsauf finds this situation so gratifying, he tells his reader, because it offers "a way to join the strict observation of *laws* and the fulfillment of her unconfessed desires" (210, emphasis added). Even the seemingly sentimental Madame de Mortsauf turns out to be driven by the quintessential realist conflict; no wonder she can give Félix such good advice.

Madame de Mortsauf's tragedy is thus pointed antisentimental polemic, of a piece with Stendhal's delineation of the female protagonist in *Armance*. Madame de Mortsauf's struggles, too, expose the great ethical vocabulary of sentimentality as repression. Her appeals to duty, virtue, and sacrifice hide her inability to confront her own participation in the "real" conflicts motivating human behavior which Balzac, like Stendhal, frames in psychological terms.

THE GOAL OF ALL HER ACTIONS

While Félix pursues his "ambitious desires," Madame de Mortsauf remains paralyzed by her "unconfessed desires." It is tempting to invoke gender in explaining Félix and Madame de Mortsauf's different relations to their desires, and certainly, realist novels privilege female characters in their campaigns to discredit sentimentality as repression. But Balzac's novels, in particular, are also filled with female characters who quickly lose their sentimental illusions if they ever had them at all: the Goriot daughters, Dinah de la Baudraye, Madame de Bargeton, the Countess Ferraud, the Duchess de Langeais, Béatrix, and so on. Both male and female protagonists prove skillful in negotiating "the culture of a world where values and meanings are always and only 'relative', because they are based solely on social relationships of power and threat," as Moretti remarks.[74] Gender does make a difference in these negotiations, but it affects the kinds of careers open to male and female protagonists, not their ability to engage in *Realpolitik*.

Moretti is eloquent on the narrative of social mobility tempting the ambitious hero. The way of the world, however, offers female characters substantially differing returns. While it opens "the possibility to become 'anything' " to the young hero, it situates the heroine squarely within "the Family and Marriage," to use Balzac's phrase from one novel of female sentimental education, *La Muse du département*.[75] This asymmetry differs

---

[74] Moretti, *Way*, 131.

[75] Ibid. *La Muse du département* ends by returning its heroine "quite simply to the Family and to Marriage" (341).

markedly from sentimentality, where there is no gender divide in the careers of the protagonists. Heroes and heroines alike struggle with the agonies of liberal subjecthood in the enclosed universe of sentimental romance.

Balzac positions *La Muse du département* against early-nineteenth-century sentimentality in a letter to Madame Hanska, claiming that his novel rewrote *Adolphe* "*from the side of the real* [*du côté réel*]."[76] And the realist plot of sentimental education might seem more "realistic" than the sentimental plot of double bind in differentiating women's careers within the family from men's access to political and professional self-realization. With this distinction, realism reveals the substantive contemporary inequality between men and women that is elided in sentimental universalism and thereby pursues the critique of sentimentality central to July Monarchy debates around the novel in progressive rather than conservative fashion.

There is some truth to this argument. But its limits are Balzac's misogyny. According to Balzac, the substance of women's ambitions is romantic gratification, like Dinah in *La Muse du département* or Madame de Mortsauf in *Le Lys* (and occasionally romantic gratification mixed with improved social position, like the Goriot daughters).[77] "To be loved is the goal of all her actions; to excite desires, that of all her gestures," Balzac wrote, defining "woman" in the *Physiologie du mariage*, where he discredited the sentimental paradigm of human relations in the years between *Sténie* and his invention of realist codes (1824–29), using a popular genre of nonfictional ethnography.[78]

If Balzac's narrative of female sentimental education is sentimental conflict "*from the side of the real* [*du côté réel*]," the "real" sentimental heroine is, in other words, the older woman [*femme de trente ans*]. Balzac was not shy about this figure as one of his great literary creations and critics from his time to the present have agreed. As Sainte-Beuve remarked: "The

---

[76] Cited in Bernard Guyon's introduction to *La Muse*, 140.

[77] Counterexamples like Renée d'Estourade, who manages a marriage of convenience as her mediated path to public success, dialogue with this fundamental truth about femininity in *La Comédie humaine*, as Renée herself dialogues with Louise, the exemplary woman according to Balzac's definition, in *Mémoires de deux jeunes mariées*.

[78] Balzac, *Physiologie du mariage*, 924. In this respect, the *Physiologie du mariage* is Balzac's equivalent to Stendhal's *De l'amour*. To open the *Physiologie*, Balzac himself makes explicit all he leaves out when he reduces woman to love. Calculating that there are perhaps fifteen million women in France, Balzac declares, "We will begin by subtracting from this total sum around nine million of these creatures that, on first glance, seem to have enough resemblance with women, but that an in-depth examination constrains us to reject." "These creatures" are women "whose hands are black as those of monkeys, with skin as weathered as old parchment" (924). Balzac's ideological arithmetic results in a definition of femininity that is both "aged" and "classed": a woman "generally is recognized by the whiteness, the delicacy, the softness of her skin" and so on (923).

theory of the older woman with all her advantages, her superior attributes, and her definite perfections only dates from today. M. de Balzac invented it, and it is one of his most genuine [*réelles*] discoveries in the realm of the novel of private life [*roman intime*]."[79] From the perspective of early-nineteenth-century sentimentality, however, the older woman is the sentimental heroine stripped of her ethical grandeur. She does particularize sentimental univeralism, but her specifically female conception of happiness is just as distanced from women's historical experience as sentimentality's use of women to embody the impasses of liberal subjecthood, as will become clear when we consider the paradoxically more "realist" representation of women's lives found in the sentimental social novel. The realist move to particularize femininity by reducing it to a desire for love has, moreover, the disadvantage of trivializing the female protagonist's suffering. Realist novels often bash their heroines for having narrow ambitions, in contrast to sentimental novels, which hold their heroines' exemplary anguish up for its readers' admiration and compassion.

WHAT I UNDERSTAND AS SACRIFICE

Mixed admiration and compassion for the protagonist are essential to the sympathetic bond sentimentality establishes between reader and text. *Le Lys* includes this bond, too, in its position-taking against the sentimental form. The sympathetic bond is the subject matter of the narrative framing Félix's sentimental education, which depicts his efforts to win a woman's hand in marriage through sharing his past. "Today you want my past, here it is," Félix tells Natalie de Manerville, the young woman whom he loves. "I have imposing memories buried in the depth of my soul . . . these old emotions . . . cause me so much pain when they are awakened" (15–16). Depicting his painful past as a secret that he divulges to promote community with his future wife, Félix acts in classic sentimental fashion. Compare, for example, his words to the way Edouard frames his story in Duras's novel of the same name. "Here . . . my promise is accomplished, you will no longer complain that there is no *past* in our friendship. . . .

[79] Sainte-Beuve, *Causeries du lundi* (1851), cited in Balzac, *la Comédie humaine* 2: 1017–18. It is striking that Sainte-Beuve, like Balzac, uses the word *réel* to compare Balzac's plot of female sentimental education to the preceding state of the "novel of private life [*roman intime*]." With such a qualification, both writers register the other realist use of the term "real," besides designating social life as relations of power. This use is the realist equation of reality with feminine sexuality so astutely analyzed in recent feminist work on nineteenth-century French realism. See, for example, Schor's *Breaking the Chain*, Emily Apter's *Feminizing the Fetish*, Dorothy Kelly's *Fictional Genders*, Janet Beizer's *Ventriloquized Bodies* and Jann Matlock's *Scenes of Seduction*.

One thinks one's memories indelible . . . and yet when one goes to the bottom of the soul to seek them, one reawakens a thousand new pains" (1012).

Félix encourages Natalie's compassion in the body of his narrative by using sentimental codes soliciting sympathy, such as the analysis of the heart and emphatic diction at moments of high moral effort. To promote his "interesting" status, he also identifies himself with sentimental protagonists as well as with the Romantic hero, whose *mal du siècle* itself owes much to sentimental suffering: "Geniuses snuffed out in tears, unappreciated hearts, saintly Clarissa Harlowes . . . you alone can know the boundless joy at that moment when a heart opens for you" (98).[80] The only problem with Félix's appeal for sympathy is the unsympathetic story he has to tell. This problem is not lost on his reader, Natalie. "You have the air of the Knight of the Sad Face [*Triste Figure*], which always interested me deeply . . . but I did not know that you had killed the most beautiful and virtuous of women in your entrance into society" (328). "You had for your beginnings . . . a perfect mistress . . . who asked you only to be faithful, and you caused her to die of sorrow; I know of nothing more monstrous. . . . Poor woman! she certainly suffered, and when you have composed a few sentimental phrases, you think you have settled your debts with her coffin" (327). From sentiments to "sentimental phrases": Natalie eloquently captures how Félix turns sentimentality from values into rhetoric; from principles into language frankly in the service of power.

But Félix's failure to incite sympathy offers consolations of its own. If his betrayal of sentimentality kills Madame de Mortsauf, its narration gives Natalie the knowledge not to repeat her mistake. "That is doubtless the reward awaiting my affection for you," Natalie responds to Félix's story, as she raises concerns of personal profit; her interest in the economic rather than the sentimental sense (327). Natalie is a good reader, for on closer consideration, this is indeed the readerly contract Félix works with all along. "I would like my confidence to *double* your affection," Félix specifies when he gives Natalie his narrative (16, emphasis added). He offers his past, not to solicit sentimental interest, but rather for personal gain: his story in return for her hand in marriage.[81] The exchange between

---

[80] Like sentimentality, Romanticism engages the aporias of liberalism, as Waller discusses in *The Male Malady*. On the relationship between Romanticism and liberalism in the English context, see Celeste Langan's *Romantic Vagrancy*.

[81] The distance between this exchange and the sympathetic bond can be measured by comparing Félix's appeal to the lines in Duras's *Edouard* when Edouard leaves his story with his reader: "Read this manuscript, but never talk to me of what it contains; do not even try to see me today, I want to be alone" (1012). Brusquely refusing the reader's sympathy, Edouard shows that he has no personal stakes in sharing his story and thereby heightens his reader's sentimental interest in his situation.

Félix and Natalie thus turns out to exemplify the realist narrative contract as it has been so eloquently explained by a critical lineage inspired by Barthes. Natalie gets knowledge from Félix's narrative, which compensates for the treacheries of deals within the narrative's plot, as well as the deal she is offered by the narrative's protagonist himself.[82]

In the narrative framing Félix's sentimental education, in other words, Balzac suggests that the realist contract between reader and text takes shape in an appropriation and displacement of sentimentality's sympathetic bond. In rewriting the sympathetic bond, the realist narrative contract emerges from a poetic structure with profound political significance. The sympathetic bond is, I have argued, aesthetic consolation for the impasses of the social contract. It is the glue forging an aesthetic community, which transforms the social contract's difficulty in accommodating negative and positive rights from political impasse into aesthetic pleasure. The realist transformation of the sympathetic bond reworks this consolation, pursuing the same conservative agenda as the realist critique of sentimentality on the level of plot. The private exchange of knowledge between text and reader is what becomes of sentimental community when the social contract does not obtain, in society conceived as "the war of interests."[83] Instead of seeking to transform this situation, the realist contract offers the reader the means to dominate it from the comfort of the armchair; it is a literary structure founded on the "interpenetration of *knowledge* and *power*."[84] The great consolation of the realist contract is its reliability. While the protagonists may succeed or fail in their worldly struggles, the reader's insight grows with every page.[85]

---

[82] Prendergast remarks that while contracts between characters are unreliable, Balzac's discourse commands "complete public confidence . . . Balzac's 'accountancy' is impeccable, everything entered in its proper place within the fully responsible balance sheet of Truth," although Prendergast also points out that at moments Balzac himself cannot keep in check the treacherous instability of values and meaning in capitalist society (*Mimesis*, 102). See, too, Richard Terdiman's *Discourse/Counter-Discourse* for a nuanced discussion of the link between semiotic instability in Balzac's narratives of education and the contemporary flowering of modern capitalism.

[83] As Prendergast observes, "the notion of '[realist] contract' signifies the exact opposite of 'sociability' and its supporting conventions of mutual trust and understanding" (*Mimesis*, 85). Prendergast also remarks that Balzac keeps sociability alive in the salon of Mademoiselle des Touches. This observation supports my argument that Balzac was well aware of the antagonistic relation between the realist contract and sympathetic community, for Félicité des Touches, a.k.a. Camille Maupin, is, of course, the George Sand stand-in in *La Comédie humaine*. Sympathetic community remains essential to the sentimental social novel's ideological performance, as we will see.

[84] Terdiman, *Discourse*, 103.

[85] For an in-depth account of the complicated relation between the realist narrative contract and the realist plot of education, see Moretti (*Way*), Terdiman, and Prendergast.

No social relation has been more important for recent criticism of realism than the relation of contract. In theorizing the realist contract, critics have looked to two models of contract in particular: the Saussurian linguistic contract and the unregulated exchanges between individuals characterizing capitalism in undiluted form. They have missed, however, the realist contract's dialogue with the social contract, not as this notion is narrowly defined by Rousseau, but as the Revolution uses it to express the project to institute a rational government respecting both negative and positive rights.[86] Their omission is surprising because Balzac himself draws attention to this dialogue in the most well-known examples of the realist credo, as well as in *Le Lys*.

"Woe to those who accept the social contract, woe to you, woe to me; at that moment man no longer exists. His will dies away, he loses his rights and society only gives them back to him broken down," we have seen Vanehrs declare in *Sténie* (134). Fifteen years later, Vanehrs's position will be that of the great rebel, Vautrin. "A convict of the mettle of Collin, here before you, is a less cowardly man than others, and one who protests against the great disappointments of the social contract" (*Goriot*, 220). Central to Vautrin's protest is his adherence to an alternative form of social relation where the realist narrative contract comes to life. This contract is the private amoral exchange between exceptional individuals to dominate society for personal profit that realism offers its readers and that Vautrin offers Rastignac.

The details of Vautrin's amoral proposal to Rastignac are well known. Vautrin cynically advises Rastignac to court "a poor unhappy and wretched girl" and seem to sacrifice his social ambitions for her love (142). Vautrin will then make the couple rich by arranging the murder of the girl's brother, who is standing between her and her father's fortune, and Rastignac can share this fortune with Vautrin. What has not been discussed is that Vautrin emphatically constructs his alternative to the social contract as a negation of sentimental values. Vautrin's deal, after all, turns around the eminently sentimental gesture of sacrifice, which Vautrin transforms from a sublime affirmation of community to a calculated strategy of self-interest unfolding with the banality of everyday life: "What I understand by sacrifice is to sell an old suit in order to go to the Cadran Bleu and eat mushroom quiche together," Vautrin specifies (143). For Vautrin, as for Félix, sentimental sacrifice is a ruse, what Vautrin calls

---

[86] Prendergast, for example, passes over the Revolution when he asserts that Balzac dismisses "[t]he Social Contract and its latter day transformation, the Napoleonic Code," as "empty fictions" (*Mimesis*, 96). Resurrecting the emergence of realism out of the sentimental paradigm makes clear that for Balzac, the fiction of the social contract, far from empty, is too full.

"good sense." "Let millions come to this young woman, she will throw them at your feet . . . 'Take them, my beloved! Take them, Adolphe, Alfred! Take them, Eugène!' she will say if Adolphe, Alfred, or Eugène has had the good sense to sacrifice himself for her" (142–43).

This imaginary scenario illustrates how thoroughly Balzac identifies the social contract with sentimentality, for Vautrin couches the fulfillment of his unsocial contract as a parody of sentimental codes. Its culminating moment is a tableau where Vautrin's heroine uses sentimentality's emphatic rhetoric at moments of high moral effort to recompense a protagonist possessing the two-syllable name starting with a vowel that often designates sentimental heroes like Eugène de Rothelin, Adolphe, and Oswald. But in the treacherous world of realism, no community guarantees the stability of the signifier; Eugène de Rastignac is not one in a substitutable chain of virtuous protagonists, despite his name. While he responds, "Silence, sir . . . at this moment sentiment is all my science," his learning will have been thoroughly desentimentalized by the novel's end (146).

Rastignac's use of the word "science" is not by chance and already indicates the violation of sentimentality to come. Realism conveys scientific, professional knowledge of society that differs as substantially from the kind of social knowledge found in sentimental novels as the form of the contract delivering it. If sentimental novels were famed for their depictions of society, I have explained this fame in light of the sentimental novel's sympathetic bond. Sentimental novels, I have argued, expose the ethical contradictions underwriting liberal society. The knowledge emerging from the realist contract is, in contrast, encyclopedic, as Barthes, Prendergast, Hamon, and D. A. Miller observe. To cite Prendergast: "Like the police file described in *Splendeurs* . . . Balzac's novels open and complete the file on modern life, they uncover and record what in the *Avant-propos* is called the 'sens caché' of reality."[87] As Prendergast's Foucauldian comparisons make clear, encyclopedic knowledge is a means of domination. The realist contract thus pursues the realist understanding of society as founded on relations of power in the kind of knowledge it delivers as well as in how it structures the reader's compensation.

I WRITE FOR MEN, NOT GIRLS

During the 1830s and 40s, writers and critics associated the realist novel with a male viewpoint. This gendering occurred when realism's encyclopedic approach to social representation was characterized with reference to professions exercised overwhelmingly, if not exclusively, by men. The

---

[87] Prendergast, *Mimesis*, 102.

Avant-Propos, for example, opens by comparing *La Comédie humaine*'s depictions of manners to the investigations of the most eminent recent scientists. The essay proceeds to annex to the novel the knowledges of the historian, the archaeologist, the philosopher, the bureaucrat, and the political theorist.

The slippage between gender and genre in such emphasis on the professions emerges vividly if we contextualize Balzac's claims in relation to the literary commonplaces they challenge. During the first half of the nineteenth century, critics associated the sentimental codes for depicting manners with an intimate, amateur observation of private life where women excelled. The previously cited review of *Vanina d'Ornano* voices a commonplace opinion: "It has been said that love, merely an episode in the existence of men, is the entire existence of women. The novel should then be for them what history is for us. . . . This branch of literature belongs to them; it exists only through them and for them. . . . if history keeps a faithful record of all the events of public life . . . private life [*la vie intérieure*] fell to the novel."[88] When the *Avant-propos* professes to write "the history forgotten by so many historians, the history of manners," it displaces private life from a discourse of female to male expertise.[89] It thus lays claim to the sentimental novel's domain at the price of women's authority over it.

The most important code in the realist transmission of encyclopedic knowledge is extensive, authoritative description.[90] And this code is particularly important in polemic associating realism's social knowledge with men. To set the scene with extensive, authoritative description at the opening to *Le Rouge et le noir*, Stendhal constructs his narrator as a

---

[88] Review of *Vanina d'Ornano*, 3–4.

[89] Victor Hugo similarly treats encyclopedic knowledge as the province of men in *Notre-Dame*, when he excludes his female readers from the novel's chapters on architecture and history. His celebrated chapter on the cathedral and the book, for example, begins, "Our women readers will excuse us for stopping a moment to seek what could be the thought hiding beneath these enigmatic words of the archdeacon: *This will kill that. The book will kill the building.*" Victor Hugo, *Notre-Dame de Paris*, 174. Hugo's stance was reiterated by reviewers who commented that while "women will understand the delicate analyses, the passion and the dreams . . . we do not think that there is one who did not skip the chapters on architecture when she read *Notre-Dame de Paris*." A. Vacquerie, "Par qui la critique devrait être faite," 67. The historical novel was another subgenre trafficking in encyclopedic knowledge, but it lost the battle to dominate the novel by the middle of the 1830s. When Hugo excludes his female readers from some of his novel's chapters, he may indicate one literary reason for the historical novel's lack of success. The subgenre alternates a Gothic or sentimental plot with encyclopedic knowledge, but never fuses these two features into a united narrative poetics. Such alternation contrasts markedly with realism, where the discovery of knowledge underpins the construction of plot.

[90] On the encyclopedic ambitions of realist description, see notably Philippe Hamon's *Introduction à l'analyse du descriptif*.

character: a blasé man of the world.[91] Balzac holds up a similar worldly Parisian man as ideal reader when he gives his authoritative descriptions a specific addressee. The "observations incomprehensible beyond Paris" opening *Ferragus*, for example, "will doubtless be grasped by those men of study and thought, of poetry and pleasure, who know how to harvest, while strolling in Paris, the mass of delights floating at all hours, between its walls."[92]

Contemporary critics, too, often focus on description when they represent realism's encyclopedic project in masculine terms. If Balzac is viewed in his time as "an anatomist, who dissects with the aid of the microscope and the scalpel: the analogy to medical science is constantly made," to cite Bernard Weinberg, Balzac's descriptions are seen to occupy center stage in his dissections.[93] Sometimes, these descriptions are credited with the entire expanse of professional expertise that Balzac claims as his own. Ten years before the *Avant-propos*, for example, Edouard Charton is writing: "Before a landscape, he describes as a geologist, as an astronomer, as a physicist, the irregularities of the terrain, the lighting of the sky, the whims of wind and clouds. Before a house, he contemplates, like an architect, a sculptor or a caster, the form of the roof, the contours of the doors and windows ... he is protean; he always has the technical term, the analytical impulse [*geste*]."[94] Description is associated with male professions, moreover, even in the rhetoric of critics who take it to task. Thus, Balzac is criticized for being a "mere auctioneer" preparing "inventories" in his excessive attention to detail.[95]

Critics also imply that realist description carries masculine connotations when they discuss novels by women without it. In such reviews, the absence of realist description indicates a novel's female authorship. "Novels written by women are clearer; they have this merit, that, if they do not always make us well acquainted with the time or country they seek to depict, they always make us acquainted with their author," proposes

---

[91] In contrast to Balzac, however, Stendhal also employs the light touch, which he admires. See, for example, Stendhal's "Walter Scott et La Princesse de Clèves," which uses Scott and Lafayette to epitomize "the two extremes when it comes to the novel. Should one describe the clothes of the characters, the countryside in which they find themselves, the shapes of their faces? or would one do better to paint the passions and the varied feelings which stir their souls? My reflections will be received badly. A great regiment of *literati* [*littérateurs*] is concerned to deify Sir Walter Scott and his way of writing." Stendhal, "Walter Scott et La Princesse de Clèves," 305–6.

[92] Balzac, *Ferragus*, 794.

[93] Weinberg, *French Realism*, 42.

[94] Edouard Charton, review of *Les Cent Contes drolatiques*, in *Revue Encyclopédique*, March 1832, cited in Weinberg, *French Realism*, 36.

[95] Weinberg, *French Realism*, 39.

a critic reviewing a sentimental social novel in 1835.[96] While this critic explains the absence of realist description with reference to an essential female personality, the absence is also a coherent poetic move: the light touch is a vital sentimental code. And the fact that women dominated sentimentality in the period before realism reinforces the feminine overtones of texts where realist description is absent. Such submerged slippage between gender and subgenre also facilitates the masculinization of texts where realist description occurs. When Girault de Saint-Fargeau, for example, contrasts novels by women distinguished for "sentiments, sensibility [*sensibilité*], even vague expression [that] were means of success for them," to novels by men containing "the sciences . . . in their most minute details or their most succinct results," he reacts to the fact that sentimental poetics have recently been the domain of women as well as to the fact that realism conveys encyclopedic knowledge associated with men.[97]

Balzac, indeed, sometimes positions realist description entirely in antisentimental terms. To take an example from his fiction, the lengthiest description in *Le Lys* is a blazon of Madame de Mortsauf that goes on for pages and pages. As in a sentimental novel, this blazon occurs at the moment in the narrative when the heroine appears as the object of the hero's desires. The blazon, however, inverts the sentimental movement from material to ideal, emphatically demonstrating that material, and particularly visual, detail holds the key both to social specificity and the truth of desire. This inversion is summed up by Félix's transformation of the sentimental commonplace that visual delineation cannot do justice to the soul. While Frédéric objects to Claire's portrait, "No, no, lifeless features will never depict Claire; and where I see no soul, I cannot recognize her" (716), Félix instead values Madame de Mortsauf's visual appearance as that compelling aspect of her person which exceeds the ability of representation: "Her visible attributes can moreover only be expressed by comparisons" (49).[98]

Balzac positions description similarly in his explicit polemic when the "Note" to the first edition of *Scènes de la vie privée* isolates "details," a term then commonly used for description, as his great literary innovation and the future of the novel as a form: "The distinctive mark [of talent] is

---

[96] Review of *Corisande de Mauléon*.

[97] Girault de Saint-Fargeau, *Revue*, 1: vi.

[98] The blazon begins: "My eyes were suddenly struck by white, plump shoulders on which I would have liked to be able to roll" (33–34). Balzac's contemporaries register the position-taking at issue in this description when they distinguish it for its incomprehensibility rather than for imparting knowledge. "This is the most stunning example of an unintelligible and stilted style that is all that is missing from Molière's *Précieuses ridicules*," comments a critic with the signature "Un ermite" in 1843. From *La Lecture*, 1843, cited in René Guise, "Balzac et le Bulletin de Censure," 279.

doubtless invention. But today when all possible combinations have been exhausted . . . details alone will constitute from now on the merit of works improperly named *Novels*."[99] The "Note" glosses a "Préface" that proclaims the *Scènes de la vie privée* as a battle to the death with the sentimental subgenre. "This work has thus been written out of hatred for the idiotic books that petty minds have offered women until now. Whether the author has satisfied the demands of the moment and of his undertaking . . . is not his problem to resolve. Perhaps the epithet that he confers on his predecessors will be turned against him. He knows that in literature not to succeed is to perish; and it is principally to artists that the public has the right to say: VAE VICTIS!"[100] In casting his "predecessors" as writing novels targeting a female audience, Balzac tacitly identifies them as writing sentimental novels, even if he does not name the form. Throughout its history, sentimentality is seen to have an elective affinity with a female audience. "This novel with its Gothic tone is best suited to women," declares Rousseau in the preface to *La Nouvelle Héloïse*, and the opinion is still commonplace in the 1830s (4). "Her romantic [*romanesque*] imagination, the fine details, the original ideas [*pensées*] of her novel, will seduce the most demanding men [*lecteurs*]: the deep sentimentality abundantly spread on all the pages of *Régina* will charm the most intractable women [*lectrices*]," a reviewer writes of Madame Tullie Moneuse's sentimental social novel in 1837.[101]

Writers and critics of the 1830s and 1840s also associate the realist novel with a male viewpoint when they distinguish realist representations of society for their immorality. "I write for men, not girls," is Balzac's response to critics who take his novels to task for their depraved characters.[102] He responds similarly to the criticisms of a female reader in a private letter: "It is perhaps unfortunate for the author that you did not resist this initial feeling, which grabs every innocent being upon hearing about a crime, upon the painting of any misfortune. . . . But how can I blame you for belonging to your sex?"[103] Balzac's equation of women with innocence is, of course, somewhat puzzling, except as a gesture of gallantry, in light of the plots of *La Comédie humaine*. Unless his equation, too, relies on the implicit slippage between gender and genre. To lay out the terms it collapses: women readers = women writers and sentimental novels = an interest in morality, which Balzac opposes to realism = immorality = the negation of sentimentality = the negation of women writers and readers = the domain of men.

---

[99] Balzac, "Note," 1175.

[100] Balzac, "Préface de la première édition," 1173.

[101] Review signed L.D. of *Régina*, 8.

[102] Conversation reported by Laure de Surville, in her *Balzac, sa vie et ses oeuvres*, 178.

[103] Letter to Laure de Surville's friend, Mme C, quoted in Surville, *Balzac*, 164.

Sand puts this spin on Balzac's opinion when she gives her rendition of it in *Histoire de ma vie*. According to Sand, Balzac declares, "You look for man as he should be; I take him as he is. I too like exceptional beings. . . . I enlarge them, I idealize them in the opposite direction, in their ugliness or stupidity. . . . Idealize in the pretty and the beautiful, this is women's work."[104] While Balzac might seem to be trivializing Sand's practice as "women's work," the literary geneaology of his comments tells a different tale. When Balzac à la Sand proclaims the novel as the inheritor of tragedy, (s)he employs a commonplace that runs back through French classicism to the *Poetics*, where Aristotle cites Sophocles on the difference between Euripides and himself.[105] Aligning Sand with the aesthetic of Sophocles, Balzac à la Sand generously casts his rival in the role of the author whose works are used to epitomize tragedy itself, from Aristotle on *Oedipus* to Hegel on *Antigone*.[106]

Stendhal, too, associates realism with a male viewpoint in discussing *Le Rouge et le noir*'s attention to corruption. The "Appendice" to *Le Rouge et le noir*, notably, claims that the "morality" of *Le Rouge et le noir* will be "horrible in the eyes of our beauties."[107]. According to Stendhal, female readers will find this "morality" repugnant because it exposes the unflattering dimensions to women's behavior as lovers and because it more generally exposes the underside of post-Revolutionary life idealized in the post-Revolutionary novels that appeal to women readers. Stendhal emphasizes that his defeminization of the novel is emphatically its masculinization when he offers *Le Rouge et le noir* to a male reader, addressing his explanatory "Appendice" to the Count Salvagnoli instead of to the sex he depicts as the great consumers of novels. By the middle of the article, Stendhal extends his male audience beyond the Count to prime candidates for the sentimental education: "Young men who want to be loved in a civilization where vanity has become, if not the passion, at least the feeling of every instant."[108] When Stendhal uses a rhetoric of

---

[104] Sand, *Histoire de ma vie*, 2: 161–62.

[105] "If the poet's description be criticized as not true to fact, one may urge perhaps that the object ought to be as described—an answer like that of Sophocles, who said that he drew men as they ought to be, and Euripides as they were," writes Aristotle in *Poetics*, 1484.

[106] The idea and ideal were terms applied to the sentimental aesthetic of condensation and purification in criticism of the time. The next chapter discusses the significance of the terms "idea" and "ideal" as they were used in debates over the novel during the 1830s and 1840s. For the moment, let Sainte-Beuve exemplify this use when he appreciates the sentimental genealogy in his previously cited article on Madame de Souza: "He who . . . thanks to the ideal . . . gives birth to a being worthy of their company is fortunate indeed" (699).

[107] Stendhal, "Appendice," 513.

[108] Ibid., 514.

masculinity to praise *Le Rouge et le noir*, he makes explicit a value judgment at issue in Balzac's masculinization of the novel as well. Stendhal is quite unabashed that the trivial femininized novels offering an unrealistic portrayal of post-Revolutionary society contrast with *Le Rouge et le noir*'s accurate depictions of immoral society addressed to men, which set a new literary standard for the genre.

The masculine connotations of the realist project are so powerful that Emile Souvestre personifies the novel itself as a man when he equates the genre with realist social knowledge in his influential essay on the novel's new cultural importance following the July Revolution. According to Souvestre, the novel's increased claim to prestige lies in its ability to portray modern society in panoramic, distanced, and accurate detail: The novel "tends each day . . . to become the camera obscura of society. . . . The more it will be faithful in tracing the world . . . the more we will give ourselves over to its authority. . . . It will give us the very [*propre*] history of our soul, like the doctor gives us that of our body."[109] Souvestre personifies the novel not only as a doctor but also as the paradigmatic realist protagonist acquiring insight into society. For the critic equating the bright future of the novel with realism's encyclopedic ambitions, "the novel . . . is a young man of great expectations . . . who makes his entrance into the world."[110]

---

[109] Emile Souvestre, "Du Roman," 124–25.

[110] Souvestre, "Du Roman," 126. Souvestre's rhetoric is all the more telling because he uses it despite himself. While he characterizes the novel's project as realist, he also praises the sentimental social novel, ranking Sand as well as Balzac at the top of the novelistic hierarchy. Theory and practice have, moreover, no obligation to coincide. Souvestre uses "Du Roman" as the preface to his own sentimental social novel, *Riche et pauvre*.

CHAPTER III

The Heart and the Code:
George Sand and the Sentimental Social Novel

WHAT WILL RULE THE NOVEL?

During the two decades that Balzac was drafting *La Comédie humaine*, women writers were prominent contributors across the spectrum of literary genres. In no genre were their works more numerous or more visible than the novel. When Narcisse-Achille de Salvandy, politician and man of letters, characterized women's recent impact on literature in general and the novel specifically, he suggested that the current literary field realized the Saint-Simonian dream of gender equality. "Our time, our country above all, is compensated for its faith in women's works. . . . At no period in society . . . have they shared so equally in the rewards for talent . . . the Saint-Simonians' wish is granted in the republic of letters."[1] Not all his contemporaries viewed women's literary prominence with such enthusiasm. Auguste Bussière illustrates the antifeminist reaction to what he called "women's novels" in an 1843 article for *La Revue de Paris*. "These ladies (whom I will certainly refrain from naming) will carry on so much they will end up making husbands interesting. Marriage is certainly a tyranny, and the tyrant must be slaughtered. This is the most sacred of duties. But as a result of these kinds of attacks, honest hearts, sensitive and gentle minds will eventually tire of seeing the sad head of what was formerly the family eternally dragged to be strung up by the levelers of community."[2]

---

[1] Salvandy, preface to Mme de Montpezat, *Natalie*, ii. "The Saint-Simonians' wish" could also refer to the Saint-Simonians' search for a "Woman Messiah" who would save the world with her message of love. The Saint-Simonians confirm women's contemporary importance as writers when they speculated on who might fill the position in the early 1830s. First considering whether the "Woman Messiah" had already come in the person of Staël, they then decided she might be Sand. Sand turned down this honor.

[2] Bussière, "Les Romans de femmes," 349. An intermediary position between Salvandy and Bussière is found in a review of two sentimental social novels by women from 1835. "However much the voices of criticism and society exert themselves against women authors, their number grows larger each day," the reviewer declared, affirming women's incontestable importance in the contemporary novel, albeit a bit reluctantly. The remainder of the review allowed female novelists complete equality with their confrères as long as it was

Women writers' recognized prominence in the novel of the 1830s and 1840s renders all the more noteworthy their absence from the generic paradigm that has become synonymous with the brilliant novelistic innovations of these years. Like Balzac and Stendhal, women were competing for top honors in the novel, and they, too, made their bids through writing works that pursued the novel's new power to intervene in public life. To assert this power, however, Balzac and Stendhal's consoeurs turned away from realist codes, preferring a subgenre also practiced by male writers that took over defining features of sentimentality in friendly rather than hostile fashion.[3]

This subgenre has been called the social novel in the only literary histories that preserve its memory, rightly identifying it as the first avant-garde literature in France.[4] I qualify it as the sentimental social novel to specify its place within a lineage that includes works as poetically diverse as the novels of Sand and Zola, as well as twentieth-century *romans à thèse*.[5] The sentimental social novel became an established generic practice in the two years following the Revolution of 1830, although its genesis can be traced back to Hugo's *Le Dernier Jour d'un condamné* if not Duras's *Edouard* and *Ourika* or Staël's *Delphine*. The subgenre flourished during

---

recognized that everyone's works left much to be desired. "To support their claims, they have furnished titles equal to those of accredited men of letters, and criticism has had to agree that there is no distinction to be made between their works and those of ordinary practioners of the novel." Review signed E.G. of *Savinie* and *Valida*.

    [3] Delphine de Girardin is, to my knowledge, the only female writer whose narratives identify with the realist position, as is suggested by their titles, *Le Lorgnon* (1831) and *La Canne de M. Balzac* (1836). The most important realist code in Girardin's texts is detailed description. In *Le Lorgnon*, for example, Girardin's narrator details character using a magic lorgnon "so perfectly in harmony with the visual rays, that reproduces so faithfully the smallest facial expressions, that shows these imperceptible details in such a marvelous fashion," that it reveals the individuals' deepest secrets. Delphine de Girardin, *Le Lorgnon* (1831) in *Nouvelles*, 7. This instrument is invented by a German mad scientist who sounds more like Balzac than E.T.A. Hoffmann's Dr. Coppelius: "at once physicist, doctor, mechanic, optician, he was everything, except a Bohemian" (7). Girardin also testifies, however, to the continued power of sentimentality when she frames the secret of character in moral rather than social terms; as "the physiognomy of your true feelings" (8). Balzac considered Girardin's novel frivolous, offering more praise for her *Monsieur le Marquis de Pontanges* (1835), whose generic identification is hybrid. While its plot represents an insoluble conflict between collective obligation and individual happiness, Girardin distances her readers from the sympathetic response by using the satirical narrative voice of the *roman gai*. Whether Girardin's most important realist writings are in fact her journalism on Parisian life in *La Presse* is a question Waller addresses in her forthcoming book on fashion journalism and the invention of the realist narrator.

    [4] See, notably, Biermann's *Avant-garde* and David Owen Evans's *Le Roman social sous la Monarchie de Juillet*.

    [5] On the *roman à thèse* in the twentieth century, see Susan Suleiman's *Authoritarian Fictions*.

the 1830s and 1840s, but fell from prestige along with the concept
of socially engaged literature more generally following the Revolution
of 1848.[6]

The sentimental social novel was the main generic practice competing
with realism for top literary and cultural honors in the novel throughout
the 1830s and 1840s. In the discursive slippage of contemporary polemic,
it was identified with a range of terms, notably as the literature of ideas,[7]

---

[6] I first discussed the sentimental social novel in "In Lieu of a Chapter on Some French
Women Realist Novelists," in *Spectacles of Realism*. There, I termed the subgenre the feminine social novel because I had not yet untangled the slippage between femininity and sentimental novels pervading literary discourse of the time. Representative titles of sentimental
social novels by women other than George Sand include Louise Maignaud's *La Fille Mère*
(1830) and *Les Etudians, épisode de la Révolution* (1831); Camille Bodin's *La Cour d'Assises* (1832), *Savinie* (1835), and *Elise et Marie* (1838); the Countess Merlin's *Histoire de
la Soeur Inès* (1832) and *Les Lionnes de Paris* (1845); Anne Bignan's *L'Echafaud* (1832);
Montpezat's *Natalie* (1833); B. Monborne's *Une Victime, esquisse littéraire* (1834) and
Deux Originaux (1835); Sophie d' Epinay Saint-Luc's *Valida, ou la Réputation d'une femme*
(1835); Charlotte de Sor's *Madame de Tercy, ou l'Amour d'une femme* (1836); Aurore Dupin's *Marguerite* (1836); the Baroness Aloïse de Carlowitz's *Caroline, ou le Confesseur*
(1833), *Le Pair de France, ou le Divorce* (1835), and *La Femme du progrès, ou l'Émancipa-
tion* (1838); Hortense Allart's *L'Indienne* (1833) and *Settimia* (1836); Tullie Moneuse's
Trois Ans après (1836) and *Régina* (1838); the Baroness de T***'s *Mystère* [signed by a
woman, I have not been able to establish the author's identity] (1837); Junot d'Abrantès's
La Duchesse de Valombray (1838); Flora Tristan's *Méphis ou le prolétaire* (1838); Madame
Charles Reybaud's *Mézelie* (1839); Virginie Ancelot's *Gabrielle* (1839) and *Emérance*
(1842), Mademoiselle Touchard-Lafosse's *Les Trois Aristocraties* (1843) and *L'Homme
sans nom* (1844); Hermance Lesguillon's *Rosane* (1843); Angélique Arnaud's *La Comtesse
de Servy* (1838), *Clémence* (1841), and *Coralie l'inconstante* (1843); Sophie Pannier's
L'Athée (1835) and *Un Secret dans le mariage* (1844); Michelle-Catherine-Joséphine Tarbé
des Sablons's *Roseline, ou de la Nécessité de la religion dans l'éducation des femmes* (1835)
and *Zoé, ou la Femme légère* (1845); Clémence Robert's *René l'ouvrier* (1841); Caroline
Marbouty's *Ange de Spola, études de femmes* (1842) and *Une Fausse Position* (1844); the
Countess Dash's *Un Mari* (1843); and Daniel Stern's *Nélida* (1846). Representative titles of
sentimental social novels by men include Victor Hugo's *Le Dernier Jour d'un condamné*
(1829); Emile Souvestre's *Riche et pauvre* (1836); Ernest Desprez's *Un Enfant* (1833) and
Les Femmes vengées (1834); Louis Couailhac's *Pitié pour elle* (1837); Armand-Ambroise
Rochoux's *Le Coeur et le code* (1839); Etiennez's *Un Droit de mari* (1834); Michel Masson's *Vierge et martyre* (1836); Félix Servan's *Maria Joubert, ou les Chagrins d'une jeune
mariée* (1836); Frédéric Soulié's *Le Conseiller d'Etat* (1835); Alphonse Brot's *Priez pour
elles* (1835); and Auguste Luchet's *Frère et soeur* (1838). For additional sentimental social
novels, see the bibliography. As should become clear, Hugo's *Claude Gueux* (1834) also
employs key sentimental social codes, albeit in highly condensed fashion.

[7] Girault de Saint-Fargeau exemplifies the July Monarchy conception of the "literature
of ideas" in the "Préface" to his *Revue des romans*: "Writers are separated in two camps,
march under two banners: here, literature is considered a means of distraction, there, a
means of direction; the former are concerned with no goal; the latter, under the influence of
an idea, march towards a demonstration." Girault de Saint-Fargeau, *Revue*, 1:vi.

the philosophical novel,[8] and the social novel.[9] Critics also called it the novel of private life [*roman intime*][10] and the novel of manners [*roman de moeurs*],[11] designations long applied to the sentimental novel in a nomenclature that continued into the 1830s and 1840s. That critics used these terms, novel of private life and novel of manners, to qualify realist works as well indicates their profound uncertainty over what poetics would inherit sentimentality's literary mantle.[12]

Given the subsequent triumph of realist codes, it may be hard to imagine that nineteenth-century audiences could prefer another literary form for depicting society. But "what will be the king of the novel," was an open question before the Revolution of 1848, as the extraordinary reputation of the form's most prominent practitioner makes clear.[13] Literary historians have long written the history of George Sand's career according to the logic of exception: as Sand's exception to women's invisibility in the nineteenth-century republic of letters, and as her exception to the triumph of realism from which women writers have inexplicably been absent. During the July Monarchy, however, George Sand was the most celebrated among notable female novelists, as well as being the most celebrated novelist altogether. "Strange that the most virile talent of our

---

[8] An announcement for forthcoming novels in *Le Siècle*, for example, qualifies Ancelot's sentimental social *Emérance* as "a philosophical work, a true painting of modern manners disguised as a novel."

[9] Thus, a review signed W. W. of Sand's *Le Compagnon du Tour de France* in *Le Constitutionnel* describes Sand's preferred subgenre as "the philosophical novel, the social novel" (2). In his *Literarische-politische avant-garde in Frankreich*, Biermann states that "the designation 'social novel' appeared for the first time in 1838, as subtitle to the novel *Méphis ou le prolétaire* [a sentimental social novel] by Flora Tristan." *Avant-garde*, 81. The subtitle was not present in the 1838 edition I consulted at the Bibliothèque Nationale.

[10] Assessing sentimental social novels by Tullie Moneuse in *Le Charivari*, the reviewer comments, "*Régina*, is like *Trois Ans après*, a novel of private life." Review of *Régina* and *Trois Ans après*.

[11] A review of Camille Bodin's *Pascaline*, for example, differentiates it from her previous sentimental social novels by stating, "*Pascaline* does not belong as specifically . . . to the genre of the novel of manners." Review signed F.T.C., 2.

[12] In "Lettre à un ami de la province sur quelques livres nouveaux," Ad. Guéroult associates Balzac with "the novel of private life," when he writes, "Three thousand years ago, Homer had discovered the novel of private life and the drama of adultery . . . and Monsieur de Balzac and Monsieur Alexandre Dumas are only two bastards of the old, blind musician of Ionia" (179). A review in *Le Siècle* draws attention to the generic imprecision of "novel of manners" when it criticizes the fact that the term is used simply as a marketing tool: "The windows of the readings rooms are cluttered with more or less boring novels which proudly parade under the title, *Novel of manners*." For the reviewer, "the novel of manners" should rather specifically pursue mimesis as envisioned by realism. It should be "the mirror of all this great society of the nineteenth century, which offers to the observer's eye so many rich and picturesque details." Review signed G. of *Magdeleine la repentie*.

[13] Gustave Planche, "Les royautés littéraires. Lettre à M. Hugo," 533.

period should be a woman's! It is obvious to us . . . that no current pen has as much vigor as hers," declared a critic in 1838, stating the reigning contemporary view.[14] The sentimental social novel constitutes the dominant generic horizon shaping most of Sand's important works across the 1830s and 1840s; works running from *Indiana*, *Valentine*, *Lélia*, and *Jacques* to *Le Compagnon du Tour de France*, *Le Meunier d'Angibault*, and *Le Peché de Monsieur Antoine*.[15] From her first novel, *Indiana*, moreover, Sand contributes much to the emergence of the subgenre out of sentimentality and against realism.

Since Sand plays a crucial role in the history of the sentimental social novel, its dominant codes could be resurrected with her oeuvre alone. Despite its accuracy, however, such a focus would do nothing to show that Sand was contributing to a densely populated generic position, that *Indiana* was not the first sentimental social novel, and that other sentimental social novelists were important and influential in their time. I have thus preferred to illustrate the sentimental social novel by referring both to forgotten works and to two works by Sand which frame the years of the form's greatest vitality: her first novel, *Indiana* (1831), and *Le Meunier d'Angibault* (1845).

Reading Sand against the horizon of the sentimental lineage (including both sentimentality and the sentimental social novel), we can better grasp not only what she shares with her contemporaries but also unique aspects of her practice that set her work apart. Through passing references to Sand, I want to suggest that she at once perfects the codes of the sentimental social novel, breaks them, and exploits their aesthetic contradictions in elegant and socially incisive fashion. While this study does not contain extensive readings of Sand's texts, its archaeology will, I hope, offer a new grid for appreciating her literary interest. Perhaps the most poignant moment in Schor's sophisticated rehabilitation of Sand is when Schor admits that she still finds Sand's work illegible in some fundamental way.[16] This way is our long-standing poetic preference for realism, which is understandable given the past 150 years of the novel and the power of realism in other media and genres. Schor makes her realist viewpoint evident when she declares that, "to read idealist fiction necessarily entails a painful renunciation of the perverse pleasure of the detail and the illusion of referential plenitude it provides."[17] But such absence of detail is a power-

---

[14] Review signed H.L. of George Sand's "*La Dernière Aldini—Les Maîtres Mosaïstes*," 1.

[15] *Consuelo* is a notable exception, taking the historical novel as its dominant generic horizon.

[16] Schor states, "My claim for Sand's oeuvre . . . is that it is a worthy conceptual object, that it is not so much readable or rereadable as it is theorizable" (*Sand and Idealism*, 216).

[17] Ibid., 46.

ful code in sentimentality, which predates realism, rather than "realism to be corrected," as Sand's contemporaries make clear.[18] For a respected critic like Philarète Chasles, realist description is "an interminable inspection that leads to boredom. Monsieur de Balzac has established himself as the great minister and instigator of this deadly imperative."[19] Chasles offers this comment in the context of praising a sentimental social novel using the light touch, which exhibits the "merit of grace and freshness that today are rare."[20]

As in the archaeology of sentimentality, I use representative examples to reconstruct the poetics of an entire subgenre, although I will not focus so exclusively on a single text. Diverse novels are, first of all, necessary to illustrate one distinctive code of the sentimental social form. If it inevitably offers an emphatic opinion on contemporary social issues, opinions in individual works range across the political spectrum. I also cite from a variety of texts as prelude to considering why women did not participate in the genesis of realism, in order to underline the number of women writing novels on post-Revolutionary society at the time of Balzac and Stendhal. For this reason, too, most of my examples are drawn from works by women, although I am describing a poetics used by both women and men. The contemporary condition of women will be the social issue that figures most prominently in my description, since the overwhelming majority of sentimental social novels by women are devoted to the subject. As in previous chapters, I am abstracting from a large number of examples and individual works fit into the paradigm according to the relation of family resemblance.

THE HEART AND THE CODE

Salvandy's enthusiasm for novels by women comes from a lengthy preface to the sentimental social novel *Natalie* (1833) by Madame de Montpezat. In his preface, Salvandy represents women's current prominence in the novel as the continuation of their extraordinary distinction in the decades following the Revolution. "What a period when, without repeating all those famous names, the author of *Adèle de Sénange* [Souza] and the writer exalting Malek Adhel [Cottin] shine among a crowd of other rival

---

[18] Ibid. Schor similarly notices two other key sentimental codes, but does not do their difference from realism justice when she observes that the idealist novel "refuses the seductive hermeneutic code that propels the classical realist text forward [the code I have termed "all should be clear"] even as it undoes conventions of characterization [the code of idealization]" (46).

[19] Philarète Chasles, review of *Gabrielle*.

[20] Ibid.

celebrities," Salvandy declares, singling out among this crowd Staël, Genlis, and Montolieu.[21]

From its opening, *Natalie* bears out Salvandy's literary geneaology. After a short frame narrative, Montpezat's epistolary work begins in medias res with the protagonist's analysis of the heart, drafted in a letter to her confidante. And from her first words, the novel's protagonist, Natalie, lays out her situation using the classic sentimental concepts of individual freedom and collective welfare. "These knots that I detested are now broken! This cold and heavy chain that froze my youth is now snapped! I am free, my dear Aglaé! The sympathetic law [*la loi compatissante*] gives me back to society, to happiness, to myself."[22] With the difference that while individual freedom and collective welfare inevitably conflict in sentimentality, Natalie seems to have found a way to harmonize them. For Natalie, there exists a "sympathetic law," a form of collective participation realizing the sentimental ideal of a community founded on sympathy. That law is divorce in this novel set in the Napoleonic period. Freeing the heroine from onerous bonds to an unloved husband chosen by her mother, divorce restores her simultaneously "to society, to happiness, to herself," as it seems to exemplify the social contract working properly (11). Has Natalie finally solved the sentimental double bind? Could Claire d'Albe and numerous other protagonists have been saved if only they had been willing to consider this option, which was, moreover, legal throughout the flowering of the sentimental subgenre?

Sentimental novels never consider divorce as an option for reasons at the intersection of poetics and ideology. From a sentimental perspective, divorce dilutes the purity of the tragic collision between individual freedom and collective welfare that is crucial to the subgenre's resolution of Revolutionary political impasse. If in *Natalie*, too, divorce turns out to be no solution, it is for social reasons internal to the plot. After her statement that she has happily resolved the tensions between the heart and social obligations, Natalie proceeds to hear stories slandering her. Despite its legality, she finds divorce brands her as an *"unprincipled woman"* "as order was restored in society, as ideas of morality and religion resumed their power" (49). Natalie's mother underscores the harmful effects of such slander in the course of telling her own story, which foreshadows the possibility that Natalie may not find the happiness she seeks. Her mother, too, the reader discovers, divorced during the Revolution and never overcame the social ostracism resulting from it. "Should I not also bless my father for having chosen such a worthy husband for me?" we

---

[21] Salvandy, preface to *Natalie*, xli.

[22] Madame de Montpezat, *Natalie*, 11. Subsequent page references will appear parenthetically in the text.

saw Claire d'Albe ask, introducing her dilemma by framing it in positive terms. With Natalie's opening comments, Montpezat's novel similarly first raises in positive fashion the conflict that the subsequent events of the narrative repeat with increasingly painful consequences.

The conflict between freedom and social norms escalates to a tragic impasse when Natalie meets and falls in love with the admirable Count Ernest de Léoville. Ernest loves Natalie and would like to marry her, but he is forbidden to do so by his prejudiced, aristocratic mother because of the scandalous rumors surrounding his beloved's behavior. Unwilling to betray his duty to his family, misled by a scheming friend of Natalie's into believing that these rumors may be true, Ernest mournfully gives in to his mother's desire that he marry the socially impeccable Blanche de Saint-Réal. At the end of the novel, he realizes that he gave credence to worldly opinion too quickly, and Natalie generously forgives him, thereby poignantly driving home to him both society's error and his own. All that is left for the two lovers is death. While Natalie pines away, Ernest finally defies his mother, who has also barred him from post-Revolutionary public life, and he is killed while displaying brilliant heroism in Bonaparte's army.

Natalie's plot structure is exemplary: like sentimentality, the sentimental social novel generates its narrative from an initial conflict between collective obligation and freedom. As in sentimentality too, the events of the plot repeat this conflict with ever-increasing force, most often culminating in disaster, if not death. "Learn, my Gabrielle, that a woman's life is one long suffering," writes a mother trying to prepare her daughter for her entrance into the world in Tarbé des Sablons's *Roseline, ou de la Nécessité de la religion dans l'education des femmes*, and the same may be said of the protagonists' careers in most sentimental social novels.[23]

The sentimental social novel also retains the sentimental principle of plot construction: "all should be clear." "I will only have a moment's pity for someone who is struck down in a moment," we remember Diderot writing. "But what happens if the blow keeps me waiting, if I see the storm brewing, and it then hangs suspended over my head or someone else's for a long time?"[24] In sentimental social novels as well, readers watch the disasters coming from afar, warned sometimes by these novels' titles (*Le Pair de France, ou le Divorce*; *Caroline, ou le Confesseur*; *Roseline, ou de la Nécessité de la religion dans l'education des femmes*) and above all by their narrators and secondary characters. The secondary

---

[23] Michelle-Catherine-Joséphine Tarbé des Sablons, *Roseline, ou de la Nécessité de la religion dans l'éducation des femmes*, 2:235. Subsequent page references will appear parenthetically in the text.

[24] Diderot, "Poésie," 227.

character proffering the warning is frequently a parent who has made the protagonist's own mistake him- or usually herself, like Natalie's mother cautioning her daughter that divorce may irreparably discredit a woman in the eyes of the world on the basis of her own bitter experience: "[S]ince that fateful day when I formed new bonds, I have not had one moment of pleasure and peace. As order was restored in society, as ideas of morality and religion resumed their power, I felt sad, ashamed, and stifled. Finally, I separated from M. d'Anglars [the man she remarried]: I thought this sacrifice would bring peace back to my soul; but to achieve it, I would have had to lose the memory of the past. . . . Whatever I do, the terrible sentence is pronounced against me! I am the remarried wife, *the unprincipled woman*! Society [*le monde*] is inflexible, pitiless, unforgiving," as Natalie unfortunately will discover too (49).[25]

George Sand makes explicit the continued authority of sentimental narrative logic when her narrator alerts the reader to expect it in the introduction to *Lucrezia Floriani*. Finely attuned to the significance of literary convention, Sand associates the principle "all should be clear" with the long-standing practice of French novelists, in contrast to the passion for suspense that is the latest vogue. "Thus, reader, to proceed in French fashion, like our worthy ancestors, I warn you that I will subtract from the narrative . . . its principal element, the spiciest seasoning in circulation in the marketplace: that is to say surprise, the unexpected. Instead of leading you from astonishment to astonishment . . . I will lead you step by step along a narrow, straight path, having you look in front and behind. . . . If, by chance, there is a gully, I will say to you: 'Watch out, here is a gully'; if there is a waterfall, I will help you cross this waterfall, I will not push you in head first to have the pleasure of saying to others: There goes one tricked reader."[26] With her contrast, Sand takes aim at realist novels for how they solicit the reader, for these works play, of course, a primary role in propagating the fashion of suspense, along with the *roman feuilleton*. Fashion may sell books "in the marketplace," Sand cautions, but its poetic worth will only emerge when the allure of novelty wanes. "Every fashion is good as long as it lasts and it is worn well; it is only possible to judge it when its reign is over" (13).

While *Natalie* certainly employs sentimental narrative construction, its founding conflict does, however, displace sentimental codes in one crucial

[25] As we will see, the sentimental social novel transforms the sentimental equation of society with the social elite, which the two subgenres identify as *le monde*, into an equation of society with the range of social classes, which the sentimental social novel characterizes as *la société*. I translate both *le monde* and *la société* with the English word society, which includes their different meanings. To clarify when a sentimental social novel is speaking of the social elite, I include *le monde* in brackets.

[26] Sand, *Lucrezia Floriani*, 12.

way. "These knots that I detested are now broken! This cold and heavy chain that froze my youth is now snapped! I am free, my dear Aglaé!" Like Claire or Frédéric, Natalie seeks freedom which she equates with the freedom of the heart. But while Claire recognizes that collective welfare, too, is a sacred duty, Natalie rather finds the relation of marriage to be a "cold and heavy chain." In the course of her thwarted love for Ernest, moreover, Natalie discovers that to be rendered to society is to be caught in bonds of convention every bit as inflexible as the ties of wedlock, her dream of a "sympathetic law" notwithstanding. Natalie emphasizes this discovery when she transfers the metaphor of the chain from her relations with her first husband to her relations with society at large. "Like an isolated link in the midst of a whole chain, I am bound to no one else's fate, and yet I am not free! . . . I believed I could run after happiness, but upon seizing it, I felt myself painfully chained," Natalie laments when she learns that Ernest's mother will never let him marry her because of her reputation (187). In the sentimental social novel, as in sentimentality, marriage thus remains a microcosm of social relations, but the sentimental social protagonist experiences both the bonds of marriage and society as oppressive rather than as a positively constituted ethical obligation.

The oppressive cast that sentimental social novels give collective welfare is epitomized by the subgenre's interest in slander, which is a common evil befalling its protagonists. In showing the power of slander, the sentimental social novel continues an important sentimental topos. In sentimentality, too, protagonists' reputations are attacked by a hypocritical community when they try to live according to the laws of the heart, as is illustrated by Montpezat's literary model for Natalie's loss of Ernest de Léoville: Delphine's loss of Léonce de Mondoville. But the different role of slander in *Natalie* and in *Delphine* exhibits the different insoluble conflicts structuring each subgenre. In *Natalie*, slander demonstrates how the implacable and repressive codes of society impinge on the laws of the heart. In *Delphine*, by contrast, slander is the false application of collective welfare, but in no way invalidates the imperative's importance nor its necessary conflict with individual freedom. This conflict, moreover, does not need slander to appear. Delphine herself initiates it with her opening gesture of giving Matilde money to facilitate Matilde's marriage to Léonce, a commitment that will subsequently make Delphine reluctant to accept Léonce's love without the blessings of the Vernon family. Rather than revealing collective welfare as oppressive, slander in sentimental novels reinforces the difference between collective welfare and collective opinion, thereby emphasizing that morality is a praxis in which every individual must engage in for him- or herself.[27]

---

[27] Thus, Delphine's indictment of Léonce's betrayal: "But Léonce! good heavens! Léonce! did Léonce need others to defend me [*qu'on me défendît*]?" (1:175, emphasis added).

The slander destroying Natalie reveals another negative displacement the sentimental social novel works on collective welfare: it comes to serve the particular interests of the stronger rather than the happiness of all. No aspect of each subgenre makes this displacement clearer than the respective characters embodying collective welfare. In *Claire d'Albe*, M. d'Albe is "such a worthy husband," "the center and cause of all the good that is done for miles around" (694, 696). Even at the end, when he abuses collective welfare, he does so from concern to keep the social microcosm intact. The character embodying the tyranny of social codes in *Natalie*, in contrast, has only selfish interests in mind. The scheming, hypocritical, Madame d'Artville first propels the young, beautiful, intelligent, and rich Natalie into society to bolster her own reputation as taste maker, and then circulates false rumors about Natalie in an effort to force Natalie to marry the vapid man of the world who is Madame d'Artville's protégé.

The particular interests governing collective obligation are embodied in especially ruthless fashion by the character who delivers the final blow to the heroine at the end of *Caroline, ou le Confesseur* (1833) by Aloïse de Carlowitz. This novel depicts the worldly and legal codes persecuting Caroline, a worthy but naive young woman, when she is seduced by a priest. Ostracized for bearing a child out of wedlock as well as for her honorable refusal to name her child's father, Caroline finds her maternal love rebuffed by society, which will give her no means to earn her living. She descends into poverty and hunger; then, unable to feed her starving child, loses her reason and kills him. Here, too, society is unforgiving and her death sentence is pronounced by a magistrate whose inflexibility is only strengthened when he realizes that the priest responsible for Caroline's seduction is his own son. Motivated by "feelings of convention and prejudice . . . less lasting than those that nature has engraved in our hearts" but "more violent," this judge sentences Caroline to death and then curses his son when the son appears to try to save the woman he has ruined (312).

Le Coeur et le code, we might term the conflict between oppressive collective obligation and individual freedom underwriting the sentimental social novel's plot. The phrase is the title of a sentimental social novel by Armand Rochoux, who glosses it with an epigraph from James Fenimore Cooper. " 'Our revered customs, our solemn decrees, the regulations of our communities, the firmness of our government, which has such good effects, are they nothing?' 'They are a great deal, for I fear they will prevail over just rights [*le bon droit*], that they will last when the tears of the oppressed have been used up, when the oppressed are forgotten, them and their misfortunes.' "[28]

---

[28] Rochoux, *Le Coeur et le codé*. In his preface, Rochoux states that he initially planned to entitle his novel *Loi contre loi* [law against law] because it is "a work where I confront

Rochoux is only one among many contemporary novelists and critics who call attention to the terms of the sentimental social novel's founding collision. When Sophie d'Epinay Saint-Luc explains the subject matter of *Valida* (1835) in her preface, for example, she states: "There definitely exists a contradiction in the character that it [society (*le monde*)] gives to women. What is asked of her? That she yield to her father, the man before whom everything bends, to her brother, the man who, often her junior in age, nonetheless prides himself on the supremacy of his sex, to her husband, the man whose reasoning is irresistible and forceful in its brevity and that is summed up with these two words: *I want* . . . But if she has listened, in this habitual submission, to the man . . . who puts forward not his rights but rather his love . . . she is guilty, lost, dishonored."[29] Similarly Sand, offering to "explain everything in this book" in her 1832 preface to *Indiana*: "Indiana . . . is woman, the weak being entrusted with representing *passions* . . . suppressed by *laws* . . . she is love bumping its blind head against all the obstacles of civilization. But . . . the forces of the soul exhaust themselves in trying to struggle against the positive in life."[30] When an 1833 review discussing *Indiana* and *Valentine* agrees, it succinctly articulates the sentimental social novel's transformation of the sentimental double bind. "In the old [*ancienne*] poetics of the novel, and we say old because everything ages rapidly, the obstacles that the lovers encountered in their path . . . came from the opposing will of unyielding parents. . . . Today, it [the novel] attacks marriage as an institution, just as it puts the blame on society."[31]

THE TEARS OF THE OPPRESSED

Rochoux isolates a third concept basic to the sentimental social novel's plot along with the heart and the code when his epigraph from Cooper identifies "misfortunes" not only with tears but with the oppressed. This concept is the social group, with social difference represented as a relation

---

two texts of the same law, one written by nature in the heart of intelligent beings, the other written in a book by selfishness and corruption" (x–xi). He chose *Le Coeur et le code* instead, he explains, because his editor reminded him that he is competing with other authors and novelistic forms for readers. In the editor's view, *Loi contre loi* sounds like a legal treatise and will do little to attract "lusty fellows who prefer *Monsieur de Balzac* . . . and *Monsieur Paul de Coq* [*sic*]" (xiii).

[29] Sophie d'Epinay Saint-Luc, *Valida, ou la Réputation d'une femme*, 1:viii–ix. Subsequent page references will appear parenthetically in the text.

[30] Sand, *Indiana*, 40, Sand's emphasis. Subsequent page references will appear parenthetically in the text.

[31] "*Valentine*, par G. Sand, auteur *d'Indiana*," signed C———r.

of power. The protagonist of the sentimental social novel suffers because she or he occupies a dominated social position, as the prefaces to these texts make amply clear. Condemning women's social inferiority, Sand likens the feminine condition to the condition of the slave in her 1842 preface to *Indiana*: "[T]he misfortunes of woman bring about those of man, like those of the slave bring about those of the master, and I have tried to show it in *Indiana*" (46). "The novelist dedicates himself less to the privileged classes than to threatened existences," writes Angélique Arnaud in her preface to *Clémence* (1843).[32] When Salvandy describes the sentimental social novelist's interest in dominated social positions in his preface to *Natalie*, he invokes a Christian model for social ills. Calling women's novels "a progress of the nun dispensing charity [*soeur grise*]," he continues, "Formerly, she [woman] did not write; now, she spreads her hand on all the wounds that fate puts the farthest from her grasp; she soothes the injuries of her brothers with her words."[33]

Sentimental social novels thus do not take issue with the realist view that power is the motor of social relations—both subgenres, after all, transform sentimental collective welfare into oppressive obligation. They do, however, contest the realist glorification of the struggle to rise to the top. The sentimental social novel dwells on those who do not enjoy the possibility of careers open to talents in a society ruled by "the respect for force, the glorification of success," to cite Caroline Marbouty's preface to *Ange de Spola*.[34] The difference between the realist and sentimental view of social life as struggle is encapsulated in how each subgenre renders the topos of lost illusions. When the sentimental social protagonist struggles with the conflict between the heart and the code, she, like the realist protagonist, realizes that sentimental ideals are impractical in a morally bankrupt society. But if lost illusions are the key to success in realism, this experience destroys the sentimental social protagonist, who remains committed to ideals against worldly *Machtpolitik*. To Lousteau's prospective "men, passions and needs are at work underneath all these beautiful imaginary things" (270), which launches Lucien on his struggle for social recognition, we can contrast Natalie's retrospective résumé of her suffering following her début into society: " 'Only six months have gone by, and my dazzling dreams are destroyed. Six months have consumed my existence; and the past, the present, and the future, all is covered in blood! My life had the span of these fragile insects which are born in spring and die in autumn' " (252).

[32] Angélique Arnaud, *Clémence*, 1:xii. Subsequent page references will appear parenthetically in the text.

[33] Salvandy, preface to *Natalie*, xlvii.

[34] Caroline Marbouty, *Ange de Spola*, 1:xlii. Subsequent page references will appear parenthetically in the text.

The most common dominated social position responsible for suffering in the sentimental social novel is the position of women across class (it is at issue in almost all novels by women and about half the novels by men), whether heroines suffer from "the injustice and . . . barbarity of the laws that still govern the existence of woman in marriage, in the family, and in society," as Sand puts it in the 1842 preface to *Indiana*, or whether, like Natalie, women are oppressed by the codes of manners (46–47). The other dominated social position prominent in sentimental social novels is the position of lower-class men, both petty bourgeois and working class, excluded from the "notables" who rule July Monarchy society.[35] In *Riche et pauvre*, for example, Emile Souvestre compares the careers of the well-placed but mediocre and sleazy Arthur Boissard and the unequivocally more worthy Antoine Larry from "that class that separates the proletarian from the bourgeoisie," who have received similar educations.[36] While Arthur prospers, Antoine cannot realize his promise because his rank gives him less access to cultural and economic capital and because he stands firm by his principles, refusing to follow the way of the world.[37] Class inequality is also at stake in the conflict between the heart and the code structuring Sand's *Le Meunier d'Angibault*. Here, male and female protagonists alike suffer because of love that is "mad [*dérangé*, literally de-ranked]," to use the term applied to the madwoman in the novel, la Bricoline, who has lost her sanity because her parents forbid her to marry a beloved who is beneath her social station.

Some novels juxtapose the conflict between the heart and the code resulting from gender and class inequality, emphasizing not only the similarities but also the differences in the dominated positions of lower-class men and women across class. Tristan's *Méphis ou le prolétaire* (1838), for example, narrates the unhappy love affair between an exceptional female singer, Maréquita, trying to live independently as an artist rather than subordinate to a man in marriage, and an exceptional proletarian painter, Méphis, producing allegorical paintings in an effort to promote "individual independence, equality of rights."[38] Maréquita is, however, not able to occupy the inspirational position Méphis assigns her in the struggle against inequality, because of her moral and legal oppression by patriarchy. In *Une Fausse Position* (1844), Marbouty compares the dominated

---

[35] On the hybrid class identity of the July Monarchy power elite, see André-Jean Tudesq and André Jardin, *La France des notables*.

[36] Emile Souvestre, *Riche et Pauvre*, 39.

[37] When Antoine's friend, the doctor Georges Randel, advises him to be more flexible, Antoine replies, "Life understood thus is but a farce." His friend responds, "And you would like to turn it into an epic poem, right? But one plays for one's public, and this century is out showing off and posing [*à la parade*]" (47).

[38] Flora Tristan, *Méphis ou le prolétaire*, 1:319. Subsequent page references will appear parenthetically in the text.

position of male workers and women and finds the latter infinitely more problematic. "I, too, . . . I will work—and . . . I will . . . have the courage of my position," the heroine Camille declares after she leaves her husband for a lover who then abandons her.[39] But in the course of a checkered career, featuring stints as a woman of letters and a nun in training, notably, Camille discovers how much harder it is for a woman to earn her living than for a man.

Occasionally, novels examine the conflict between the heart and the code structuring other dominated social positions. While Carlowitz devotes *Caroline* to the conflict between maternal love and the oppressive moral codes that condemn maternity outside of marriage, the novel's preface rather prepares us to consider the suffering of priests. In Carlowitz's rendition, the code ordaining the celibacy of the priesthood deprives these men of their sacred rights to personal happiness. If priests "still snatch our wives and daughters from us," Carlowitz's narrator explains in the preface, it is "because you forbid them to have wives and daughters of their own. Yet God and the Scripture allow it and morality demands it as well; why then do you not want it?" (xxvi). Clémence Robert treats the same question in *L'Abbé Olivier* (1839). In Hugo's *Le Dernier Jour d'un condamné* (1829) and Anne Bignan's *L'Echafaud* (1832), the suffering social group is those criminals condemned to death, cut off from humanity by the unjust harshness of the penal code.

Early examples of a form often highlight its continuity with a preceding literary historical moment and Hugo's novel is no exception. It sets up the conflict between the heart and the code as a variation on the sentimental conflict between opposing forms of rights. Portraying the moral suffering of the condemned man in a work that is one long analysis of the heart, Hugo opposes "the great matter of the right of humanity argued and pleaded for loudly and clearly before society" to "the criminal code."[40] But this opposition differs from the conflict at issue in sentimentality because only one of its terms preserves human rights. Hugo's narrative pits the "right of humanity" against the abuse of collective welfare worked by capital punishment, which unjustly turns the criminal into a "wretch who lost, through murder, the right to be counted among men," as Nodier put it in his discussion of Hugo's text.[41]

---

[39] Marbouty, *Une Fausse Position*, 1:242. Subsequent page references will appear parenthetically in the text.

[40] Hugo, 1832 preface to *Le Dernier Jour d'un condamné*, 368. Subsequent page references will appear parenthetically in the text.

[41] Nodier, cited in Roger Borderie's "Notice" to Hugo, *Dernier Jour*, 411. Anne Bignan structures her sentimental social novel against capital punishment around a similar transformation of the sentimental double bind. "The social body has no more the right to cut off one of its members with the sword of the law, than an individual has the right to raise his

Hugo's approach to the sentimental discourse of rights is characteristic. The sentimental social novel continues the sentimental novel's interest in the conflict between "social right [*le droit social*]" and "human right [*le droit humain*]," to take Sand's terms from an 1842 general preface to her works. The subgenre does not, however, translate this conflict into a balanced opposition on the level of plot. Rather, these novels pit "human right" against the code, which abuses "social right," enthroning "the inequality of rights and of means of development," as "the last word of the social order and the wisdom of laws," to cite Sand's 1842 general preface once more.[42] When sentimental social novels represent the code using a vocabulary of rights, they transform right into might, "the right of the stronger." " 'Indiana! . . . who has hurt you so?' " Ralph exclaims when he sees the mark her husband's boot has left on her forehead. " 'You ask?' she answered with a bitter smile; 'who else has the right to but *your friend*?' " (270, Sand's emphasis).

In identifying moral authority with the heart against the code, sentimental social novels dissolve the insoluble conflict that gives the sentimental plot its tragic grandeur. Rather than being torn between two equally valid options, the protagonist resists the code in the name of the heart, but no matter how strong this resistance, the code inevitably reasserts itself. Natalie's discomfort with the power of worldly demands when she first enters society contains in miniature the experience of all sentimental social protagonists: "Madame d'Artville seems a whirlwind who carries me off; she is always there to snatch me from my mother, from my reading, from my harp. I am annoyed when my study or our treasured intimacy is disturbed; but she has gained a kind of influence over me that I cannot resist" (43–44).

The sentimental social novel's poetic loss vis-à-vis sentimental tragedy may also be viewed as a shift in the political tensions to which the form responds. When the sentimental social novel transforms the conflict between "opposing duties" into the heart against the code, it no longer engages Revolutionary tragedy but rather the same contemporary social contradiction at issue in the realist plot of *Bildung*. This is the contradiction between the July Monarchy's symbolic foundations in Revolutionary ideals and its political and economic organization favoring the privileged classes, which I have summed up as the problem of unequal social divi-

---

hand against his own life: an execution and a suicide are two equal crimes in the eyes of the creator; for individual lives matter to the collective life of peoples. Break the links, what would become of the chain?" writes Bignan in her preface, refunctioning the image of society as a chain common in the sentimental social novel to describe the bonds of humanity that join individuals rather than the codes that oppress them. Anne Bignan, *L'Echafaud*, 55. Subsequent page references will appear parenthetically in the text.

[42] Sand, 1842 "Préface générale," 19.

sion. Sentimental social novels underscore the problem of social division when they represent their protagonists as abused by the code because they belong to an oppressed social group. Montpezat's Natalie is unable to enjoy individual freedom because the novel shows moral codes to be harsher on women than on men, and the same is true for Arnaud's Clémence. Tristan's *Méphis*, Sand's *Indiana*, and Marbouty's *Une Fausse Position* represent their heroines as unable to pursue life, liberty, and happiness because of women's legal and economic subordination along with the moral double standard.

THE POLITICAL IDEA, THE SOCIAL IDEA

The sufferings of individuals in dominated social positions are the "ideas [*idées*]" that led contemporaries to qualify the sentimental social novel as a literature of ideas. In this use of "idea," the term designates an openly proclaimed stance on political and social issues.[43] "The author can today unmask the political idea, the social idea, that he wanted to popularize under the guise of this innocent and ingenuous literary form," Hugo declares in his 1832 preface to *Le Dernier Jour d'un condamné*, making clear that he can now reveal the politics of his novel since he need not fear censorship following the Revolution of 1830. "He thus declares, or rather he admits openly, that *Le Dernier Jour d'un condamné* is nothing other than a plea, direct or indirect, as one will, for abolishing the death penalty" (367–68). Thirteen years later, Sand uses the term "idea [*idée*]" in similarly politicized fashion when she discusses how her publisher refused to publish *Le Meunier d'Angibault* on account of its politics: "Monsieur Véron faulted me for having promised him a novel of manners and given him a novel of ideas."[44]

The politicized use of *idée* during the 1830s and 1840s extends to the term ideal, with which it is often coupled. As Schor observes, the notion of the ideal has historically had two diverging meanings, indicating both a retreat from the real and the goal towards which it should tend.[45] When July Monarchy critical discourse coupled the term ideal with the novel, it was in the latter fashion. This meaning is captured in the review of *Le Meunier d'Angibault* by Eugène Pelletan cited by Schor, which describes the novel as offering "an ideal which guides us across mountains and

---

[43] Schor misses this usage when she defines Sand's idealism by referring to nineteenth-century philosophical discourse.

[44] Cited in Schor, *Sand and Idealism*, 108, Schor's translation. "I could not and will never understand the distinction," Sand continues, turning the slippage in contemporary terminology around the novel to her advantage.

[45] Ibid., 84.

rivers to the cradle of nascent truth."[46] The figure of the ideal as guide was common at the time. "All those who have received gifts from heaven that they can use to influence men . . . should navigate like the pilot, who has his eyes on the heavens, who looks for his route up above and not around him, at his feet, on this ocean, where his poor visibility would soon lead him astray," writes Salvandy in the preface to *Natalie* when he describes the writer's imperative to pursue social transformation.[47]

Sentimental social novels express their underwriting idea (or ideas—sometimes they have more than one) through the comments of narrators, characters, and authorial personae. Their comments highlight one of the subgenre's major transformations of sentimentality. With such explicit political and social position-taking, sentimental social novels focus the reader's attention on the public sphere, in contrast to the private emphasis in sentimental stories of love.[48] The subgenre also pursues this focus in its plots representing social injustice.

Sentimental social novels voice ideas that cross the political spectrum. To stick with sentimental social novels devoted to the feminine condition, ideas range from the promotion of pious, domestic womanhood to the call for complete gender equality. *La Duchesse de Valombray* (1838), by Junot d'Abrantès, is a sentimental social novel formed around a conservative idea. The work narrates the sufferings of the "sensitive [*sensible*]" and upright heroine, Suzanne, who languishes subordinated in marriage to a worldly egotist interested only in pleasure. The idea driving this novel is that women, oppressed by materialist society, can best resist through exercising private, feminine duties as well as through devoting themselves to religion. For Abrantès, woman is "this weak being, so great, so affec-

---

[46] Ibid., 108–9, Schor's translation.

[47] Salvandy, preface to *Natalie*, xlvi.

[48] Sentimental social novelists demonstrate their political inflection of sentimentality when they offer readings of their sentimental predecessor, Staël. For novelists concerned with the feminine condition, Staël's novels primarily portray women's oppression by unjust legal and moral codes. Most often, sentimental social novelists approve of Staël's feminism. Dupin, for example, authorizes numerous chapters in her novel on divorce, *Marguerite*, with epigraphs from Staël like, "Nature has decided that all women's gifts would be intended for the happiness of others and of little use to themselves." Aurore Dupin, *Marguerite*, 1:137. "Madame de Staël painted women dying for prejudice; our time, more advanced, paints women who defy prejudices," writes Allart in the preface to her sentimental social novel, *Settimia*. Allart, *Settimia*, 1:ix. Subsequent page references will appear parenthetically in the text. Carlowitz's *La Femme du Progrès* is one of the few sentimental social novels that takes a negative stance towards Staël's feminism, and, as is common in antifeminist attacks, the target is Staël's person along with Staël's works. Carlowitz here shows the importance of the separate spheres through depicting the heroine's sentimental oppression by the *femme du progrès*, a woman who is a feminist for supposedly humanitarian reasons that turn out to derive from profound egotism. Carlowitz's worldly feminists promoting women's rights for their own glory model themselves on Staël and her Corinne.

tionate," given not only her natural fragility but her social subordination. "Slave of all changes, constant plaything of the most conflicting variations, who will help her, if not God? Save her, holy religion, release her from society [le monde] and from herself."[49]

The redemptive power of religion also shapes Charlotte de Sor's *Madame de Tercy*, which depicts the unhappy lives of several worthy women who are alternately "the plaything or the slave" in marriages where they have been sacrificed "to fortune, to pride."[50] "My share," writes Sor in the preface, "is the thought of spreading some balm on the painful sufferings of the heart. . . . I will say to us weak women: have faith in order to bear with the betrayal, the disappointment of our noble dreams [nos généreux chimères]; to suffer the injustice and the demands of society, which has made us so wretched. . . . it is for us, disinherited of joys and prosperity, to believe in God to leave life quietly" (1:viii–ix). As Abrantès's and Sor's comments indicate, sentimental social novels voicing conservative ideas are in conflict with themselves, for they both indict society and do not propose transforming the status quo. A pointed moment of conflict in *La Duchesse de Valombray* occurs when the narrator suggests that women suffer more intensely over betrayals in love because of their confinement within the private sphere, which the novel nonetheless defends. "A man is free to go find the woman who does not come; a man is free to do something crazy. A woman dares not even think about it. She must remain upset alone, in the grip of her anxieties, for her place is in the bosom of her family, and in the secret of her home" (1:291).

In contrast to such restrained portrayals of women's dominated social position, Sand's *Indiana*, Arnaud's *Clémence*, Tristan's *Méphis*, Marbouty's *Ange de Spola* and *Une Fausse Position* insist that women's flagrant inequality must be remedied with thoroughgoing legal and social transformation. Sand attacks "the injustice and . . . the barbarity of the laws that still govern the existence of woman in marriage, in the family, and in society," in her 1842 preface to *Indiana* (46). Similarly, Marbouty calls for laws transforming the condition of women in the preface to *Ange de Spola*: "[A]s we have previously said, women's education is too often like a costume for them, it tends too often to mislead them. . . . Should not this moral mutilation of woman, doubtless necessary in former times, stop with progress?—And could not and should not contemporary legisla-

---

[49] Abrantès, *La Duchesse de Valombray*, 1:110. Subsequent page references will appear parenthetically in the text.

[50] Charlotte de Sor, *Madame de Tercy, ou l'Amour d'une femme*, 1:51; 47. Subsequent page references will appear parenthetically in the text. Other sentimental social novels presenting conservative *idées* include Tarbé des Sablons's *Roseline, ou de la Nécessité de la religion dans l'éducation des femmes* and *Zoé, ou la Femme légère*.

tion know how to remedy institutions that are so cruel and so unfavorable to the happiness of all?" (1:8–9).

A number of sentimental social novels propose ideas between these conservative and radical poles. Following the July Revolution's revitalization of Revolutionary ideals, there was hot public debate around whether to reestablish divorce, which, it was widely recognized, would promote women's emancipation.[51] A position in favor of divorce was a common idea in sentimental social novels, which identify women with the private sphere while suggesting that private life should protect individual happiness rather than subordinate women to tyranny. The moderate character of this idea emerges in *Une Victime*, for example, when Monborne identifies her call for divorce with a limited rather than an unrestrained notion of freedom: "I am not asking to reestablish Divorce as it was practiced in '93; its frequent misuse made the law immoral. I do not even include mismatched temperaments. . . . But where there is disgrace, dishonor, bad behavior, abandonment; I demand Divorce."[52] In *Le Pair de France, ou le Divorce*, Carlowitz champions divorce from the perspective of a highly tempered feminism, valuing it as the foundation of domestic happiness. "Next to the coffin of Francesca, next to the coffin of the duke, I cursed the fanatical obstinacy which has refused to allow the re-establishment of divorce. You force me to curse it again; it is more guilty than you!" declares one of the spokespersons for the novel's idea to a woman who has committed adultery to escape from what these novels call a *mariage mal assorti*. "How many existences has it already broken! How many people who would have been able to become virtuous husbands and wives have found themselves drawn into crimes!"[53] Montpezat's *Natalie* is one of the most ambiguous novels taking a position on divorce, for it exceptionally does not clearly state its informing idea. Is it a novel against divorce? Natalie's mother as well as her confidante criticize divorce as a "fault," and the novel represents divorce as precipitating women's sufferings from moral codes (7). At the same time, *Natalie* condemns these codes as hypocritical and underlines the merit of both the heroine and her divorced mother, emphasizing Natalie's efforts to "keep the respect of the public and the peace of her heart" (17).

Whatever their differing gender politics, sentimental social novels on the feminine condition are united by one idea that is sometimes fused with the idea of women's oppression and sometimes stated as an idea of its

---

[51] On July Monarchy debates around divorce, see Francis Ronsin, *Les Divorçaires*.

[52] B. Monborne, *Une Victime, esquisse littéraire*, 5–6.

[53] Aloïse de Carlowitz, *Le Pair de France, ou le Divorce*, 3:366. Subsequent page references will appear parenthetically in the text. Other novels promoting divorce include *Marguerite* by Dupin, *Un Mari* by Dash, *Settimia* by Allart, *Mézélie* by Reybaud, and *Trois Ans après* by Tullie Moneuse.

own. This idea is an indictment of materialism as "the greatest evil, which risks swallowing up our period," to cite Marbouty's preface to *Ange de Spola* (1:xliii). By materialism, novels designate a society where individuals pursue self-interest and where all social relations turn around power and money. Marbouty's diagnosis is exemplary: "[M]oney will sum up everything, and society, overrun by that which is the lowest in this world, the respect for force and the glorification of success, will seek an antidote in vain" (1:xlii–xliii). Sentimental social novels also agree that women suffer from contemporary materialism more than men because they are in a dominated position and thereby inevitably lose out in a morality rewarding success and strength. Novels voicing radical ideas further stress that women have no way to escape from this domination because they have been denied all access to the foundations of contemporary social power: "The law-maker having separated women from all positive interests, having given their rights to their husbands," has left to women only "family life and feelings," writes Marbouty in her preface to *Ange de Spola* (1:xxi).

Sentimental social novels pursue their critique of materialism in their delineation of character as well as in their stated ideas. The magistrate who condemns Caroline to die in *Caroline*, Madame d'Artville in *Natalie*, and Suzanne's self-centered husband in *La Duchesse de Valombray* are only three of the "selfish people" populating these novels. Raymon de la Ramière exemplifies one preferred way sentimental social novels embody materialism: as the young man of great expectations who is the hero of the realist sentimental education. From the vantage point of the sentimental social novel, such a young man is an unprincipled, hypocritical, self-aggrandizing seducer who subjects the protagonist to extreme suffering if not destruction. In *La Cour d'Assises* (1832), Camille Bodin underlines the realist source of this sentimental social type. The character who finally murders the heroine after a tortured passion is one Julien, the adopted son of Beaumarchais, who gets his start as an aide-de-camp to Napoleon before entering into politics during the Restoration and rising to the pinnacle of rank and power, including ennoblement as the Count de Berville.[54]

VICTIM OF AN UNJUST LAW

Like sentimentality, the sentimental social novel solicits the reader's sympathy with its plot of a worthy protagonist caught in an insoluble conflict. The sentimental social novel's transformation of the sentimental double

---

[54] Other versions of this character are Paul in Carlowitz's *Le Pair de France* and Auguste Bervil in Monborne's *Une Victime*. When Stendhal has his heroine coldly pay one Jean Berville for her first sexual experience in *Lamiel*, is he countering the sentimental social novel's attack on a character type he originates with Julien Sorel?

bind, however, also transforms the protagonist's claim to our interest. In sentimental plots, we admire and sympathize with protagonists in moral anguish, as they struggle to respect the conflicting imperatives they can neither escape nor resolve. In the sentimental social novel, we sympathize with protagonists suffering from injustice. "He is a victim . . . struck down by an unjust law!" declares a character in Louise Maignaud's *Les Etudians* of a protagonist who receives an unreasonably heavy penalty for an unwitting crime, and the same can be said of sentimental social protagonists more generally.[55]

Sentimental social novels show an engagement with melodrama in transforming the protagonist from moral exemplum to victim and in constructing their plots around a clear-cut opposition between good and evil. They also are fascinated by melodramatic excess so important in realism too. While realism celebrates this excess, sentimental social novels, in contrast, identify it with social injustice.[56] Their Manichean struggles pit, specifically, "just rights [*le bon droit*]," as Rochoux puts it citing Cooper, against "an unjust law." To quote Bignan's preface to *L'Echafaud*: "This dramatic conflict between our good and our bad principles will produce educational scenes [*tableaux instructifs*] inspiring in us love and respect for the former, hatred and scorn for the latter" (24). The sentimental social novel differs from melodrama, however, in giving the "dramatic conflict" a tragic, which is to say sentimental, ending; a point Sand underlines in her 1832 preface to *Indiana*: "Then you will say that you have not been shown virtue rewarded in a sufficiently resounding fashion. Alas! it will be answered that the triumph of virtue is no longer seen except in popular plays [*théâtres du boulevard*]. The author will tell you that he has not committed himself to showing you society virtuous, but rather necessary, and that honor has become as precarious as heroism in these days of moral decadence" (41).

When Sand depicts her novel's distance from the melodramatic dénouement, she draws attention to another crucial difference separating the sentimental social novel not only from melodrama but also from sentimentality: virtue is not the protagonist's prime heroic attribute.[57] "Virtue is strength," we have seen Claire d'Albe declare, and in the sentimental social novel, too, the protagonist exhibits strength in the face of trial. But sentimental social novels more often depict this strength as what they call "courage," perseverance against oppression, rather than as "virtue,"

[55] Maignaud, *Les Etudians, épisode de la Révolution de 1830*, 4:67.

[56] On the realist immersion in melodrama, see Peter Brooks's *The Melodramatic Imagination*.

[57] Virtue, I have argued, means something rather different in melodrama and in sentimentality. While melodrama opposes virtue to persecuting vice, sentimentality validates virtue as the protagonist's own moral combat.

moral rectitude.[58] Indiana has no reservations about calling on Raymon in the middle of the night, although her gesture flagrantly violates manners. When Raymon reproaches her for her "madness," Indiana replies "I would have called it *courage* myself" (216). In *Le Meunier d'Angibault*, Sand's narrator similarly praises the heroine who flouts social convention as the "affectionate and courageous Marcelle."[59] The protagonist of Marbouty's *Une Fausse Position*, too, asserts "the courage of my position" as she struggles to support herself, braving the censure of society (1:242). When Epinay Saint-Luc's *Valida* defends one heroine, Eléonore, for giving herself to a man she loves without being married to him and for devoting herself unselfishly to the child born from this union, the preface qualifies Eléonore as showing "courage, even heroism" (1:x) in contrast to the "easy virtue" of those women who have never been tried by suffering (1:xi) and to society's hypocritical "conventional virtue" (1:122). The subgenre's use of "courage" to describe heroism is well suited to the conflict it portrays. Courage is force deriving from the heart, *cor*, the organ epitomizing subjectivity in the sentimental social novel as in sentimentality.

As Indiana and Eléonore illustrate, sentimental social protagonists can display their courage while transgressing morality. These transgressions usually take the form of what the subgenre calls "faults": romantic sex outside of marriage. If sentimental protagonists, too, sometimes consummate love outside of marriage, the significance of this gesture differs markedly in the two subgenres. For sentimental protagonists, sex outside marriage violates the sentimental double bind and thereby threatens the entire social order, particularly if it is adultery. It thus most often concludes the sentimental plot, as is the case with *Claire d'Albe*, although it can also get the plot going; in Rousseau's *Julie*, it plays both roles. For sentimental social protagonists, in contrast, sex outside of marriage illustrates the heart striving for fulfillment against the code; the heroine's fault is one incident in a long career of oppression. The harshness of this career can, moreover, exacerbate the gravity of her transgressions. In *Caroline, ou le Confesseur*, Caroline murders her son born out of wedlock after she has been rejected by society. In Bodin's *La Cour d'assises*, a Corinne-like heroine stabs the Lucile character, who is engaged to the Oswald-like man she loves, in a scene where she had originally planned to kill herself, frustrated by stultifying social conventions that give her no outlet for her imagination.

---

[58] Sentimental social novels voicing conservative *idées* are those most likely to continue the sentimental approbation of virtue.

[59] Sand, *Le Meunier d'Angibault*, 17. Subsequent page references will appear parenthetically in the text.

Whether fault or crime, sentimental social protagonists' trangressions only heighten their "interesting" status as the victims of unjust codes. The preface of *Valida,* for example, defends women who, "throwing themselves out of the circle of their customary duties, push this deviation to the point of defying the most caustic barbs of malicious gossip. Readers, if you know anyone who has shown this deplorable energy, do not rush to blame her: rather pity her; compassion is her due. . . . Who knows if it is not virtue that leads her astray?" (1:xii). According to Bodin's narrator, the Corinne-like heroine of *La Cour d'assises* is "placed in the class of women who is the most to be pitied."[60] When Hugo takes a murderer as hero of *Le Dernier Jour d'un condamné,* he declares that he pleads for "all possible defendants, innocent or guilty," underlining that all humans deserve mercy, whatever their guilt (368).

"Madame de Staël painted women dying for prejudices; our period, more advanced, paints women who defy prejudices," Allart writes in the preface to *Settimia* (1:ix). Surveying sentimental social novels, it is hard to be so optimistic; the protagonists succumb to the founding collision as often as their sentimental counterparts. Allart's statement does, however, register the fact that the subgenre supports its protagonists who defy society. Contemporary critics did not always agree with this stance. When an 1839 review reads a novel by Jules Sandeau as reacting "against the novels of a certain school of female literature," it censures the "school" on account of its heroines' revolt: "For one of these heroines, of these *Lélias,* who, relying on her exceptional strength, can wage war against manners and place herself above ordinary judgments, how many will encounter only shame and isolation, instead of fame and freedom!"[61]

The sentimental social novel's turn away from virtue is in keeping with its transformation of the sentimental double bind. When the codes are unjust, can one speak of someone who upholds them as virtuous? At the same time, is it virtuous to defy social obligations, particularly if the obligations broken are not only oppressive laws but such fundamental Judeo-Christian tenets as "thou shalt not kill"? In obscuring virtue, the subgenre also confuses other Enlightenment abstractions in the sentimental moral universe, notably the notions of duty and sacrifice.

There is, moreover, one aspect of society as it is depicted in the sentimental social novel that disqualifies the notion of virtue from relevance to the subgenre. "Free! Great word which indeed contains all human dignity; no virtue without freedom," writes Michelet in *Le Peuple,* stating a fundamental tenet of republican political theory.[62] At the crux of the

---

[60] Camille Bodin, *La Cour d'assises,* 67.

[61] Review signed H. L. of Jules Sandeau's *Mariana.*

[62] Michelet, *Le Peuple,* 85.

sentimental social novel is the absence of such freedom; the subject's dominated social position. As Arnaud puts it in the preface to *Clémence*: "Independence is necessary to rise to virtue" (1:xiii).

I AM THE SLAVE AND YOU THE LORD

The sentimental social novel heightens the reader's interest in the narrative with other sentimental conventions for soliciting sympathy besides
the plot of a protagonist caught in an irreconcilable conflict. The subgenre's use of these other conventions, too, bears the mark of its transformation of the sentimental double bind. Like their sentimental forbears,
the protagonists of sentimental social novels use the analysis of the heart
to underline that they suffer intensely. These analyses, however, do not
emphasize the protagonists' moral dilemma but rather their longing for
freedom and the tyranny of the codes.

"The objects I hold dearest are those I shun with the greatest terror!...
Even you, Frédéric, I find you unbearable because I adore you; your presence kills me because I no longer have the strength to resist you; and my
love only seems a crime to me because I am burning to yield to it," Claire
declares in a letter to Frédéric, emphasizing the contradiction between
individual freedom and collective welfare producing her moral anguish
(740). Natalie offers the sentimental social novel's version of this analysis
when she realizes that Ernest's mother opposes her love. "I think that I
can no longer be happy. Madame de Léoville would always be there to
vie with me for her son. And in society [*le monde*], what feeling could I
admit for Ernest? I would never be allowed to say how dear he is to me.
I could never vaunt his love, and yet Ernest's love is a reason to be
proud. . . . I envy the fate of all women who have a husband and children.
Like an isolated link in the midst of a whole chain, I am bound to no one
else's fate, and yet I am not free!" (187).

The sentimental social novel's transformation of the sentimental double
bind also marks its use of the tableau. In sentimentality, the tableau occurs
when the two conflicting moral imperatives confront each other with full
force in the protagonist's soul. At this moment, language breaks down,
the protagonist stages the confrontation with gesture, and solicits sympathy not only with the intensity of his or her reaction but by sacrificing
individual freedom for collective welfare. In the sentimental social novel,
in contrast, the tableau occurs at a moment when the code oppresses the
heart with a violence making evident the scope of its brutal domination.
This oppression can occur in the soul of the protagonist, as in sentimentality, or it can take the form of a confrontation pitting a character embodying the heart against a character embodying the code. More often, the

code overpowers the heart in the physical gesture after the breakdown of language. Such tableaux heighten the reader's sympathy by painting the protagonist as sacrificed rather than sacrificing.

"Yes, I love you, ardently, violently; and in this very moment, when I forget my most sacred duties to tell you this, I delight in the excess of weakness which proves to you my love," we have seen Claire declare as her conflict between collective welfare and individual freedom reaches an unbearable pitch (735). When Frédéric subsequently kisses her, she falls at his feet, imploring him to respect collective welfare and not exploit her weakness. Here is an equivalent tableau in *Indiana*, when Delmare orders Indiana to depart with him for the Ile Bourbon after she has spent the night at Raymon's: "I know that I am the slave and you the lord," responds Indiana. "The law of this country has made you my master. You can tie up my body, shackle my hands, govern my actions. You have the right of the stronger, and society reinforces this; but over my will, sir, you can do nothing, God alone can curb and subdue it" (232). Delmare responds, "Shut up, you stupid and impudent creature, we are sick of your language out of a novel," implying that the novel is a genre fleeing reality although he himself figures in a work that is anything but escapist romance. His efforts to impose silence failing, Delmare resorts to physical force, "bruising her hand between his index finger and his thumb" (232). Sand will repeat this tableau with heightened brutality when Delmare bruises Indiana's forehead with his boot.

The sentimental social novel's transformation of the sentimental double bind affects, in addition, its use of the narrator to underscore the protagonist's interesting status. The sentimental social novel is most often recounted by an omniscient third-person narrator who uses sentimentality's economical, neoclassical diction. As in sentimentality, too, the narrator switches to emphatic rhetoric and the present tense of heightened emotion, sometimes accompanied by general maxims and direct reader address, when the founding conflict reaches a crisis.[63] In the sentimental novel, the narrator turns emphatic at a moment of moral impasse. In the sentimental social novel, in contrast, he or she does so at a moment pitting the code's extreme oppression against the heart's maximum effort of resistance.

The substance of the narrator's emphatic commentary evinces the sentimental social novel's politicization of the sentimental private sphere.

---

[63] The subgenre intensifies the tendency already visible in the sentimental novel to subordinate private writings to third person narration. *Natalie*, along with Allart's *Settimia*, Desprez's *Les Femmes vengées*, and Sand's *Jacques* are among the few sentimental social novels written in the epistolary form. Both *Les Femmes vengées* and *Jacques*, moreover, underline the epistolary novel's outmoded character, for they justify their narrative structure as a citation of the sentimental legacy.

When the sentimental social narrator calls on the reader to pity the protagonist in the throes of conflict, she or he transforms sentimentality's psychological or social maxims into a political or social idea.[64] In *Valida*, the narrator offers the sentimental social equivalent to the maxim when Eléonore provokes social scandal by publicly glorying in her new position as unmarried mother. Breaking with the action, the narrator explains that Eléonore's behavior results from women's relegation to the private sphere. "To quench his passions, man has an immense field opened to all excesses, all hazards, all perils, and all glories," the narrator declares. "But to what object can an impassioned woman's soul transfer its profusion of energy, when even her love is turned into a crime!" (1:256). A similar social indictment occurs in Tristan's *Méphis* when the hero, Méphis, offers to be Maréquita's lover on the condition that she freely assert her love for him. While Maréquita knows that this relationship would bring her happiness, she is unable to accept Méphis's offer because the pressure from the code of manner is too intense. Halting the narrative, the narrator comments, "Alas! poor Maréquita was far from capable of feeling all that is superior and truly religious in the action of the woman who chooses her lover and gives herself instead of letting herself be *taken*. . . . Oh! that is because in order to give oneself, a woman has to feel quite strong! In letting herself be taken . . . she saves herself an excuse for society [*le monde*]" (2:144–45). Tristan goes on to project a time when woman will "free herself from the approval of others" (2:145).

THE HEART THAT DIRECTS HER CONDUCT

The sentimental social novel also follows sentimentality in downplaying material appearance to intensify the reader's sympathetic response to the suffering protagonist. Like sentimentality, sentimental social novels prefer the light touch, detailing physicality, whether of people or places, with a few stock adjectives so as not to distract from the reader's attention to the soul.[65] Natalie is introduced as "the most charming of women" (2),

---

[64] Sentimental social novels also evince their politicization of the sentimental private sphere in the transformation of the sentimental title. As Genlis's titles illustrate, sentimental titles frequently use "or" to join a proper name or dramatic description with a concept that pertains to manners and/or private life: *Adèle et Théodore, ou Lettres sur l'éducation; Alphonsine, ou la Tendresse maternelle; Les Mères rivales, ou la Calomnie*. In the sentimental social novel, "or" introduces a concept invoking a political or social idea; thus, Carlowitz's *Le Pair de France, ou le Divorce* and Tristan's *Méphis ou le prolétaire*.

[65] Abrantès makes the sentimental emphasis on the soul apparent when *La Duchesse de Valombray* offers its version of Stendhal's celebrated figure for the novel as the mirror of external reality. In Abrantès's reworking, the soul, rather than the novel, reflects experience:

endowed with "beauty" and "extreme youth" (4). All we learn about the heroine of *La Duchesse de Valombray* is that "Suzanne, at eighteen years of age, was one of the most graceful and attractive types of women" (10). When Arnaud first presents Clémence, we know nothing about her physical aspect. Marcelle, the heroine of Sand's *Le Meunier d'Angibault* is introduced as "the blond Marcelle"; she has "beautiful golden hair," "alabaster hands," and a small "foot shod in satin" (6).

Sentimental social novels also pursue the sympathetic effect with the sentimental codes of description that deviate from the light touch, like the sentimental blazon. *Natalie* is of no use to exemplify the sentimental blazon, perhaps because the hero does not want to tax the heroine, who is fed up with physical description after only a brief experience of society: "I am tired of the same worn-out praise; when they have said: She has beautiful eyes! they have said everything. Do they even know what feelings they express? Have they sought a soul in their gaze?" (64). Other sentimental social novels use the sentimental blazon to make the same point. Clémence enters the narrative when she debuts in the salon of the Hôtel du Lac, an oasis of uncensored conversation during the Restoration. After she leaves the gathering, Arnaud depicts her heroine with a blazon that summarizes the collective judgments of the men who find her desirable: "[I]t was an explosion of praise: how beautiful she is! what a slender, elegant and graceful figure! what delicate coloring! what a penetrating gaze! what a harmonious voice! what gorgeous chestnut hair!" (1:24). The hostess at the salon, Clémence's protectress, gives the blazon its sentimental moral. "You think you know my Clémence because you have seen her pass by, attractive and radiant, and you are left stunned with admiration!—What would it be like, if you could have appreciated, like me, her boundless charms, the countless nuances of her mind, the exquisite whims of her heart?" (1:25–26).

When Sand finally characterizes the physical aspect of *Le Meunier d'Angibault*'s heroine, Marcelle, she assigns a class to the social microcosm whose focus on materiality needs to be corrected. Severing Marcelle's description from the viewpoint of a desiring man altogether, she ascribes it to the young bourgeoise, Rose, spoiled by cold, parvenu parents interested only in self-satisfaction and gain. Rose starts detailing Marcelle's body from the capitalist motive of competition: "asking herself if this Parisian beauty would outshine hers at the village festival" (189). Rose is, however, worthy, and Marcelle's appearance would seem to be persuasive enough to lead her to the sentimental moral on her own. Moved by Marcelle's "inner liveliness," Rose concludes, "She is however

---

"Our soul is a mirror on which all the most diverse disturbances pass by, each one successively tarnishing its glass in turn" (2:330).

not as beautiful as I thought! . . . why then do I want to resemble her?" (190–91). With her attraction to Marcelle, Rose begins her moral and social education, as the utopian socialist aristocrat helps develop "her nature stifled by external circumstances" (191).

Sand's description of Marcelle, moreover, shows her virtuosity in manipulating the codes of the entire French novelistic tradition. In fact, it is not quite accurate to speak of Sand's break with the light touch as a sentimental blazon. Rather, she delineates Marcelle's description using the codes of the *portrait moral*, as Sand indicates when she titles her chapter, "Portrait." Like the *portrait moral*, Marcelle's description joins physical appearance and spiritual qualities into a moral and psychological whole, in contrast to the blazon which breaks the heroine's beauty down into discrete, physical features, dwelling in particular on these features' visual appeal.

In substituting a *portrait moral* for a blazon, Sand intensifies the social significance of her exception to the light touch. As Brooks has observed, the *portrait moral* offers description using "an exact, elegant, and general language of psychological and moral analysis" that reflects a "constituted, closed, and ordered society which alone can create such a language and give it meaning."[66] This order is society as constructed by the ruling elite, whether that elite is the court of Louis XIV or the eighteenth-century salons bringing together court and town. When Sand couches Marcelle's description as a *portrait moral*, she thus invokes the question of hegemonic social values, but corrects the significance of the *portrait moral* in the worldly tradition. In Sand's hands, the *portrait moral* exposes the imperfections of the hegemonic construction of society rather than celebrating it. If Marcelle's *portrait moral* remains a topos of education, as in the worldly tradition, it leads the reader along with Rose from society as it now is to society as it should be.

The beautiful young person overly concerned with material appearance is a stock character in the sentimental social novel, although not necessarily a member of the bourgeoisie. Nor do all these characters share Rose's moral worth; most commonly, they lack soul and fritter away their time in idle, worldly pleasures. In *La Duchesse de Valombray*, the heroine falls for a handsome count, but "[h]is exterior aspect was completely opposed to his character. His dark and stern face gave him the appearance of a man engaged in serious and gloomy thoughts, while he was only occupied with the most insignificant things" (1:75). The heroine of Tarbé des Sablons's *Roseline, ou de la Nécessité de la religion dans l'éducation des*

---

[66] Brooks, *Worldliness*, 92. Brooks points out that such description, starting from a "given ethical totality," contrasts with realist description, proceeding to its encyclopedic social knowledge through "fragmented details of the real" (92).

femmes offers a similar lesson before she has learned to abjure the code and follow her heart. "Roseline only seemed to be beautiful to prove once again that regular features and figure are nothing, if grace does not give them life. The first glance was enchanting, the second almost caused annoyance: people do not like to go back on their admiration, like a jeweler who is ashamed to have mistaken a rhinestone for a diamond" (1:33). Through such characters, the sentimental social novel reinforces its warning against excessive attention to the material.

Sentimental social novels also turn the reader's attention from external appearance to interiority with the sentimental code I termed the "image of the heart." This code occurs when narrators break with the light touch in their treatment of setting, turning landscape into an allegory of interiority. I took the phrase from the description in Carlowitz's *Caroline, ou le Confesseur* that opens the scene when Caroline throws her starving child into a lake, driven mad by social abuse.

> Holding her sleeping son in her arms, she goes down the hill slowly, comes near the lake, stops, and stares in silence at a long column of fire, which seems to emerge from the water at the spot where the last rays of the setting sun are now falling.
>
> Soon, however, this phenomenon vanishes . . . and a soft and melancholy glow now illuminates the whole countryside; the strangely variegated nuances of the pine forests and birch woods, of sterile rocks and fields dotted with flowers, clashes without blending and seems an image of the human heart—it, too, brings together the most opposing contrasts, for in this abyss, which the philosophy of so many centuries has not yet been able to sound, crime adjoins virtue, madness reason, fanaticism the mild confidence in divine goodness. (103–104)

Soliciting sympathy for Caroline by turning the reader's attention from exteriority to interiority, the novel corrects the mistreatment that has destroyed her. Carlowitz depicts society's overemphasis on the external trappings of morality as leading its members to neglect her heroine's fundamentally worthy soul.

Sentimental social novels sometimes give their attack on contemporary materialism a literary point, for they direct it against realist description, which is the most celebrated contemporary novelistic code valuing material aspect. In the preface to *Roseline, ou de la Nécessité de la religion dans l'éducation des femmes*, for example, Tarbé des Sablons condemns "literary monstrosities that pervert even good sense, that annihilate even sensibility [*la sensibilité*]," along with the excessive materialism of post-Revolutionary society (viii). In 1835, the year Tarbé's novel was published, critics brought the charge of monstrosity against Balzac above all, catalyzed by his publication of *Le Père Goriot*, as Weinberg explains.[67] Tarbé goes on to associate this literature of monstrosity with an excess of description, which she differentiates from her own focus. "If we have allowed ourselves *useful* reflections, we will spare the reader descriptions." Rather, it is "the soul," which attracts "our attention . . . this poor, neglected soul" (xv).[68]

Sand, too, indicts realist description in the chapter of *Le Meunier d'Angibault* where she rewrites the *portrait moral*. Introducing Marcelle's portrait by posing description as a subject of aesthetic debate, Sand's authorial persona criticizes "the storytellers of our time" for having "somewhat misused the fashion for portraits in their narratives" with their efforts to "describe meticulously the features and clothing of the people they represent" (188). The authorial narrator goes on to assert that she lacks the force to deviate from the "beaten path," as she capitulates to the expectations of contemporary readers epitomized by "the opinion of Rose," the young bourgeoise (188). But if Sand gives in to Rose and her ilk with some hesitation, she projects a future moment when realist description will no longer be necessary: "future masters, condemning our attention to detail [*minutie*], will sketch their characters in broader and more clearly defined strokes," although she does not explicitly link this departure from bourgeois aesthetic expectations with the advent of egalitarian postbourgeois society, which her novel promotes in its ideas (188).

Attacking realist description, sentimental social novelists condemn one of the most celebrated inventions of the nineteenth century, which went on to a long and successful career. To counterbalance the seemingly self-evident appeal of this code, it is useful to remember that the sentimental approach to material aspect retained great prestige in the July Monarchy, the invention of realism notwithstanding. When *La Revue des Deux Mondes* assessed Madame Charles Reybaud's sentimental social novel, *Mézélie*, for example, Reybaud received praise for evoking surroundings without succumbing to excessive detail: "The characters that are met and left behind, the places that are passed through and described on the way, all seemed completely natural and simple. Madame Reybaud does not get overly bogged down in detail, although she lets things be seen ade-

---

[67] Weinberg, *French Realism*, 43–44. Thus, the critic Hains declared, "I look for man throughout his works, and I find only exhausted natures or weird anomalies. They are the monsters of the species" (43–44). Similarly, Jacques Chaudes-Aigues called *Le Père Goriot* "one of the 'monstruosités morales qu'on doit laisser dans l'ombre [moral monstrosities that should be left in shadow]' " (44).

[68] Tarbé, however, engages in some slippage, for she also qualifies description in terms evoking the Romantic picturesque rather than Balzac's encyclopedic social overviews, as "description of the moon, woods, *ruins*, etc." (xv).

quately."[69] We have seen Philarète Chasles not only appreciate the beauty of the light touch but contrast it with Balzac's "interminable inspection, which leads to boredom," in his review of Ancelot's sentimental social novel, *Gabrielle*.[70] According to Gustave Planche, who took early-nine-teenth-century sentimentality as his literary ideal, however, even *Gabrielle* came too close to realist description. "It is unfortunate that Madame An-celot, in drawing Gabrielle . . . thought herself obliged to emphasize all the visual details of her model . . . these details, which charm me in a painting, which I find pleasing in an English vignette, have little interest for me in a narrative. The most beautiful woman should not be described like a thoroughbred horse . . . Madame Ancelot . . . has sinned through an excess of reality. We know too much about Gabrielle's body [*per-sonne*], we know too little about the heart that directs her conduct."[71]

HUGE HEAPS OF MANURE

In criticizing *Gabrielle* for its excessive description, Planche makes evi-dent one significant difference between the sentimental social novel and early-nineteenth-century sentimentality: sentimental social novels some-times include more detail. Their interest in detail extends from a more fleshed-out light touch to occasional descriptions of historically specific social types that focus on their material aspect. While short by realist standards, these descriptions are lengthy when measured against senti-mental poetics, which is characterized by extreme descriptive restraint.[72]

Sometimes the descriptions of social types make a sentimental point, deflating material appearance even as it is invoked. Arnaud's *Coralie l'in-constante*, for example, contains one exception to the sentimental light touch.[73] In portraying the idle bourgeoise, Adine Genevois, Arnaud pro-ceeds in realist fashion. Adine is "a twenty-eight-year-old woman, beauti-ful and well built, but whose waist was starting to thicken with the plump-ness that comes from a comfortable and lazy life, and whose cheeks, like flowers grown in hot-houses, lacked life and freshness; but this complex-

[69] Review signed Y. of *Mézélie*, 419.

[70] Chasles, review of *Gabrielle*.

[71] Gustave Planche, review of *Gabrielle*, 834. In associating *Gabrielle* with a realist con-vention, Planche may also be reacting to the fact that it is one of the rare sentimental social novels to resolve the conflict between the heart and the code with the realist morality of compromise.

[72] The sentimental social novel shares its interest in the social type with realism as well as with contemporary nonfictional genres of popular ethnography like panoramic literature and the physiognomies.

[73] Sand praised Arnaud's novel for its handling of description. See George Sand to Angélique Arnaud, Paris, beginning of June 1843, in Sand, *Correspondance*, 414.

ion, slightly pallid and nuanced, with blue veins, suited her tired features, and heightened the brilliance of her beautiful eyes; she was half leaning on the back of a loveseat facing a mirror, and was passing her fingers slowly through the curls of her fine black hair, all the while throwing a satisfied and languishing gaze on her graceful image."[74] Calling on physical aspect to depict Adine's overinvestment in materiality, Arnaud gives her description a sentimental moral, which resembles the sentimental invocation of other nonsentimental descriptive codes. Even as Arnaud exhibits the characteristically realist attention to material detail, she represents such attention as a specifically bourgeois form of narcissistic vanity rather than as a privileged tool for uncovering social truth.

Sometimes, however, sentimental social novelists use realist description without qualification. Indeed, Arnaud offers one of the lengthiest examples of unreconstructed realist description when she characterizes a compelling habitué of the Hôtel du Lac in *Clémence*. "The oracle of taste and propriety" at the Hôtel is the Marquise de Mont Brun, a.k.a. Madame Palmer, an ancien régime aristocrat who allied herself with Napoleon and who has lost all her fortune by the time the novel opens (1:8). A few lines should convey the realist texture of the Marquise's description, which goes on for several pages: "The marquise was plump. On her full and highly colored face, the traces of small pox hid those of age; her hair was silky and of a beautiful silvery grey; she wore it short and curled. Her head, ordinarily bare, was remarkable for the beauty of its form and the flexibility of its poses; her hands looked like those of a woman of thirty, and her well spaced and full set of teeth, had lost nothing of their whiteness" etc. (1:11). Carlowitz, too, uses physical detail to portray the historically specific types who people *Le Pair de France, ou le Divorce*, although her descriptions are restrained in comparison to Arnaud's portrayal of the Marquise de Mont Brun. These types include a peer of France, a coachman, "the type of the woman of the world," and the type of the grisette, as well as a "young lawyer taken in by the July Revolution" (1:28). When Sand justifies her use of description in *Le Meunier d'Angibault*, she is referring not only to her *portrait moral* but to her novel's procedure for delineating social types like the worthy peasant, Louis, and the newly parvenu Bricolins. To describe such figures, Sand offers extensive material, and particularly visual details on character and setting, down to the Bricolins' "huge heaps of manure sunk in their square freestone pits and still rising up to ten or twelve feet in height [from which] foul streams poured off that were expressly left to flow in all freedom towards the lower grounds to warm up the vegetables in the garden" (67).

---

[74] Angélique Arnaud, *Coralie l'inconstante*, 1:41. Subsequent page references will appear parenthetically in the text.

Nothing could be more antisentimental than manure; when Sand breaks with her novel's dominant generic horizon, she goes all the way. Her heaps of manure do not simply convey information but underline her flagrant defiance of sentimental poetics, as they draw the reader's attention from the content of the description to its literary significance. Such a citation of realist description, emphasis added, resembles Sand's critical comments on description in the chapter "Portrait." In both cases, Sand invokes this crucial realist code, but does not seamlessly integrate it into her practice.

In a writer highly attuned to the significance of convention, such ambivalence is revealing; specifically, it reveals one of the great poetic challenges facing the sentimental social subgenre. The sentimental social novel's literary foundations are sentimentality's purified tragic aesthetic, where all inessential details are subordinated to the progress of the action, which is inseparable from the movements of the soul. As we have seen, these inessential details include representations of social specificity. Sentimental purification is, however, in conflict with the sentimental social novel's need to depict differences among social groups as part of its political project to represent unequal social division. Calling on realist description, Sand, like other sentimental social novelists, finds a way to fulfill this need. The depiction of social difference is also at stake when sentimental social novels continue the sentimental light touch, but fill it in with somewhat more material detail.

The sentimental social novel's appeal to realist description, however, introduces social difference at the expense of the sentimental effect. Detailed attention to exterior aspect transgresses the sentimental subordination of materiality to the soul and establishes a distance between reader and narrative conflicting with sentimental sympathy. The sentimental social novel finds a similar partial solution to the problem of representing social difference when it includes the distinctive speech patterns of differing social groups. Heteroglossia disrupts sentimentality's neoclassical diction, which helps remove unnecessary distraction from the insoluble collision driving the sentimental plot.

Sand's ambivalence about realist description is constant from her first novel *Indiana*, which starts with a detailed, encyclopedic overview of character and setting, emphasizing visual aspect. But *Indiana* then proceeds to undermine the authority of realist descriptive codes in two diverging ways. Sand's first tactic is to destroy the credibility of her realist narrator. While he astutely grasps the character of Raymon, he is unable to give Indiana's courage its full due because he is crippled by sexism; in the case of women, his supposedly penetrating observations on human nature reduce to generalizations like "woman is an idiot by nature" (251). Failing to do justice to his heroine, the narrator defaults on the realist contract to serve as trustworthy guide, and the reader must read through his prejudice to grasp the significance of the novel. Sand also undercuts the authority of realist description by moving away from this code in the course of the narrative, until she does away with her realist observer entirely, giving the last word to a first-person traveler, who describes character and setting using the light touch and the image of the heart.

PHYSICAL AND MORAL BEAUTY'S
DIVERSE AND CONTRASTING FORMS

The sentimental social novel's attention to historically specific social types transforms sentimental codes of character as well as sentimental description. While sentimental novels set their plots among the nobility with at most a bourgeois interloper, characters in sentimental social novels range across the spectrum of French society. This diversity is greatest among the protagonists, as Sand's *Le Meunier d'Angibault* makes clear. Here, heroes and heroines embody the most important classes comprising contemporary French society, from the aristocratic Marcelle and the bourgeois Rose to the proletarian Henri and the peasant Louis. Similarly, Carlowitz's *Le Pair de France* represents the effects of the law forbidding divorce on a middle-class woman unhappily married to a coachman as well as on a Duke, a Duchess, a grisette, and a lawyer.

In realism, characters from different classes further the project of encyclopedic knowledge. The sentimental social novel, in contrast, uses its panorama of protagonists both to continue and to complicate the function of social identity within sentimentality. When sentimentality sets its plots among a single social class, I have argued, it abstracts social difference for political reasons. Eliding attention to social division, it suggests all protagonists are equal before the tragic conflict of rights. The sentimental social novel's broad social panorama at once exposes the illusions of sentimental equality and substitutes another form of social leveling in its place. Including socially diverse protagonists, the subgenre shows that the conflict between the heart and the code can occur in a wide range of social groups and classes. It also underlines the notion that courage is distributed across the social spectrum. Arnaud puts this conclusion in moral terms when she explains why she has given *Coralie l'inconstante* two heroines who contrast in physique, temperament, and social identity.[75] "[E]qually

---

[75] While the fair, tall, buxom Hélène is the melancholy, over-educated, hard-working daughter of a poor widow supporting herself through a lending library, her cousin, the dark, small, and slender Coralie is the only child of an aristocrat who married the sister of Hélène's mother on a whim. Despite her young-lady's education, Coralie, too becomes impoverished when her father dies ruined.

chaste and graceful, appealing to [*intéressant*] the soul and the eyes, but charming in such different ways, these young women seemed to have the mission to prove that physical beauty, like moral beauty, takes different and contrasting forms, and that men have been stingy in interpreting divine thinking, every time they have wanted to delimit in one type alone, the good, which is immense, from the beautiful, which has an infinity of aspects" (2:220).

The use of socially diverse figures to vindicate "diverse and contrasting forms . . . of moral beauty" may explain why there is little variation among secondary characters embodying the code, in contrast to the protagonists standing up for the heart as well as the worthy characters who support them. Proponents of the code come in three breeds: egotistical, materialistic, hypocritical society men and women, like Madame d'Artville in *Natalie*; unprincipled arrivistes, often young men, scheming to "succeed [*parvenir*]," like Julien de Berville in Bodin's *La Cour d'Assises*; and cruel, if not crooked, agents of the law, like the magistrate in *Caroline, ou le Confesseur*.

If the sentimental social subgenre makes a political point through its panorama of protagonists, such diversity carries a poetic risk. In sentimentality, I have argued, social homogeneity has a poetic as well as a political function, eliding accidental details that might distract from the ethical collision underwriting the sentimental plot. This code of character also facilitates the unity of place, another tragic strategy for focusing all attention on the founding collision. The sentimental social novel risks disrupting such focus with its characters from all walks of life, for these characters bring in their wake social details that may or may not directly relate to the sentimental social novel's structuring conflict between the heart and the code. In addition, these characters can dilute the plot's spatial unity, for they often live in different places. Carlowitz makes the poetic dangers of social diversity evident in *Le Pair de France*, where her protagonists are scattered across the map of Paris. Provoking their interactions through spatial coincidence instead of through the ineluctable progress of the heart against the code, Carlowitz's lengthy, episodic novel is at the furthest remove from the tragic suppression of "incidental actions and characters in a subplot" (*A*, 2:1167), or from the dictum that the protagonist should not be "debased in the chance of events," which Sand formulates when she explains "the theory . . . I have generally followed" in composing her novels.[76]

Sentimental social novels avoid this danger most successfully when they continue the sentimental practice of cutting plot to the measure of the family. Sand is particularly skillful at turning the family into a unit incor-

[76] Sand, *Histoire*, 2:161.

porating social diversity, as she finds a way to represent social difference while respecting tragic compression. In *Indiana*, for example, Sand gives her aristocratic heroine a "foster sister [*soeur de lait*]," Noun, a servant of lower-class origins, possibly of color.[77] Precipitating both sisters into suffering through their love for the same hypocritical man, Sand generates her novel's conflicts between the heart and the code from a limited number of characters and situations, even as she shows that women's social subordination ranges across class.

In *Le Meunier d'Angibault*, Sand uses the sentimental family to concentrate action among socially diverse characters, capitalizing on the sentimental family as a unit of place. All the novel's events are situated in and around the aristocratic family estate, which constitutes the classic sentimental topography. In this work, a family incorporating social diversity is not the origin of narrative but its goal. Bonding together aristocrat, bourgeois, peasant, and proletarian into one idealized community devoted to the education of the next generation, *Le Meunier d'Angibault* replaces the oppressive aristocratic-bourgeois notion of the family built on ties of blood and money with a collective based on freely chosen bonds of affection, just as her characters transform the crumbling Blanchemont estate, littered with heaps of the Bricolins' manure, into a "pretty country cottage" (376).

Sand was, moreover, not the only sentimental social novelist to respect tragic condensation while representing social diversity by keeping the narrative all in the family. In *Coralie l'inconstante*, for example, Arnaud suppresses unnecessary social details and spatial dispersion by making her petty bourgeois and aristocratic heroines cousins who live together when the aristocrat falls on hard times. Like *Indiana*, Arnaud's novel further limits subplots and incidental actions by generating the novel's structuring conflict between the heart and the code from both cousins' love for the same man.

THE NOVELIST IS THE REAL LAWYER OF ABSTRACT BEINGS

When sentimental social novels disrupt sentimental poetics, they threaten their ability to resolve contemporary political and social conflict. Realism, as we have seen, compensates for unequal social division with the private

---

[77] Like Indiana, Noun is a *créole*. At the time, *créole* could mean either a white settler in the colonies or a colonial subject of mixed race. Sand suggests Noun's racial otherness when her narrator describes Noun's physique, comparing, for example, Noun's beauty "full of creole blood" with "the pale, fragile beauty of madame Delmare" (60) and noticing Noun's "cool, brown arms" (104).

realist narrative contract that gives the reader the knowledge to dominate social struggle. The sentimental social novel, in contrast, counters the spectacle of social division with the spectacle of sympathetic community.

From their prefaces, sentimental social novels make clear that their goal is to solicit the reader's sympathy for their narratives of suffering. Epinay Saint-Luc's previously cited appeal on behalf of her heroines at the beginning of *Valida* is typical: "Readers . . . do not rush to blame them: rather pity them; compassion is their due" (1:xii). Pursuing the sympathetic response with sentimental codes like the light touch, the plot of insoluble conflict, the sentimental blazon, and the emphatic narrator, sentimental social novels set up the reader's relation to the text as a bond of disinterested sympathy, which is in profound contrast to the self-interested relations of power reigning both within the sentimental social novel's plot and in society at large.

"Come, we shall weep together over the unfortunates in his stories," Diderot invites Richardson's fellow readers.[78] The sentimental social novel, too, constructs its audience as a sympathetic collective, personifying its reader in markedly different fashion from the realist text. What greater contrast to Balzac's idle consumer in the comfort of the private interior opening *Le Père Goriot*, "you who hold this book in your white hand, you who sink into your comfortable armchair, saying, 'Perhaps this will entertain me' " than *Indiana*'s portrait of the reader as both suffering protagonist and judge, who meet in the courtroom of the novel to listen to the case made by the novelist (50). "Bending over the victims, and mixing his tears with theirs, serving as their interpreter to his readers, but, like a prudent defense attorney, not trying to mitigate his clients' faults too much, and addressing himself to the mercy of the judges rather than to their rigor, the novelist is the real [*véritable*] lawyer of the abstract beings who represent our passions and sufferings before the bench of force and the jury of opinion" (44).

In the sentimental social novel's idealized sympathetic community, unequal social divisions disappear. Compassion knows no rank or gender; all readers are equal before the suffering narrated and in their potential to be an object of such compassion themselves. Sentimental social novels sometimes mention this ideal collective beyond inequality in appealing to the reader's sympathy. Sand includes both those in dominating and dominated subject positions when her 1842 preface depicts the readers as implicated in *Indiana*'s "cause": "It is that of half the human species [*genre*], it is that of all humanity, for the unhappiness of woman leads to that of man, like the unhappiness of the slave leads to that of the master. . . . Enough cries of pain and sympathy have answered mine so that I

---

[78] Diderot, "Richardson," 85.

now know what to think about the supreme bliss of others" (46). Occasionally, however, novels exclude the ruling elites or classes as unfit for the sympathetic response. In her preface to *Madame de Tercy*, for example, Sor offers her idea of religion "to young men . . . to us weak women . . . to all who suffer," but leaves aside "men of the times": "why do they need to hope for another future?" (1:viii–ix).

Sentimental social novels all invoke sympathetic community as the response to unequal social division, whatever their stated politics. In answering diverse political critiques of social division with sympathetic community, the sentimental social novel resembles the political and social theory of its time. During the July Monarchy, as Furet observes, "The *idea* of forging a new community beyond individual interests and class divisions . . . is found all over the place . . . it will be shared by two stars as distant as Tocqueville and Marx."[79]

There is, moreover, direct dialogue between sentimental social novelists and political theorists interested in a community beyond social division, as Karl Marx's conclusion to *The Poverty of Philosophy* (1847) makes clear. "It is only in an order of things in which there are no more classes and class antagonisms that *social evolutions* will cease to be *political revolutions*. Till then . . . the last word of social science will always be: '*Le combat ou la mort; la lutte sanguinaire ou le néant. C'est ainsi que la question est invinciblement posée* [Combat or death; bloody struggle or nothingness. Thus is the question insurmountably posed].' "[80] Marx's "last word" in social science is written by George Sand, as he offers eloquent testimony to the contemporary political importance of sentimental social representations of unequal social division, their distance from realist mimesis notwithstanding. Marx takes his citation from Sand's *Jean Ziska* (1843), a work that Sand characterizes as "history from the standpoint of sentiment."[81] For Sand, history from the standpoint of sentiment is historical events narrated with sentimental social conventions, in particular the plot of subjects in dominated social positions. In *Jean Ziska*, the narrative driving history is "the struggle of equality, which strives to establish itself, against inequality, which strives to maintain itself, the struggle of the poor against the rich, of the honest against the cheat, of

---

[79] Furet, *Révolution*, 149. Emphasis added to underline Furet's retention of the nineteenth-century usage of "idea."

[80] Karl Marx, *The Poverty of Philosophy*, 175.

[81] Sand, *Jean Ziska*, 19. Sand explains that she directs her work to a feminine readership, in particular, because women are the dispossessed of contemporary society: "[T]he history of heresy should interest and touch you particularly; because . . . you are all heretics; you all protest in your heart; you all protest with no success. . . . You are all *poor* like the eternal disciples of evangelical poverty; for according to the law of marriage and the family, you own nothing" (19).

the oppressed against the oppressor, of woman against man . . . of the worker against the master, of the laborer against the exploiter, of the free thinker against the priest," and so on.[82] "Women, it is always your struggle of feeling against authority," Sand continues, reducing the essence of history to the heart struggling against the code.[83]

If Sand's narratives appeal to Marx, it is in keeping with their aesthetic project. Sand addresses her sentimental social novels to a socially conscious audience, and this is a characteristic feature of the subgenre. The sentimental social novel's socially conscious audience constitutes one crucial way it displaces the consolations of sympathetic community. Sentimentality resolves political tensions at a distance. An idealized version of the liberal public sphere, sentimental community allows readers to enjoy the difficulty reconciling negative and positive rights as the dissension of taste. In the sentimental social novel, in contrast, the transformation of unequal social division into an ideal community is a first step, but it is not a solution on its own. Throughout these works, narrators and authorial personae mobilize the sympathetic community, urging their readers to intervene directly in social if not political change.

Novels with conservative ideas frame this social intervention as a private moral transformation. In *Madame de Tercy*, for example, Sor counsels, "we, disinherited of joys and prosperity," should take comfort in "the hope of a better life . . . a belief in heaven" (1:ix). Novels promoting moderate and progressive ideas, in contrast, exhort their readers to reform manners if not laws. In her 1842 preface to *Indiana*, Sand hopes that sympathy will lead readers to change their opinions, for it is opinion "that slows or encourages social improvement" (47). Hugo declares that he will have achieved his goal in *Le Dernier Jour d'un condamné* if, "with no other tool than his thought, he has searched deeply enough to draw blood from the heart that beats under the magistrate's robe! happy if he has made pitiful those who believe themselves just!" (369). In the preface to *Ange de Spola*, as we have seen, Marbouty too focuses the reader's attention on changing the legal code: "Should not this moral mutilation of woman, doubtless necessary in former times, stop with progress?— And could not and should not contemporary legislation know how to alleviate institutions which are so cruel and so unfavorable to the happiness of all?" (1:9). Sentimental social novels sometimes stress their social mobilization of sympathetic community by including idealized versions of such communities within their novels. Sand, notably, portrays these communities in her works with happy endings, like *Indiana*, where Indiana and Ralph pursue the abolition of slavery, or *Le Meunier d'Angibault*,

---

[82] Ibid., 20.
[83] Ibid., 24.

where a peasant, a proletarian, a bourgeoise, and a marquise work together for the education of the next generation.

One great attraction of sentimentality's idealized liberal public is the interpretive freedom it offers the reader. "I have seen how the diversity of judgments gave rise to secret grudges, hidden contempt, in fact the same divisions between united friends [*personnes unies*] as if they had been involved in some serious dispute [*l'affaire la plus sérieuse*]," Diderot declares, and I have argued that such reader disagreement is crucial to the sentimental novel's ability to mediate the conflict between individual freedom and collective welfare at an aesthetic distance.[84] The sentimental social novel, in contrast, might seem to restrict the reader's freedom with its emphatic condemnations of the code. But in fact, the sentimental social novel leaves room for disagreement on "the conduct of the characters," which Diderot places at the crux of sentimental response.[85] While the sentimental social novel opposes the heart and the code in a Manichean struggle, its protagonists are not above reproach. They commit faults deserving censure, if not crimes, as Sand makes clear when she compares the novelist to a defense attorney, "not trying to mitigate his clients' fault" (44).

If dispute over the protagonists remains constant from sentimental to sentimental social problem-solving, its significance shifts in keeping with the sentimental social novel's mobilization of sentimental community. Carlowitz explains the substance of such dispute in the sentimental social novel when she introduces *Le Pair de France*. Her preface takes the form of a dialogue between a female authorial persona and a benevolent, worldly man, Monsieur Niçaise. The novel has "a central, irreparable flaw," Niçaise tells the author, "none of the persons you represent is completely right" (1:25). He goes on to enumerate the different kinds of critics *Le Pair de France* will displease. While the royalists will object that it does not glorify Charles X, their adversaries will find that it fails to "paint this same king as a ferocious beast. . . . The republicans will reproach you for not having endowed them with all virtues, all perfections. The centrists [*juste-milieu*] will never excuse your second volume and above all your conclusion" (1:30). "I am pleased with this criticism," responds Carlowitz's author (1:26). "All my characters, even the republicans, seek the triumph of their opinions only through the channels of discussion" (1:31). Rather than discussing the poetic construction of the novel and the morality of the characters, like Diderot's readers, Carlowitz's readers enter into the specifics of current political and social debate.

When the sentimental social novel introduces its reader into the liberal public sphere in action, it exhibits its foundations in the Revolution of

---

[84] Diderot, "Richardson," 88–89.
[85] Ibid., 88.

1830. It assumes that writers and readers have the power to transform society, and this assumption both produces and depends on the July Revolution's abolition of censorship. Sentimental social novels, moreover, sometimes call attention to the importance they accord 1830 by setting scenes where the heart comes into particularly intense conflict with the code against its backdrop. When Indiana finally runs away from Delmare in extreme defiance of his authority, "what were her surprise and alarm, in landing, to see the tricolor flag floating over the walls of Bordeaux!" (290). Languishing in unconsummated love for a revolutionary devoted entirely to his social duty, Arnaud's Clémence meets death on the barricades of 1830 by shielding her beloved from a bullet. The adultery between Carlowitz's unhappily married middle-class woman and her peer of France reaches its crisis during the Revolution of 1830 when the Duke, entirely consumed by his love, "neglects . . . the duties towards his country that are required of him by his rank as peer" (1:276).

No texts make the sentimental social novel's foundations in the July Revolution more vivid than Hugo's differing introductions to *Le Dernier Jour d'un condamné* (1829) before and after 1830. When the narrative was first published, Hugo did not exhort his readers to social action. Rather, in "Une Comédie à propos d'une tragédie," he portrayed his work as misunderstood by a group of frivolous readers in a private salon. When Hugo republished *Le Dernier Jour d'un condamné* in 1832, he included the 1829 "Comédie" with the apologetic note, "It must be remembered, in reading it, among what political, moral, and literary objections the first editions of this book were published" (249). He also added a new preface where he "unmasks" "the political idea, the social idea, that he wanted to popularize using this innocent and ingenuous literary form," positioning his narrative and his reader within contemporary debates over the abolition of the death penalty (367–68).

The sentimental social novel's active participation in the liberal public sphere may help explain why authorial personae frequently defend their novels against public criticism. In the preface to *Le Pair de France*, we have seen Carlowitz mention the different political groups her novel will offend. When Sand defends *Indiana* in her 1842 preface, she is concerned with charges brought by professional reviewers running from "certain journalists who currently set themselves up as representatives and guardians of public morality," to "conservatives," "innovators," and "unjust and malicious critics" (43, 45, 47). In the conclusion to her preface, however, Sand makes clear that persuading all her critics is less important than the sheer existence of the controversy. Indeed, her novel ends not by reiterating its central idea but rather with a paean to freedom of opinion that might seem surprising if we do not recognize that this freedom underwrites Sand's very ability to promote social improvement through literature. "Let not these reproaches that . . . I have just directed against most journalists of my time be seen as any kind of protest against the right of control [*droit de contrôle*] with which public morality invests the French press. . . . Freedom of thought, freedom of writing and speech, sacred victories of the human mind! what are the minor sufferings and passing cares resulting from your mistakes or abuses, in comparison with the vast benefits you offer the world?" (47).

The sentimental social novel is the most influential among numerous July Monarchy literary and visual art forms taking positions in public political and social debate. These art forms are the first modern avant-gardes.[86] Like other contemporary avant-garde forms, sentimental social novels describe their intervention as participating in the march, if not the battle, for progress.[87] Auguste Luchet, a respected sentimental social novelist, emphasizes the rhetoric of battle in his preface to Elisa Billotey's sentimental social novel, *L'Agent de change* (1837): "The writer has one and only one task left, one duty, which is to battle . . . the horrible God of our times, selfishness, it is boldly to go attack it and strike it down everywhere. . . . [T]he novel no longer makes merry, morals torn asunder call out to it, social ills implore it . . . it is no longer a matter of entertaining us but of saving us."[88] Allart similarly compares socially progressive writers to soldiers in the opening lines of her preface to *Settimia*: "In a period of political and moral reconstruction, our books all discuss religion, manners, or affairs of state: our novels are protests, and address general questions, most often without intending to. Courage! Let us not tire; let France, victorious and still active, use in its new investigations this genius it has shown in its conquests of all types . . . while 400,000 soldiers in arms ensure peace in this restless nation . . . it is women's task above all to demand moral reform, and their works and their novels will be cries directed towards this desired goal" (1:i–ii). Salvandy, too, gives women a leading role in moral reform when he incorporates the novel in the march of progress, although *Natalie*'s preface figures women as advisors rather than the vanguard. "It is to be expected, in all careers, that if

---

[86] On the French invention of the avant-garde during the 1830s, see, notably, Biermann, *Avant-garde*.

[87] To my knowledge, Olinde Rodrigues first formulates the modern notion of the avant-garde in his Saint-Simonian dialogue, "L'Artiste, le Savant, et l'Industriel" (1825). "We, the artists, will serve as your avant-garde," declares the artist, "the power of the arts is in fact the most immediate and the fastest" (210). The artist goes on to describe his function, using the figure of progress as a march that was common in avant-garde declarations throughout the 1830s and 1840s. Once artists grasp their importance in promoting social improvement, the artist declares, "We will see them march with their times, and take back the importance they have always had when they worked, not for a few men, but for the masses; when they were the guides and the moral expression of society" (225).

[88] Auguste Luchet, preface to Elisa Billotey's *L'Agent de change*, i–ii.

the genius of peoples strides in the vanguard, opening new routes and adding progress to progress, theirs [women's genius], like a prudent and retiring advisor . . . will warn of dangers. . . . The ancients had personified the alliance of wisdom and literary genius using the features of a woman."[89]

Sentimental social novels sometimes underline their avant-garde ambitions by including avant-garde artists as characters in their works. A Romantic painter, Arnaud's Clémence is inspired to social art by the brooding revolutionary with whom she is in love. "Her mind, nourished until then on poetic enthusiasm, raised itself to noble conceptions of social vocation" (1:217). "I, too, will live for an idea!," Clémence declares, "I, too, will ask myself why people suffer, why there is a class of men condemned to serfdom and parasite classes who bring nothing to the masses. . . . I, too, will study wisdom and justice, after having studied grace and beauty" (1:218). In Tristan's *Méphis*, both protagonists, the singer, Maréquita, and the painter, Méphis, view the artist as protecting the weak against the strong and dream of an ideal society where artists make social policy. To cite Maréquita, "[I]t would perhaps be unwise today to name them ministers or prefects, but if society was organized as it should be, artists would be its leaders and its guides, for it is necessary to be impassioned about the beautiful, to have a sense of harmony, to be able to conceive all that is great and useful for the people" (1:33).

No aesthetic has been more antithetical to the avant-garde since Baudelaire than sentimentality. Belying the avant-garde's history of itself, the sentimental social novel shows all that this pivotal modern notion of art owes to the sentimental relation between art and politics minus sentimentality's Enlightenment separation of "art" from "life," to use Peter Bürger's terms for the avant-garde gesture. If avant-gardes from the mid-nineteenth century on deny their sentimental origins, it is to flee a history of failure. The July Monarchy version of the avant-garde evidently steeped in sentimentality will be discredited during the Revolution of 1848, when writers like Sand and Hugo do become "ministers or prefects," as Tristan put it, and stumble into the chasm separating the aesthetic from the political. In Flaubert's realist response to 1848, the failure of the first French avant-gardes is called the sentimental education.

---

[89] Salvandy, preface to *Natalie*, lv–lvi.

CHAPTER IV

A Compromised Position:
French Realism and the *Femme Auteur*

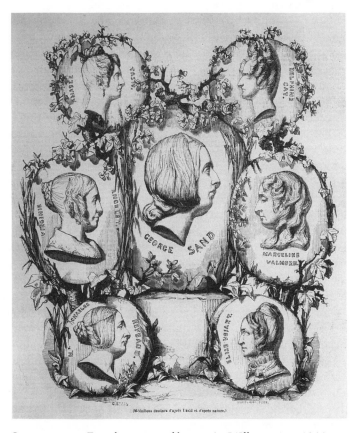

Contemporary French women of letters, in *L'Illustration*, 1844.

HE SAID, SHE SAID

In 1836, Balzac took a trip to Torino to help out a friend with some business pertaining to a lawsuit. His contact there, a count and lawyer, was at least as interested in Balzac's secretary, Marcel. "Please give my regards to your charming traveling companion," wrote the Count Sclopis to Balzac shortly before the writer returned to Paris. "Our sex would not seriously dare claim him for fear of losing him in the other. Tell him to clear up the mystery for us. . . . If you are not averse to this courtesy, we will find the solution to the puzzle [*enigme*]."[1]

"You are a fine and noble soul," Balzac replied. "You will not be surprised to see me wish you a good trip and all the pleasures you desire. I would, in these cases, like to have the power of God to fulfill the dreams of those I love. As for my traveling companion . . . he is certainly not what you think he is. . . . (So) I will tell you never to recognize him, because she is an attractive, witty, and virtuous woman who, never having (had) in her life the chance to breathe the air of Italy, and being able to cheat on her household cares for a few weeks, has placed her confidence in my absolute discretion and Scipio-like self-control. . . . Relying on these, she has enjoyed the life of a young man for the one and only time in her life. . . . The novel is at its last chapter. The term of three weeks is that of Cinderella's glass slipper. Marcel has to take up her woman's diadem and leave his student's riding crop!"[2]

"Marcel," a.k.a. Caroline Marbouty, has left her version of the adventure, too. "Torino, August 2, 1836. The date of this letter will surprise you, dear mother. You are far from thinking me in Italy, two hundred leagues away from my usual home. . . . I will thus tell you that, through Jules Sandeau, Balzac invited me to have dinner with him. I had the plan . . . to seduce him. . . . In short, someone spent three sleepless nights . . . someone came to propose to take me to Torino, from there to Genoa, perhaps to Florence. I hesitated a great deal, but I gave in. . . . I am alone with Balzac without a servant. He had me dress as a man and I am delighted with this costume, which suits me well. It keeps me from being recognized and gives me an endless number of new, attractive freedoms. . . . In Torino, I pass for his secretary. . . . Balzac is, like all superior men [*gens supérieurs*] very concerned with his ideas and not very nice. But he has such force and intellectual power, he has such superiority in all his being, that he is appealing. . . . He thinks I have a lot of talent . . . and wants to try to put me to work in order to earn 20,000 francs [*livres*] of income. But I should tell you that he is a man who likes to make plans and that only the present should be reckoned on with him. I am therefore not counting on it. It would involve working together on plays. . . . Back in Paris, I do not know what will become of this acquaintance. I have

---

[1] Frédéric Sclopis de Salerano, letter to Balzac, Torino, August 9, 1836. Cited in Henry Prior, "Balzac à Turin," 383.

[2] Balzac to Sclopis, Torino, August 9, 1836. Cited in Prior, "Balzac à Turin," 383–84.

kept the right of freedom for myself. . . . I need health, happiness, action: I have no prejudices, I let myself go with the current."[3]

The Italian journey according to Balzac? A virile but self-possessed man of the world enjoys the minor indiscretions of a charming *femme comme il faut*, who is cross-dressed as a student to flee her household cares, but who is admirable and virtuous despite appearances. The last "chapter" of a realist "novel," too, where an omniscient if not God-like male narrator clarifies what the male reader presciently calls "the puzzle [*l'enigme*]" to realize his reader's desires and thereby cement their affective bond. As Sclopis guessed, the "he" was in fact a "she," but Balzac perpetuated the tease by refusing to reveal that he had had an affair with his housewife, even while he presented her as highly desirable, to say nothing of irregular in her behavior.

And the Italian journey according to Marbouty? An aspiring writer takes off for adventure to escape the tedium of domestic duties. Masquerading as the quintessential ambitious hero of realist upward mobility narratives, she plays young secretary to an older man, who masters the profession she would like to enter, seducing him with an ambiguously erotic yet professional camaraderie. A sentimental social novel, too, where the conflicted protagonist first hesitates, then rebels in the name of "freedom" against the codes that constrict women. Confessing her transgressions, she asks a sympathetically disposed female reader to understand the emotional and material oppression that motivates them.

Balzac and Marbouty never confronted their different views of their trip directly. These accounts contain in miniature, however, a subsequent conflict between them over gender and novelistic genre that proved sufficiently bitter to end a friendship forged in an entertaining escapade. Let these two accounts hence also figure this book's concluding speculations on why there were no French women realists at the time the powerful poetics first emerged. One revealing perspective on why French women may have eschewed realist codes is what two players immersed in contemporary novelistic struggle had to say about the situation themselves.

THE MUSE OF LIMOGES

When Balzac and Marbouty returned to Paris, they did not pursue their vacation intimacy, but they remained cordial, frequenting some of the same Parisian literati such as Jules Sandeau, who had collaborated with

---

[3] Caroline Marbouty, letter to her mother, Torino, August 2, 1836. Cited in Prior, "Balzac à Turin," 376–77.

Sand on her first novel, as well as the influential critics Gustave Planche and Charles-Augustin Sainte-Beuve.[4] Sainte-Beuve was particularly helpful in facilitating Marbouty's access to the people and institutions that controlled the flow of symbolic capital, giving her contacts in the prestigious reviews publishing his works, and introducing her to Planche. As was typical of many contemporary writers, Marbouty pursued the profession of letters both from ambition and financial need. In her case, the need arose when she separated from her husband in 1831 and confronted raising two daughters supported only by a modest pension.

In contrast to Sainte-Beuve, Balzac played little role in furthering Marbouty's literary career. In the letters between the two in the Lovenjoul archive, it is a question of his works and his need for money, a theme present from their first relations, for, as Marbouty explained to her mother, "Balzac does not have a cent . . . he is riddled with debts," and it was her 500 francs that took them across Italy.[5] When Balzac did exceptionally turn his attention to Marbouty's place in literature, it was in a dedication he added to an 1842 reedition of *La Grenadière*: "*To Caroline—the poetry of travel, from the grateful traveler.*"[6] Identifying Marbouty with the first name poets use to conjure up their muse, Balzac here cast her in the traditional feminine posture of the "medium of the divine or poetic word" inspiring the great artist.[7]

While Balzac was transforming Marbouty into a muse, however, Marbouty was honing a voice of her own. Between 1836 and 1842, she drafted several unproduced plays as well as co-authoring a play with Emile Souvestre that saw the light of performance and collaborating with

---

[4] In his informative introduction to *La Muse du département*, Bernard Guyon observes, "After the Italian escapade, relations of trusting friendship [between Balzac and Marbouty] persisted for quite awhile. In 1838, Caroline went to visit les Jardies; in 1840, she was present at the opening night of *Vautrin*." Bernard Guyon in *La Muse*, 108. On the details of Marbouty's relations with Balzac, see, too, M. Serval's more misogynistic *Une Amie de Balzac* as well as the materials by and on Marbouty in the Lovenjoul archive at the Bibliothèque de l'Institut de France, which are the principal sources for Guyon and Serval as well as for Prior. Marbouty also frequented such important figures in the contemporary cultural elite as the playwright and novelist Virginie Ancelot, the novelist Aurore Dupin, and the painter Elisabeth Vigée-Lebrun.

[5] Marbouty, letter to her mother. Cited in Henry Prior, "Balzac à Turin," 376. In a posthumously published piece entitled "Portrait de Balzac," Marbouty represents Balzac's need for money as such an important piece of their relationship that she formulated "the principle never to advance him money." The portrait appeared in the *Gazette anecdotique* of October 9, 1891, as Serval mentions.

[6] Anne-Marie Meininger discusses the dedication in her notes to *La Grenadière*, 1379. As Meininger observes, Balzac suppressed the dedication after his relations with Marbouty fell apart.

[7] Christine Planté, *La Petite Soeur de Balzac*, 247.

the prominent dramatist Scribe.[8] She also produced journalism and a collection of short stories for children, *Les Jolis Contes vrais*, usually writing under the pen name Claire Brunne. In the year Balzac rededicated *La Grenadière*, her efforts were crowned with three short sentimental social novels, published together under the title *Ange de Spola, études de femmes* (1842).

That Balzac was well aware of Marbouty's literary career, his representation of her as passive inspiration notwithstanding, emerges in *La Muse du département* published the following year (1843). The only work in *La Comédie humaine* to represent the struggles of the female author (Camille Maupin enters onto its stage after she has made it), this novel employs the term muse as it was was then sometimes used satirically, to designate women who were de trop in the feminine contributions to the arts because they wanted to be the poet instead of the poem. "Tenth Muse," such women were also called, as well as blue-stocking [*bas-bleu*] and superior woman [*femme supérieure*]. These designations make their way into *La Muse du département* along with Balzac's own invented diagnosis, "Sandism [*sandisme*]": "This sentimental leprosy [that] has spoiled many women who would have been charming without their pretentions to genius" (154). And to model *La Muse du département*'s fictional example of the woman suffering from such a corrosive disease, Balzac used the life of the "Muse of Limoges," to cite an epithet coined for Marbouty at the time of their Italian journey.[9]

As Bernard Guyon points out, Balzac's Dinah is, like Marbouty, a provincial from a Protestant background, but "so many other features make the two women comparable!"[10] Like Marbouty, Dinah was married young to an older, unattractive man from a local family with land, although in Marbouty's case, the husband was not a scheming arriviste but rather an unambitious legal clerk. Like Marbouty, Dinah stuck with her husband through her twenties and finally broke with him when she was twenty-eight. In the summer of her twenty-eighth year, Marbouty had an affair with a native son made good in Paris, who had returned to Limoges

---

[8] According to Marbouty, she collaborated with Scribe on the plays *Une Chaîne* and *La Calomnie* (Prior, "Balzac à Turin," 371). The play written with Souvestre was *La Protectrice* (1841). It received a negative review from Jules Janin in the *Journal des Débats* of May 24, 1841. Souvestre also wrote the influential piece on the contemporary novel, "Du Roman" (1836), which I used in the title to Chapter 2. As I mentioned at the end of that chapter, "Du Roman" prefaced Souvestre's own well-received sentimental social novel *Riche et pauvre* (1836).

[9] The epithet is the title of a gossipy article on Balzac and Marbouty in the satirical newspaper *Le Vert-Vert*. See Prior, "Balzac à Turin," 377.

[10] Guyon, introduction to *La Muse*, 108. I am endebted to Guyon's introduction for drawing my attention to these features.

while he unsuccessfully ran for office: Guillaume Dupuytren, the celebrated chief surgeon of the Hôtel Dieu. Marbouty followed Dupuytren
to Paris and when their relationship fell apart, she became friends, possibly lovers, with Sandeau, another successful native son. In *La Muse du
département*, who are the two conquering Parisians who return to their
roots during Dinah's twenty-eighth summer and end up transforming
her life? Bianchon, "already chief doctor of a hospital, officer of the Le-
gion of Honor, and member of the Academy of Sciences," and the trend-
making journalist Etienne Lousteau, whose similarities with Sandeau
range from the sound of his name and his debts to his baldness and his
elegant dress (154).

Was Marbouty pretentious, pedantic, and self-centered, like Dinah
when the novel opens, intelligent and attractive, certainly, but without
sufficient charm, elegance, and sensitivity to display these qualities in an
appealing way? Luckily, Dinah has Balzac to write her story. The upshot
of Marbouty's encounter with Dupuytren and Sandeau was that she left
her husband and eventually the provinces to try her hand at a literary
career in Paris. *La Muse du département*, in contrast, has Dinah leave her
literary ambitions behind when she takes off for Paris to follow Lousteau.
In this hub of civilization, she strips herself of her provincial mannerisms
and intellectual pretensions, discovers the proper place for the woman
writer, which is to ghostwrite pieces for one's lover in financial difficulties,
bears the children her impotent husband is all too pleased to recognize as
his heirs, and when Lousteau tires of her, returns to her family transformed from a tedious *bas-bleu* into a charming *femme de trente ans*. The
difference in Dinah's dress between her first and last meeting with Lousteau says it all. The provincial *femme supérieure* initially wears a "dress
of light black kerseymere . . . like a riding habit without a train" [*amazone
sans queue*] and "a beret of black velvet à la Raphaël," framing "beautiful
eyes and beautiful eyelids almost withered by the troubles of life" (197).
What a contrast between "the enormous pretentions in this excess of sim-
plicity" (197) and Dinah's final appearance as the Countess de la Baudraye: "[S]he had put on a delightful dress in straw yellow silk brocade
interspersing flowers with matte stripes. Her trimmed gloves with tassels
revealed her shapely white arms. . . . Her hairstyle à la Sévigné gave her
a discriminating air" (338–39). From Raphaël to Sévigné: no longer a
somewhat grotesque imitation of the male artist, Dinah resembles the
exemplary feminine author, a loving mother who writes in a private genre
for her intimate family, and it comes as no surprise when the novel ends
by returning "the Muse of Sancerre quite simply to the Family and to
Marriage" (341).

For Balzac to derive *La Comédie humaine*'s types from historical figures is not uncommon, as Lousteau's similarities with Sandeau or Bian-

chon's similarities with Dupuytren make clear. But Balzac's delineation of Dinah using Marbouty entails more than historical authenticity, for biography here warms up ideology with flesh and blood. As Christine Planté explains, the *femme auteur* was a conspicuous figure in nineteenth-century debate around the bourgeois construction of the social formation because her profession transgressed such fundamental tenets of bourgeois ideology as the gendered divide opposing public/private and production/reproduction.[11] Geneviève Fraisse agrees when she analyzes the discussions around women's literacy that were prominent as bourgeois notions of the res publica emerged to hegemony during and after the Revolution. In these discussions, as Fraisse underlines, women's ability to read and write was placed on a continuum with their participation in public intellectual and artistic production.[12]

Controversy around the female author is particularly pronounced during the 1830s and 1840s for a reason Balzac himself isolates when he attacks the figure in *La Muse du département*. He ascribes the rise of this type to "the Revolution of 1830," which spawns "[S]trange doctrines . . . on the role that women should play in society," in other words the first modern feminisms (189). As I have discussed, the July Revolution relegitimated Revolutionary ideals, and there was serious debate concerning whether the doctrine of the separate spheres did justice to women's Revolutionary birthright of liberty, equality, and fraternity. In positions for and against women's exclusion from public life, the *femme auteur* took center stage as a figure visibly transgressing the tenets of domestic ideology.

This relegitimation of Revolutionary ideals further heightened the significance of the *femme auteur* in authorizing other second-class citizens to demand their place in the July sun. As Joan Scott observes, the gendered separation of the spheres underpinned the bourgeois subordination of workers along with women. Scott shows, for example, that the unstable ideological oppositions supporting this separation (production/reproduction, public/private, etc.) were crucial in denying the possibility of worker exploitation. Thus, when socialists asserted that "the sale of labor power was no different from the sale of women's bodies, that economic and sexual exploitation were of a piece," political economists countered by insisting on the division between "work and sex, productivity and waste-

---

[11] See Planté, *La Petite Soeur de Balzac*.

[12] No text makes this point better than Sylvain Maréchal's *Projet d'une loi portant défense d'apprendre à lire aux femmes* (1801), which Fraisse uses to open her argument. "How contagious is reading: as soon as a woman opens a book, she believes herself capable of writing one," declared Maréchal in his ambiguous piece, written in a register somewhere between irony and polemic. Cited in Fraisse, *La Muse de la raison*, 22. On the psychosocial anxieties informing nineteenth-century debates around women's literacy, see Matlock's *Scenes of Seduction*.

fulness [as well as reproduction] . . . male and female."[13] Scott also suggests that domestic ideology helped criminalize working-class social structures where women were not relegated to private life and hence helped justify working-class oppression on the grounds that workers were inferior. Scott offers these observations when she analyzes the public preoccupation starting in the 1840s with the working woman, another female type visibly transgressing the gendered division of the spheres.[14] The woman writer, too, is of such contemporary interest because her transgressions reverberate even beyond the social situation of women.

In his delineation of Dinah de la Baudraye, Balzac typifies representations of the *femme auteur* in discourse across the social formation promoting domestic ideology. As Planté and Fraisse show, the portrayal of the blue-stocking as an unattractive, pedantic monstrosity misled from happy feminine destiny is found in medical and pedagogical works, in political writings, in nonfictional ethnographic and sometimes satirical descriptions of modern France, in literature, in literary criticism, and in caricatures. To illustrate that Balzac's depiction of the woman author was a commonplace outside as well as inside literature, consider Dinah's point by point correspondence with the most celebrated representations of the *femme auteur* contemporary with *La Muse du département*, which are found in Daumier's "Bas-Bleu" series, first published in *Le Charivari* (1844).

Dinah's career exemplifies how women authors are "the slightest feminine talents . . . diverted from a peaceful life by a mirage of fame" (189). Here is Daumier's visual rendition of the same topos, which depicts the scribbling lady writer perpetrating unwitting child abuse while lost in her overheated imagination: "La mère est dans le feu de la composition, l'enfant est dans l'eau de la baignoire! [The mother is in the heat of composition, the baby is in the bathwater]." Like Balzac, too, Daumier accompanies a woman's rise as a blue-stocking with her corporeal decay. Dinah's feminine advantages ruined, she becomes "emaciated . . . a dressed-up skeleton," adopting "without realizing it, masculine manners," when she frequents men for their conversation (181, 182). In Daumier's equivalent, the *femme auteur* is an unsexed, withered aberration whose body is ruined for the constitutive feminine activity of reproduction: "C'est singulier comme ce miroir m'applatit la taille et me maigrit la poitrine que m'importe? Mme de Staël et M. de Buffon l'ont proclamé... le génie n'a point de sexe [It is odd how this mirror flattens out my figure and reduces my

---

[13] Scott, *Gender and the Politics of History*, 146.
[14] Indeed, Scott and Planté independently arrive at the same word, disorder, to characterize the threat posed by the working woman and the woman author. See Scott, *Gender*, 141, and Planté, *Petite Soeur*, 41.

La mère est dans le feu de la composition, l'enfant est dans l'eau de la baignoire!

Honoré Daumier, "The mother is in the heat of composition, the baby is in the bathwater!" 1844.

C'est singulier comme ce miroir m'applatit la taille et me maigrit la poitrine que m'importe? Mᵐᵉ de Staël et Mʳ de Buffon l'ont proclamé. le génie n'a point de sexe.

Honoré Daumier, "It is odd how this mirror flattens out my figure and reduces my bust, what does it matter? Madame de Staël and Monsieur de Buffon proclaimed it ... genius has no sex." 1844.

Honoré Daumier, "So you find that my last novel is not completely up to those of Georges Sand ...! Adélaïde, I will see no more of you!" 1844.

— Ma bonne amie, puis-je entrer !.... as-tu fini de collaborer avec monsieur ?.......

Honoré Daumier, "My dear friend, may I come in! ... have you finished collaborating with the gentleman? ..." 1844.

Honoré Daumier, "It is odd... I now only have ideas when I am in the Bois de Boulogne and I am riding with Monsieur Edouard!..." "So what ideas can come to my wife when she is riding with Monsieur Edouard?... this interests me... I am annoyed she has become an amazon... I would have preferred she simply rode her hobby horse of virtue!" 1844.

bust, what does it matter? Madame de Staël and Monsieur de Buffon proclaimed it... genius has no sex]." According to Balzac, "the fame of George Sand" is to blame for this lamentable turn taken by French womanhood (189). Similarly, Daumier: two vain, unattractive, and implicitly untalented *femmes auteurs* squabble among themselves: "Ah vous trouvez que mon dernier roman n'est pas tout à fait à la hauteur de ceux de Georges Sand... ! Adélaïde, je ne vous reverrai de la vie! [So you find that my last novel is not completely up to those of Georges Sand... ! Adélaïde, I will see no more of you!]."

Somehow, however, despite their physical disadvantages, these *femmes auteurs* use literature to introduce adultery into the home, thereby further disrupting the domestic sphere. To Lousteau and Dinah's mutual seduction through literature, compare one of the favorite activities of Daumieur's *femme auteur*: "Ma bonne amie, puis-je entrer!... as-tu fini de collaborer avec monsieur?... [My dear friend, may I come in!... have you finished collaborating with the gentleman?...]". And for Balzac and Daumier, once women find that great feminine occupation, erotic love, they are rejuvenated, abandoning their intellectual pretensions along with sentimental ideals like virtue. To Dinah's metamorphosis from superior woman into older woman [*femme de trente ans*], compare Daumier's plumper, if not pregnant, version of the skeleton admiring herself in the mirror: "C'est singulier... il ne me vient plus d'idées maintenant que lorsque je suis au bois de Boulogne et que je trotte avec M. Edouard!..." "Quelle idées peuvent donc venir à ma femme, quand elle trotte avec M. Edouard?... ceci m'intrigue... je suis faché de voir qu'elle s'est faite amazone... j'aurais mieux aimé qu'elle restât simplement à cheval sur la vertu!..." ["It is odd... I now only have ideas when I am in the Bois de Boulogne and I am riding with Monsieur Edouard!..." "So what ideas can come to my wife when she is riding with Monsieur Edouard?... this interests me... I am annoyed she has become an amazon... I would have preferred she simply rode her hobby horse of virtue!"].

The "Bas Bleu" series consists of forty images published in *Le Charivari* during the space of six months. That this leading cultural periodical would focus with such intensity on a single social type is remarkable and underscores the *femme auteur*'s great contemporary fascination.[15] If the

---

[15] Planté is right that the years surrounding *La Muse du département* saw a rash of negative representations characterizing the *femme auteur*, although she overstates the case when she concentrates these representations in the early 1840s for the *femme auteur* was a contested ideologeme throughout the July Monarchy. Planté speculates that the early 1840s were a time of backlash against "the effervescence which dominated the first years of the regime" (*Petite Soeur*, 44). There was, however, no reduction of that effervescence when it came to women actually writing. As the rest of this chapter explains, women remained prominent and powerful members of the literary scene through the end of the July Monar-

femme auteur was so compelling, it was not only because her activity resonated in contemporary social and political debate but because there were many women writing at the time and these women along with their products were highly visible. Whatever the actual numbers, it was a commonplace for both critics and writers during the 1830s that women were publishing as never before.[16] "The number of women writers was still rather sparse in 1828; they could be counted, which is a calculation that would be lengthy and almost difficult to do nowadays," declared the renowned author Mélanie Waldor in 1836.[17] "The opinion of critics and that of society inveigh against women authors to no avail, every day their number grows," is a more grudging acknowledgment of the same phenomenon from 1835.[18] Balzac too agrees, albeit disparagingly, when he

---

chy, and the proliferating negative representations of the *femme auteur* could simultaneously be an index of women writers' genuine literary and cultural influence. Planté also overstates the authority of attacks on the *femme auteur* by neglecting the fact that these attacks were hotly contested both within the literary field and in cultural discourse across the social formation as they were appearing. Louise Colet's "La marquise de Lambert" exemplifies how negative representations of the *femme auteur* were contested within literary production. Beginning with the fact that "[s]ince Molière, an attitude of systematic denigration has always hounded women authors," Colet then used a discussion of seventeenth-century women writers to refute the various arguments made against women's participation in the profession of letters. Louise Colet, "La marquise de Lambert," 5. Nathalie de La Jolais's *Education pratique des femmes* exemplifies an extraliterary refutation of arguments against women writers, as a section excerpted in *Le Constitutionnel*'s favorable review of the book illustrates. Disputing a long-standing tradition attacking women's imagination, this chapter praises imagination as a vehicle of education if properly tempered with reason, suggesting its usefulness in developing, notably, women's writing styles and their "poetic sense [*sens poétique*]." Cited from an unsigned review of Nathalie de La Jolais's *Education pratique des femmes*, 6. *L'Illustration*'s desexualized, dignified neoclassical medallions portraying important *Femmes de lettres contemporaines françaises* (1844) constitute the visual counterpart to arguments defending the *femme auteur* (see illustration on p. 163). Janis Bergman-Carton's *The Woman of Ideas in French Art, 1830–1848* details both positive and negative representations of the *femme auteur* in contemporary visual culture.

[16] In Planté's view, "the Revolution of 1830 . . . represents a true break," inaugurating a new era of women's literary prominence (*Petite Soeur*, 43). Planté continues, "The reasons for it are numerous and of different kinds: the development of education for girls, even if it is substantially behind that for boys; the central place of the woman question in debates across numerous political currents, in particular the Fourierist and Saint-Simonian ones; the birth of the first collective movement promoting women's emancipation . . . the influence of Romantic ideals; the unavoidable fame of George Sand" (44).

[17] Mélanie Waldor, *Pages de la vie intime*, 2:248–49.

[18] Review signed E.G. of *Savinie* and *Valida*. In an even less favorable acknowledgment, another review of *Savinie* counted "one hundred twenty-five women authors alive and well in the year of disgrace 1835." Unsigned review of *Savinie*, 1. The only disagreement I have found with the perception that the July Revolution inaugurates the explosion of women writers is the occasional opinion that this explosion dates to the Revolution. Salvandy advanced this view in his "Préface" to *Natalie*. "At no time in society have they given the arts

comments that "after the Revolution of 1830 . . . many Tenth Muses were seen in France, girls or young women diverted from a peaceful life by a mirage of fame!" (189).

Women authors were not only visible but considered quite influential by those critics who viewed their presence favorably, although critics objecting to them insisted, rather, on these tenth Muses' threats to domestic ideology. Emile Deschamps exemplifies the positive reaction to the proliferation of women writers when he stresses their literary and cultural influence in his contribution to the *Biographie des femmes auteurs contemporaines françaises*. "Do women have genius in arts and poetry? Should women devote themselves to literary studies? Are women suited to strive for the hazards of fame and the perils of public life?" Deschamps queried. And he then dismissed these questions, which are "now ridiculous, or rather not real questions.—While men in the profession discuss seriously or dispute bitterly the rights and claims of female authors . . . they [female authors] . . . have taken over countless thrones in the republic of letters; splendid republic where all citizens are kings!"[19] That Balzac's animosity

---

of thought so many disciples at once; never, either, have they had such an equal share in the recognition offered talent," Salvandy declared, tracing women's cultural importance to 1789: "This new character of civilization certainly is worth noting. How can we ignore that it is intimately bound to the great revolution that has been realized in the past forty years in our interests, our opinions, our manners?" Salvandy, preface to *Natalie*, ii; ii–iii. Where contemporaries most often differed was not on the proliferation of women writers but rather on the value of their works. A review in *Le Charivari* discussing a collection of writings exclusively by women exemplifies a respectful stance towards the proliferation of *femmes auteurs*: "It will be a distinction for our period to have had at one time enough women of wit to suffice for a publication of this scope. More than twenty-five names figure there, without counting the reputations that were not included." Unsigned review of *Heures du soir*, Oct. 29, 1833. But a review of the same collection in the same periodical several months before downplayed the importance of women's contributions to contemporary literature by comparing women to children: "Today . . . literature has become secularized as an industrial profession, even while keeping the morality of its aim, and . . . it has sufficiently widened its thoroughfares so that everyone can enter there, even women, even children, without publicity, disturbance or sensation." Unsigned review of *Heures du Soir*, May 28, 1833. Despite Sainte-Beuve's enthusiasm for individual female novelists, he agreed. "We must resign ourselves . . . to the invasion of literary democracy, as with the advent of all other democracies. . . . With our voting and industrial practices, everyone, at least once in his life, will have had his printed page, his speech, his advertising, will be *toasted*, will be an *author*. . . . There is a family, a marriage for love, woman too will write under a pseudonym." Sainte-Beuve, "De la littérature industrielle," 681. Why a change in voting "practices" should encourage women writers is, of course, a bit puzzling since women were excluded from political participation at the time.

[19] Emile Deschamps, "Mme B. d'Altenheym," in *Biographie des femmes auteurs*, 339. When a *Charivari* article compared contemporary women writers to Saint-Simonians in search of the Woman Messiah, it looked on their literary influence with similar enthusiasm. "Look at Madame George Sand, Madame Camille Bodin, Madame d'Abrantès, Mademoi-

to the *femme auteur* may as much concern her power in the republic of letters as her violation of domestic ideology emerges if we examine *La Muse du département*'s dialogue with Marbouty in more detail.

"RATHER DEATH." "RATHER LIFE."

When *La Muse du département* sends women writers back into the home, Balzac is not just revising Marbouty's biography but rewriting one of her works. Balzac sets up the sufferings of his *femme auteur* through echoing the plot of Marbouty's *Cora*, a short sentimental social novel published in her 1842 collection *Ange de Spola*.[20] Like *La Muse du département*, *Cora* tells the story of an ambitious provincial *femme supérieure*. "Dangers... elation... boundless pleasures [*jouissances*]... setbacks... then an intoxicating success... fame perhaps" (2:43), is how Marbouty's Cora explains her aspirations at an age when Balzac's Dinah is converting to Catholicism "only from ambition" (158). Both Dinah and Cora marry men interested only in money, following the advice of their mothers, and both find themselves enmeshed in a conflict between the code and the heart as a result of their submission to collective demands.

Like Marbouty's Cora, busy with "organizing her interior," Balzac's Muse first seeks an exit from the emotional vacuum of her marriage by refurbishing her chateau; then both heroines take refuge in study and writing (2:70). Nonetheless, they continue to suffer, childless, unfulfilled, until the possibility arises for an affair. In each case, the seducer is a successful, cultivated, and corrupt Parisian. In *Cora*, he is the polished politician, M. de Mervanne, a "man of the times" (2:85), "[s]hrewd, flexible, clever" (2:88), possessed of "great self-control . . . having only his interest for guide" (2:86). Both Mervanne and Balzac's Lousteau enjoy the heroine's hospitality and make love to her in the course of deep conversations about literature and society. " 'But what, then, becomes of women like you, Ma'am?' " asks Mervanne, "placing himself opposite her, one elbow gracefully leaning on the mantelpiece, and his gaze fixed on hers" (2:113). Lousteau recapitulates Mervanne's gesture in more obviously gallant

---

selle Gay [Delphine de Girardin], Madame Desbordes-Valmore, Madame Tastu. . . . [T]o let the world know they were undertaking the Rehabilitation of woman . . . they put aside all theory, all discussion, and they wrote. . . . Is this method not worth that of Father Enfantin?. . . In truth, I tell you, and this is nothing less than reassuring: the century belongs to women, there is women's fame in the air, we are taking a turn towards the amazon. It is no longer a question of man's supremacy, let us simply try to keep up." Review signed Ed. L. of *Savinie*.

[20] Guyon is, to my knowledge, the first critic to elaborate this relation in his introduction to *La Muse du département*.

fashion: "How could a woman who is as beautiful as you are and who seems so intelligent [*supérieure*] have remained in the provinces? What do you do to withstand this life?" (198). Both Marbouty's Cora and Balzac's Dinah would seem to have the same response. "There are only two routes, submit or be broken," Cora answers sadly (2:116). Similarly, Dinah, "One does not resist. A deep despair or a dumb resignation, one or the other, there is no choice" (198).

But with this comment, Balzac's recapitulation of *Cora* ends and his antagonistic rewriting of the novel begins. For Marbouty's sentimental social heroine, adultery does not solve the conflict between the heart and the code but instead offers only its recapitulation. When Cora explains why her options shrink to "submit," resign oneself to social norms, or "be broken," transgress social norms in search of freedom and be destroyed, she ascribes her bleak fate to women's social inequality. In the course of studies undertaken during her marriage, Cora "reached a sufficient level of general knowledge to judge the position of women, to weigh the laws that set it up, to appreciate the prejudices that maintain it. . . . After long reflection, Cora felt all hope leave her soul," and her story ends in death (2:81). While Dinah, too, would seem to have arrived at Cora's conclusions, her tragic "[a] deep despair or a dumb resignation, one or the other, there is no choice," turns out to be tactics rather than truth (198). With this phrase, Dinah inaugurates a biting satire on provincial women that completely disarms and charms Lousteau, "[S]tunned by the brilliant maneuver with which Dinah handed over the provinces," since he had been preparing to dismiss Dinah with such a satire himself (199).

Dinah's transformation of tragedy into tactics ("maneuver" is Balzac's military word) is only the first step in her transformation of the sentimental conflict into a sentimental education ending in tragicomic fashion rather than death. In the course of her sentimental education, Dinah learns to finesse the conflict between the heart and the code in order to further her own interests, which Balzac identifies with Parisian refinement, sex, love, and children. If Dinah can escape the tragic clash of the heart with the code, it is because Balzac reduces both the political and the poetic to the personal. Dinah has no trouble abandoning *Cora*'s sentimental social plot and the novel's feminist ideals, once she realizes they impede her own satisfaction.

Appropriately, Dinah hones her skills at manipulation in a relationship to Lousteau, who purveys the lesson of compromise throughout Balzac's oeuvre. When Lousteau describes to Lucien the hypocritical flattery of idiots necessary to survive in the Parisian literary slime, Lucien exclaims, "Rather death." "Rather life," counters Lousteau (*Illusions*, 322). Dinah, too, learns to live, in contrast to Marbouty's Cora, and she opposes the realist lesson of life to sentimental tragedy even before she begins her sentimental education, upon encountering a girlhood friend who has been transformed from one Anna Grossetête into a charming baronne de Fontaine through Parisian high society and adultery. "Anna . . . was learning to live while I was learning to suffer," Dinah sighs, qualifying her existence moldering away in the provinces with that verb most closely associated with the protagonist's conflict both in the sentimental novel and in the sentimental social novel (183).

When Balzac rewrites not only Marbouty's biography but also her work, he is thus taking a position against realism's major poetic competition throughout the July Monarchy for how the novel should pursue literature's engagement with public life. The critic Molènes noted *La Muse du département*'s polemical tone, explaining it as Balzac's overreaction to the fact that his works received mixed and often hostile reviews. *La Muse du département*, Molènes wrote, is filled with "a bile that becomes tiresome. Monsieur de Balzac's pride has been so bruised that it has now become excessively swollen and painfully sensitive."[21] That Molènes would view Balzac's portrait of Dinah as polemic is all the more telling since he was himself no great friend of the *femme auteur*.[22]

In taking aim at sentimental social poetics along with a negative delineation of the *femme auteur*, Balzac was not alone; such slippage was common in opinions censuring both. We have seen Bussière conflate emancipated women's threats to the foundations of the family with the proliferation of "women's novels" in an essay which was, it is now the moment to point out, written on the occasion of reviewing *Cora*, along with the other texts collected in Marbouty's *Ange de Spola*. Similarly, an article entitled "La Femme Libre" condemned the free woman for destroying her husband's authority, engaging in ridiculous feminist politics, and writing novels of women's victimization. "In general, the free woman is an author," the article charged. "She composes novels where the heroine is always an angel adorned with all the virtues and the hero is a scoundrel too low even for prison," in other words, the hero is the realist protagonist as he appears from the vantage point of the sentimental social novel.[23] As these examples suggest, critics censuring the sentimental social novel reduced it to works promoting women's full social equality, although the subgenre's politics were substantially more varied.

When a review of Sandeau's *Mariana* described how women as well as the family suffer when women's novels threaten the separate spheres, it included George Sand as a target of its polemic. "Jules Sandeau was frightened by this fickle heart, by this agitated brain, by the giddiness that takes

---

[21] P. Gaschon de Molènes, review of *La Muse du département*, 997.
[22] See, for example, Molènes on "Les femme poètes."
[23] "La Femme libre," signed L.Cc.

hold of so many women, casting them out from the shelter of marriage, and leading them in their wake to blast the young souls that their breath caressed for a brief moment. For one of these heroines, of these *Lélias*, who, relying on her exceptional strength, can wage war against manners and place herself above ordinary judgments, how many will encounter only shame and isolation, instead of fame and freedom!"[24] Invoking Sand's heroines and implicitly her life to emphasize the extravagance of women who overstepped the boundaries of domestic femininity, the review risked, however, discrediting its position-taking, for it bucked the prevalent view that Sand was the most significant novelist if not writer to emerge following the Revolution of 1830, whatever her personal irregularities. George Sand was "[t]he most evident, the most original, and the most celebrated individual to emerge in the past twenty years," according to Sainte-Beuve (1840), and similar judgments pervade literary criticism of the time.[25]

Whether Balzac reached the heights of Sand was an open question; in important cultural periodicals like *La Revue des Deux Mondes*, *L'Artiste*, and *Le Charivari*, his novels consistently received less favorable reviews. When Paulin Limayrac ranked first "Madame Sand and to a lesser degree, Monsieur de Balzac" as "[t]hose among our novelists who best possess the feeling for art" in *La Revue des Deux Mondes* (1845), he summed up the view emerging not only from these periodicals but also from the essays of the noted literary critics Planche, Sainte-Beuve, Jules Janin, and Jacques Chaudes-Aigues.[26] That critics often praised Sand's preeminence by belittling men currently writing exacerbates the prominence of gender in her threat to Balzac. Sometimes, Sand was cited as "the most virile talent of our period,"[27] sometimes she made clear the inferiority of "so many *virile* stupidities . . . [that] bring shame on our literature."[28]

When *La Muse du département* denigrates Sand's preferred novelistic poetics along with women writing, it, too, attacks the author who offered the greatest challenge to Balzac's authority over the novel of his time. And

---

[24] Review signed H.L. of *Mariana*.

[25] Sainte-Beuve, "Dix ans après en littérature," 695.

[26] Paulin Limayrac, "Du roman actuel et de nos romanciers," 957. To be even more precise, Chaudes-Aigues excluded Balzac from the top tier of novelists altogether, as did other critics favorable to the sentimental tradition. A review in *Le Charivari* of 1837, for example, suggested the successes of George Sand and Madame Charles Reybaud as "certainly the most brilliant that our literature has offered since 1830. The Revolution of July has definitively precipitated women's emancipation." Unsigned review of *Le Château de Saint-Germain*.

[27] Review signed H.L. of Sand's "*La Dernière Aldini—Les Maîtres Mosaïstes*," 1.

[28] The context runs, "Madame Dudevant is ranked first among our writers . . . where so many *virile* stupidities bring shame upon our literature." Review signed E.S. of *Régina*.

in implying these conclusions while he explicitly targets the life and writing of Marbouty, Balzac finds a more effective strategy for diffusing Sand's threat than confronting it head-on like the Sandeau review. With this gesture, Balzac reduces sentimental social poetics to a work that is less complex than the major novels of Sand and to a minor woman author who commands less respect than his major competition. He is thus able to deny the importance of the sentimental social subgenre and mobilize fears around the *femme auteur* without mentioning the counterexample who would expose his poetic critique as tenuous and his gender politics as irrelevant to a work's literary importance.

Balzac further defends his polemic against the counterexample of Sand by himself suggesting her as counterexample in the fashion that best makes his case. Paying homage to "the fame of George Sand," Balzac mythologizes her as literary genius, severing her both from her social identity and the poetics she was celebrated for forging (189). In Balzac's rendition, Sand is the extraordinary exception that proves the rule of women's literary inferiority and thus implicitly disproves the possibility of her own existence. While making this point, Balzac takes the opportunity to bash Sand for encouraging the corrosive proliferation of the *femme auteur*, "and indeed it is true, morally speaking, that the good almost always has an evil lining," since Sand's inimitable example leads other women to think they can escape the inevitable limitations of their gender (154).[29]

---

[29] Balzac has already taken a position against Sand with a similar strategy in his *Mémoires de deux jeunes mariées*, published the year before. This novel is prefaced by a dedication to Sand praising her celebrity. At the same time, however, it offers a realist plot of feminine sentimental education that Balzac constructed in a hostile takeover of two short sentimental social novels representing women's domestic sufferings by the well-known novelist Camille Bodin. These novels are *Elise* and *Marie*, which Bodin published together under the title *Elise et Marie* (1838). Once we realize the tension between the dedication of *Mémoires de deux jeunes mariées* and the novel's poetics, the dedication's hyperbole becomes equivocal. "Dear George, this will not add anything to the splendor of your name," runs the dedication's opening, although Balzac does not explain why that should be the case. Balzac, *Mémoires*, 195. Is Sand's prominence so great it cannot be amplified, or does Balzac's work not in truth add to Sand's fame, since it attacks the foundations of her novelistic poetics along with her feminist politics? "I thereby want to testify to the true friendship that has continued between us," Balzac continues, "despite our works" (195). Why should these two authors' friendship be disrupted by their work? Do their careers detract from their ability to spend time together or does the problem relate to what they are writing? Every line of the dedication can be read as equally ambiguous, down to Balzac's vague mention of unattributed "criticisms incurred by my threatening fertility" (195). Do these reproaches come from critics, or might Balzac be anticipating Sand's response as he abrogates to himself a female metaphor of creativity often used to praise Sand's oeuvre? Chaudes-Aigues, for example, mentioned Sand's "fertile pen" when he applauded her oeuvre's variety in discussing "George Sand.—Alexandre Dumas," 43. Similarly, Planche: "How does Georges Sand conceive such essentially diverse works at the same time? How come this powerful brain, far

In using Marbouty to attack the poetics dominated by Sand, Balzac chooses a figure who has close links to Sand in his imagination: one of his letters identifies Marbouty as having made "the famous trip under the name of George Sand."[30] Meeting Marbouty through Sandeau, dressing this aspiring writer as a man (at least in Marbouty's letter to her mother, she credits Balzac with the idea for this disguise), taking off with her on a trip to Italy, which is, of course, Sand's privileged romantic geography, did Balzac dream of playing out a "novel," as he put it in his letter to Count Sclopis, with a George Sand cut to his measure?

That Marbouty, however, would not accept the confines of Balzac's imagination became public when she riposted to *La Muse du département* with her own representation of the *femme auteur*. It is, indeed, from Balzac's reaction to this representation that I cite his association of Marbouty with Sand. To contextualize his comparison in more detail, Balzac's 1846 letter to Madame Hanska described Marbouty as "a horrible blue-stocking, who made the famous trip under the name of George Sand and who writes books against me."[31] The books, or rather book, is Marbouty's sentimental social novel *Une Fausse Position* (1844), which narrates the struggles of Camille Dormont, a writer of considerable talent, when she aspires to break into the contemporary literary field.[32] *Une Fausse Position* made a splash when it appeared, receiving, notably, a twelve-column review from Janin in *Le Journal des Débats*. "In my view, it has been a long time since a book has been published that is more deserving of attention," Janin declared. "The narrative is filled with truths and lies, but I do fear that truth prevails over fiction."[33]

---

from getting tired, rather seem more fertile and more inexhaustible, as it were, the more it labors and produces?" Gustave Planche, "Revue littéraire," 220. Sand's rejoinder to Balzac's dedication was appropriately prickly: "I admire the heroine who procreates, but I *adore* the one who dies of love. That is all you have proved and it is *more* than you wanted to." George Sand, cited in Roger Pierrot's "Introduction" to the *Mémoires de deux jeunes mariées*, 191. Validating the heroine who dies from the conflict between the heart and the code, Sand frames *Mémoires de deux jeunes mariées* as signifying despite Balzac's intentions rather than in accordance with them. Rose Fortassier observes the resemblance between Bodin's *Elise et Marie* and *Mémoires de deux jeunes mariées* in "Balzac et le roman par lettres."

[30] Balzac, letter to Madame Hanska, December 24, 1846. Cited in Guyon's introduction to *La Muse*, 110.

[31] Ibid.

[32] In naming her heroine Camille, Marbouty underlines her engagement with Balzac's polemic against the sentimental social novel and women writers. Camille is the first name of *La Comédie humaine*'s George Sand stand-in, Camille Maupin. Camille Maupin figures prominently in *Béatrix*, another Balzac novel that attacks the pretensions of the female intellectual along with the sentimental lineage.

[33] Jules Janin, review of *Une Fausse Position*.

UNE FAUSSE POSITION

Une Fausse Position is most obviously "against" Balzac the way *La Muse du département* is "against" Marbouty: in its disparaging allusions to Balzac, the man. Marbouty appropriates Balzac's tactic of modeling distinctive contemporary social types on historical figures, and Balzac appears in Marbouty's panorama of the July Monarchy literary scene as Ulric, a brilliant novelist who has made it as a result of great talent and "the excessive strength of his will," but who is ruined by his struggle for success (1:101).[34] Ulric is completely materialistic: "Ulric walked with his century; he understood everything through gold, with gold, and coming from gold, only he had the naiveté to confess it, to recognize it, to make a principle out of it" (1:102). He is also entirely self-interested: "[T]his forced struggle had ruined the harmony of his fine nature and had given his mind such precedence over his character that it alone directed his actions, without any other rules than his personal interest. Popular and sought-after, he was intoxicated with his belated successes, to such an extent that he did not know how to carry them, and his dreams, his hopes became gigantic, like the opinion he had of himself. This vanity ended up having its absurd and monomaniacal side" (1:101). Ulric's only concern vis-à-vis Marbouty's heroine, Camille, is therefore what their relationship offers him. "In studying her [Camille], he realized that her character would hurt her success. She put feelings before needs, the idea [*la pensée*] before the fact, poetry before analysis, duty before desire.— They were not to agree on anything, it would thus be impossible for him to exploit her; either for his profit alone, or in the common interest" (1:103).

Needs instead of sentiments; facts instead of ideas: desire instead of duty. As these oppositions suggest, *Une Fausse Position* also resembles *La Muse du département* in targeting Balzac's literary innovations along with Balzac, the great man of letters. Even when Marbouty looked back on *Une Fausse Position* through the veil of old age and possible mental instability, she was lucid concerning her novel's poetic *parti pris*: "It is a novel of manners, a philosophical novel, which is no longer related to those from this period . . . of the school of Staindal [*sic*]."[35]

---

[34] Other historical figures invoked in the novel include Scribe, who appears as Brices, a famous playwright; Sandeau, who becomes the writer, Henri; Dupuytren, who takes the form of Ubert, the doctor; and either Sainte-Beuve or Planche, who serve as models for the critic, Samuel.

[35] Marbouty, letter to Ch. Spoelberch de Lovenjoul (1885). Cited in Prior, "Balzac à Turin," 370. Both Prior and Serval assert that Marbouty became mentally unhinged, but their judgments require further investigation since they are so evidently clouded by misog-

Une Fausse Position takes its distance from the school of Balzac along with Stendhal throughout its description of Ulric. In a conflation refreshingly subverting the reduction of a woman's work to her life that was then commonplace, Marbouty's narrator blames the defects of realist codes on the personal weaknesses of its inventor. "He took his sense for observing material things to a hitherto unknown level. No one went as far as him in the explicit details of external vices. If such an agile intelligence had had a higher point of departure, that of the idea [*la pensée*] or the analysis of the feelings of the soul, he would have been at once the greatest poet and the greatest metaphysician of his time and of all time. But the need to satisfy his senses or his vanity continually turned him away from the noble paths to which he was called by the superiority of his talents" (1:102–3). Ulric's self-centered investment in material pleasures and immediate satisfaction degrades the idea, the soul, and the analysis of feeling into the overvaluation of external aspect found in realist description and into an overemphasis on what the narrator calls "vice," like many contemporaries, and what Moretti calls compromise.

Une Fausse Position also targets realist poetics by attacking the realist plot of feminine *Bildung*, which Marbouty rewrites from sentimental education back into sentimental tragedy. The novel opens with Marbouty's heroine, Camille, sacrificed by her father in "a rich marriage" and then dumped by the lover who consoles her for her unhappy lot when she follows him to Paris (1:50). Contemplating her options, Camille ponders Dinah's capitulation to *Realpolitik* along with domestic ideology, elaborating "this life of intrigue, of ruses . . . the innumerable machinations, the innumerable detours, the countless details," were she to accept her mandated social place (1:17). "Can I not go back to my household and flatter the man there who was offending me until, with hypocrisy and skill, I had established a faction against him in society to condemn him for it?—Could I not, behind some rigorous principles, which would cost me only a few women's reputations cleverly sacrificed,—only a few lying words and appearances, win public opinion in my favor and make myself an honor guard from the men I would choose for lovers?" and so on (1:15–16). "Yes!—this role is great, it is just," Camille concludes, "because it is all *they* have left me" (1:17, emphasis added). But Camille then regrets the reduction of morality and sentiment to opportunism and self-interest were she to accept this fate: "But the heart . . . but the soul, who would fulfill them?" (1:17). Seeking to preserve her soul as well as her freedom, Camille decides to try supporting herself as a *femme auteur*.

---

yny. Thus, Serval brings as evidence for Marbouty's madness the fact that she published a political tract during the Second Empire entitled *"De l'unité de pouvoir, concordat politique*, which prefaced a play, *Le Mariage*." M. Serval, *Une Amie de Balzac*, 76.

In the course of thwarted efforts to find satisfactory venues for her writing, however, Camille discovers that this is no easy task, her considerable talent notwithstanding. Whether she knocks on the door of the newspaper or the publishing house, the theater or the salon, Camille's efforts are undermined by a version of the sentimental social conflict, which Marbouty represents as specific to women who seek recognition outside the domestic sphere. Camille finds the products of her independent self-realization repeatedly judged not for their merit but for how her behavior conforms to the dominant code of manners. In Marbouty's terms, "woman is judged by public opinion, man by his acts" (1:95). Since the dominant code of manners promotes domestic femininity, a woman seeking public recognition structurally defies its tenets, whatever her morality or talents. Marbouty underlines this point when she represents society's readiness to accept slanderous gossip circulating about Camille with no other proof than the fact that Camille was already inherently suspect because of her choice of careers.

The *femme auteur*'s violation of domestic ideology is the *fausse position* [compromised position] that gives Marbouty's novel its name. In contemporary usage, the *fausse position* described a compromised social situation that transgressed the reigning code of manners and possibly laws, but that was tolerated. In Marbouty's refunctioning, the *fausse position* describes the compromised gender politics of this code, which punishes any woman infringing on its authority. When Marbouty elaborates the sexist double standard defining men and women's claims to social standing, she continues, "It is what gives men such a great power, and what, in contrast, hampers the position of women when they disastrously leave the ordinary path [*la route ordinaire*]. Condemned by prejudices, checked by all etiquette and custom, their life is spent in a scramble, where victory is only a way station on the way to another combat until their faded charms, their lost youth, plunge them back into the general oblivion which other women never left" (1:96). The *fausse position* giving Marbouty's novel its name is, in other word, the gender-specific obstacles preventing women from making good on the century's promise of a career open to talents. It is a way to designate how much more difficult it is for Camille, although she may be endowed with an equal measure of ability, to become a Lucien de Rubempré or a Lousteau, let alone a Rastignac or a Julien Sorel, simply because she is a woman.

When Planté surveys the situation of the woman writer at the time of Balzac, she agrees with Marbouty that women writers were structurally in a *fausse position* because their activities violated hegemonic notions of femininity. As Planté puts it, the "position" of women authors, "often envied by other women, is an untenable position," because women authors are caught in a contradiction between "*the social code* of the requisite feminine virtues, and *their individual behavior*," which affronts "the woman who writes with the moral principles of her time."[36] In diagnosing the *fausse position* of the *femme auteur*, Marbouty was, moreover, not alone among her contemporaries, as Planté's citation illustrating the "untenable position" of the woman writer makes clear. "A woman who dedicates herself to literature or the arts thus accepts a whole life of suffering, and this suffering will be greater, more continual for her than for a man, simply because she is a woman," declared the author S.U. Dudrezène, a.k.a. Ulliac Trémadeure, in a nonfictional piece on "Les Femmes auteurs," which appeared in *Le Conseiller des Femmes* (1834).[37] "As a woman, she finds herself condemned by social laws, prejudices, duties themselves, to meet obstacles unknown to men every step of the way. It must be said, because it is the case: for the woman of letters and for the artist, existence is a continual struggle against herself, against the condescending or arrogant protection offered by those [men] who are stronger, against crude envy and perversity."[38]

In the course of detailing Camille's specific struggles, Marbouty cites the overwhelmingly masculine character of the institutions controlling a writers' access to the public as a second factor exacerbating a woman writer's difficulties in gaining recognition for her talent. Consumed by sexism, the men in charge of the newspapers, the publishing houses, and the theater see the *femme auteur* as a woman as well as an author; indeed as more of a woman than an author. Once they decide her work will sell, they pay no more attention to it, preferring to speculate on her sexual appeal and availability. In Marbouty's representation, these men's atten-

---

[36] Planté, *Petite Soeur*, 173. Emphasis added to stress that Planté formulates the *femme auteur*'s social dislocation using the terms of the sentimental social conflict.

[37] S. U. Dudrezène, "Des femmes dans les diverses conditions de la vie. 1. Les femmes auteurs," cited in Planté, *Petite Soeur*, 173. Planté uses the compromised position of women authors to explain a striking contradiction in many of their self-representations. While these women are evidently leading public lives, they often justify their activities with recourse to domestic ideology. Marbouty's writings do not display this contradiction nor does it trouble the radical sentimental social novelists, but it runs through writings by sentimental social novelists whose feminist politics are more moderate. That the contradiction might have a strategic dimension was, moreover, noticed by a reviewer of Carlowitz's *La Femme du progrès*, a novel that targets the *femme supérieure* for her intellectual pretensions and her politics. The reviewer declared, "Madame de Carlowitz . . . represents for us the blue-stocking, with all her ridiculous ways and her peculiarities of language and behavior, the older woman [*femme de trente ans*] in short, just as she was born from Monsieur de Balzac's imagination. There is some cleverness on the part of a woman who writes, to put on trial women pedants who are too often confused with women authors. It is a way to establish firmly the dividing line and thereby get rid of an annoying solidarity." Unsigned review of *La Femme du progrès*. The reviewer substantiates the link I have drawn between Balzac's *femme de trente ans* and his polemic against women writers.

[38] Dudrezène, cited in Planté, *Petite Soeur*, 173.

tion to the *femme auteur*'s gender impedes their attention to her writing all the more because the *femme auteur*'s structural *fausse position* strips her of respectability, encouraging their advances. When Lucien dashes off his first brilliant theater review and is received into the newspaper, his new colleagues accept him for his merit, even as they consider how to take economic advantage of it. " 'There are no more children,' said Blondet . . . 'I must tell you quite simply that you are a man of wit, heart, and style.' 'The gentleman belongs to the paper,' said Finot, thanking Etienne [Lousteau] and throwing him the shrewd glance of the exploiter" (*Illusions*, 400). When Camille first places her writing in a newspaper directed by one Vermot rather than Finot through the intermediary of Henri, a character modeled on Sandeau, like Balzac's Lousteau, the journalists recognize its merit and then turn to the more compelling matter of her desirability.

> — She has surpassed her teacher on the first try— said one of Henri's enemies. Henri blushed.
> Ulric drew closer to him.— Is she really attractive?
> — Who?—said Henri, preoccupied.
> — The Muse—Madame Dormont.
> — How should I know,—said Henri impatiently.
> — That's to say, how should you still know!...Happy man —said Vermot; the director— Maurice saw her once and he drew a delightful portrait.
> — He's trying to hide her— said Ulric?
> — Even if she's a blue-stocking, I'll help her if she's pretty—said Vermot.
> — Why don't you introduce me to her, Henri—said a conceited young man.
> — I'll go see her myself —said Ulric.
> — Madame Dormont doesn't want to see anyone —said Henri angrily. (1:86)

Une Fausse Position here recapitulates the negative stereotype of the *femme auteur* as sexually available. But rather than ascribing this immorality to the *femme auteur*, Marbouty shows it to be an abusive male fantasy attempting to capitalize on her *fausse position*. Indeed, every man who offers to help Camille publish her work asks for sex in return, although Marbouty lacked a term for sexual harassment. In the salon, too, the only institution of literary production Marbouty represents as partially dominated by women, the society ladies making taste are not reluctant to traffic in the *femme auteur*'s sexual status in the eyes of the powerful literary men.

The society ladies feel secure as they manipulate Camille because they adhere to what Marbouty calls "the ordinary path" of domestic femininity in their outward behavior, if not necessarily in their private lives (1:96). The discrepancy between their outward behavior and their private lives, however, points to another meaning Marbouty develops for her novel's title in the secondary women surrounding her heroine. These women are characters who seem to follow "the ordinary path," but they cannot live up to the domestic idealization of woman, because they suffer from their inequality with men. Thus, Marbouty represents Camille's treacherous friend, Caroline Delmarre, as engaging in adultery to compensate for her unhappy subordination in marriage; it is her "compromised and dependent position which had led her to the vices of the slave" (2:5–6).

A woman who reacts with the opposite strategy to Caroline, by trying to embody the domestic ideal even in the face of her husband's brutalization, finds it equally inhospitable. This woman is a working-class wife whose husband has abandoned her during a fourth pregnancy, although she has scrupulously followed both the code of manners and the code of laws. As she explains to Camille, "I have fulfilled all my duties . . . I have submitted to all society [*le monde*] has asked and ordered of me. . . . And I still have nothing! . . . I ask for support, and everyone says to me: There is nothing to be done" (1:297–98). This woman is emphatic that women's sufferings derive from their inequality before the law, which is nowhere more evident than in the institution of marriage. While her husband assured her the "protection necessary for a woman my whole life long . . . now he has taken possession of everything, he has left me!... I have no protector, I have no support, my contract is null, the law can do nothing for me. I have no more rights, and I still have responsibilities! Oh! Ma'am, suffering teaches women many things.—I am only an unfortunate woman who knows nothing, but I have suffered so much in the past four years, that I ask myself what we call the law; if it has been created to help us or to deceive us, we poor women who know nothing about it" (1:296–97).

With such characters, Marbouty develops an idea (in the July Monarchy sense of the term) she has already sketched in the preface to *Ange de Spola*. There, she defines the *fausse position* as the discrepancy between women's social inequality and Woman's importance as a vehicle of ideological work. In Marbouty's terms, women suffer from the "[p]eculiarities of man, who places the being whom he does not even want to recognize as his equal in the most difficult position in society. To this being fall responsibility, deprivation, hardship, suffering, poverty; to her lot fall the *positions* that are *compromised* [*positions fausses*], difficult, inextricable. The true junk-room [*capharnaüm*] of society, where all that has no recognized place in this world is left, woman must satisfy the most conflicting needs, the most dissimilar temperaments. Is it necessary, in the interests of society, that the family survives?—Woman keeps it going in sacrificing herself for it.—Are manners necessary? They are demanded of women.— Is it necessary that one will alone maintains and regulates order in families?—Woman is deprived of hers" (1:xxxvi–xxxvii, emphasis added). No text better confirms the truth of Marbouty's statements than Balzac's rejoinder to the novel where they appear. While *La Muse du département* unwrites *Cora*'s feminist politics to snatch domestic femininity from the menace of the *femme auteur*, Dinah's unhappy marriage also exposes the domestic ideal's emptiness, for she undertakes her sentimental education as the only way to palliate her indissoluble bond to a tyrannical husband.

Like most sentimental social novels, *Une Fausse Position* offers neither the novel's secondary characters nor its heroine any exit from their compromised situations. While Camille first resists the code of manners in the name of freedom, she sees no other choice than to "submit," as Cora put it, by the time the novel is two-thirds over (2:116). Destitute, ill, and on the brink of suicide, Camille finally accepts that she must exploit her compromised position if she is to have any hope of literary success. She decides to live off the old doctor, Ubert, offering him a vague hope of sexual compensation, which he seeks to make more concrete as her health improves. She also agrees to sleep with the playwright Brices if he will produce their play, deferring his reward until after the play's first performance.

This strategy brings material success, but at a price. Following a successful opening night, Camille attends a dinner in her honor until the time comes for her to satisfy Brices as the celebration draws to a close. Unable to imagine how to escape succumbing to the oppressive codes she has manipulated, Camille defers sacrificing her freedom a final few minutes by entering into a long diatribe on the corruption of the century, which she equates with the ethics of realism, " 'which has made a *morality* from selfishness, a law from *self-interest*, a strength from *calculation* [*intrigue*]!' " (2:304). This diatribe skids into madness when Brices, busy admiring her charms rather than listening to her words, comes forth to claim his reward. "The clock struck two. Camille counted the strokes and trembled. Brices took her hand and kissed it tenderly. 'Camille,' he said, 'It is quite late, come' " (2:309). But Camille will not be silenced: " 'Oh, oh, oh! we are acting a play [*une comédie*] . . . I will pose for you all, gentleman, I will be the victim. Oh, oh, oh, oh, oh! the victim,' she continued, laughing, 'let us drink to the victim!' The guests look at each other in fright.—'The victim will be virtuous,' she continued after having emptied her glass, 'the victim is always virtuous' " (2:310–11)]. "Camille was mad," the narrator concludes (2:312).

WOMAN IS THE STYLE

Why were there no French women realists? Balzac's Lousteau would be the first to advise that writers use literary strategies promising maximum return. When Bourdieu systematizes Balzac's depiction of the nineteenth-century literary field, he agrees, adding the clarification that this return can be financial and/or symbolic. In Bourdieu's terms, "the field of possible position-takings is open to the *sense of placement* (in the double sense, incorporating the meaning of investment) in the guise of a certain structure of probabilities, probable profits or losses, as much on the material plane as on the symbolic plane."[39] Symbolic capital is principally what is at stake in July Monarchy battles over how to use the novel's new power to address public affairs. And the literary struggles surfacing in the hostile dialogue between Balzac and Marbouty foreground why realism might have seemed to offer women writers so little symbolic yield.

As *Une Fausse Position* suggests, gender was an inevitable aspect of a woman author's identity as a literary producer, whatever other social parameters might define her subject position. In showing why the woman author cannot escape from her gender, Marbouty is above all interested in the fact that men dominate the institutions structuring the literary field. There are, however, additional factors reinforcing the woman author's inescapable feminization as *femme auteur*. Carla Hesse points out that women writers had a gender-specific relation to literary property, along with other forms of property in the first half of the nineteenth century, because the law defined their rights to ownership depending on their relations to men. As a result, women writers did not enjoy "the authorial signature" as "the legal basis by which the origins, claims, limits, meaning, and fate of the text were determined," in contrast to their confrères.[40] For married women, notably, their "legal standing in relation to their texts was entirely contingent upon the nationality and authorization of their husbands."[41]

The woman author's identification in terms of gender was reinforced by the critical reception of her works. "One would like to recognize women in everything and everywhere, and above all in their style," is an axiom characterizing every review of writing by women I have read from the time, although its converse does not apply to writings by men.[42] In the

---

[39] Bourdieu, *Rules*, 238.

[40] Hesse, "Reading Signatures: Female Authorship and Revolutionary Law in France, 1750–1850," 483.

[41] Ibid.

[42] Unsigned review of *Heures du Soir*, April 17, 1833. Every dominant view has its dissenters. When a review of Bodin's sentimental social novel, *Savinie*, addressed the gendering of style, it declared that in the eighteenth century, "style . . . was a mirror that reflected its author" both for women and men. Now that books have become industrial products, however, "books are produced quickly," and "style has lost its freshness, its original character, its gender [*genre*]. . . . Men and women of letters write in this fashion: after this, present the work to the cleverest expert, he will not recognize the sex of the author any more than a manufacturer would recognize in two pieces of fabric the one that has been woven by the hand of a man and the one that has been woven by the hand of a woman." Review signed E.G. of *Savinie* and *Valida*.

case of sentimental social novels by women, no review is complete without some comment on the gender of the author's style, whether the reviews are written by women or men, whether they appear in mass dailies, literary and cultural periodicals, or the feminine press. "We ask that we be allowed to give a sex to the author: we need to do so, first to facilitate the narrative, also, and this will be seen, for the very propriety of our ideas," one critic went so far as to remark, suggesting that ascribing a gender to a text filled a basic conceptual need.[43] "The style is the man himself," runs Buffon's famous phrase, cited ad infinitum throughout the first half of the nineteenth century. For women writers of the time, in contrast, "woman is the style."

During the July Monarchy, a feminine style was associated with sentimentality. As the author Félicité de Choiseul-Meuse put this critical consensus: "Men who write do so with what they think; women with what they feel."[44] In reviews of novels, feminized codes included neoclassical diction, analysis of the heart, the light touch, and a pared-down plot. Thus: "It is one of those rare and delicate works that women alone know how to write and that truly escapes analysis, not due to the multiplication of situations and the confusion of incidents, but rather due to a completely opposing cause: it is easy to retell the action of the novel; but when one isolates from it the mere data, one sees a thousand delightful nuances of grace and feeling fade; one might as well dissect a flower."[45] Similarly: "The style of Madame de Constant is pure, limpid, harmonious; it is woman-style, this style of the Cotins [sic] and Genlises, whose tradition had, I believed, been lost, now that some of our blue-stockings have their sentences do all manner of great athletic feats."[46]

As this comment indicates, while reviewers always asked whether novels by woman writers evinced a feminine style, they did not always answer yes. Poetics sometimes identified as masculine in novels by women include such sentimental social codes as a plot characterized by high dramatic intensity, some attention to social specificity and description—even if less than in realist novels—and the engaged narrator taking a public, judgmental stance on contemporary social issues. Madame Reybaud was an author whose style was frequently associated with men: "This writer has nothing, either in her touch or coloring, that could have betrayed her sex. Aside from a few scenes depicting the heart, for which women alone have the instinct, everything else is composed of vigorous and firm hues; bold and clear lines, carefully composed effects full of contrasts, which few

[43] A. Granier de Cassagnac, "*Jacques* par George Sand," 69.
[44] Félicité de Choiseul-Meuse, "De l'esprit chez les femmes," 94.
[45] Review signed H.M. of *Adélaïde: Mémoires d'une jeune fille*.
[46] Review signed L.C. of *Deux Femmes*.

men have known how to attain."[47] But the gendering of poetics was unstable; its details were less important than the fact that it occurred. Reybaud was also praised for her "energetic and brilliant style, which seems to have become the privilege of women in our century."[48]

The important role played by gender in orienting the reception of women's works helps clarify the specifically poetic advantages Sand derived from her sexually ambiguous literary identity.[49] Signing with the name of a man, even while she flaunted the fact that she was a woman, Madame George Sand, as some reviewers called her, abrogated to herself the attributes of both literary masculinity and femininity, whatever they might be, along with challenging the binarism of the divide. The success of her strategy is evident in critical evaluations, which frame her writing as transcending sexual categorization. "The style of *Jacques* is, like the book, eminently *human*," declared Planche, refusing the gendering of poetics dogging women writers in the name of a common humanity.[50] When Janin began his entry on "Mme George Sand" for the *Biographie des femmes auteurs contemporaines françaises*, he developed the subversive implications of Sand's bisexual literary identity in detail. "Who is he or who is she? Man or woman, angel or demon, paradox or truth? . . . How all at once has she found this marvelous style, which takes countless forms, and tell me why he has thus set himself to covering all of society with his contempt, his irony, and his biting scorn? What a puzzle this man, what a phenomenon this woman! what an interesting object of our sympathies and our terrors, this being of a thousand differing passions, this woman, or rather this man and this woman! And what critic in this world, would dare confront them head on and explain them?"[51] Sand was, however, exceptional in her ability to destabilize reigning cultural clichés. "A book by a woman should be before all else a woman's book, and women know it well," to cite Charles Nodier's opinion in the *Biographie*, and that Janin read Sand's bisexual identity as disruptive confirms Nodier's point.[52]

During the years framing the emergence of realism, I have been suggesting, the woman author's identity as a *woman* writing was inescapable. This identity was also contested, because the woman author was a light-

---

[47] Review signed I.C.T. of *Le Château de Saint-Germain*.

[48] Review signed H.L. of *Teresa*.

[49] On Sand's ambiguously sexed identity, see Schor's *Sand and Idealism*, and Sandy Petrey's "George and Georgina Sand: Realist Gender in Indiana," in *Sexuality and Textuality*, eds. Michael Worton and Judith Stills.

[50] Planche, review of *Jacques*, 21.

[51] Janin, "Mme George Sand," in *Biographie des femmes auteurs*, 439.

[52] Nodier, introduction to *Biographie des femmes auteurs*, 8.

ning rod in disputes around gender central to the construction of the contemporary social formation. As a result, a woman writer had no choice but to write as a woman, and yet she needed simultaneously to legitimate the fact that, as a woman, she wrote at all. In such a situation, the woman writer faced an added burden to her male counterpart. Not only were her works bids for symbolic and/or economic capital; they had to authorize their existence as the products of a female pen.

For the woman novelist interested in accumulating symbolic capital, it was evidently legitimating to build on the previously dominant sentimental practice of the novel, given that women were preeminent in this practice, that women writers' contributions to early-nineteenth-century sentimentality were widely recognized, and that the sentimental novel continued to be accorded critical respect by major taste-makers of the period like Sainte-Beuve, Janin, and Planche. How much more difficult it would be to exploit the realist position, whatever its symbolic rewards. From their emergence, realist works assert their claims to literary importance by identifying the novel with men, by forging a poetics associated with masculine forms of knowledge, and by undercutting the authority of the woman writer along with sentimental codes.[53] To make good on realism's symbolic promise, Balzac's consoeur would need to perform the tricky move of short-circuiting those aspects of the realist position challenging her authority without, however, dismantling the position itself. From the standpoint of the canon, it is incomprehensible that Balzac and Stendhal's female contemporaries did not leave their mark on one of the most successful and influential practices of the novel ever invented, and this lacuna has long bolstered suspicions concerning the inferiority of women writers as a class. From the standpoint of the imbricated politics around gender and genre defining the July Monarchy practice of the novel, in contrast, realist poetics first emerged for the woman writer as *une fausse position*.

---

[53] The most explicitly masculinized code is realism's professional and scientific approach to description. This treatment of description differs markedly from British realism, which emerges in continuity with the British sentimental tradition. Whether imparted by Austen and Eliot's gossips or Dickens's *flâneurs*, description in British realist novels is the province of a keen amateur observer who can be either female or male.

Select Bibliography

Primary Texts

French Novels Consulted

All Balzac, Stendhal, Hugo, and Sand novels are relevant to my study. As a guide to further reading, I list those uncited novels that best exemplify the writers' engagement with the sentimental tradition. When I used editors' comments to an edition of Balzac other than the Gallimard *Comédie humaine*, I have referenced the novel by that edition instead. When editors' comments appear in my argument, I include the editor's name in citing the primary text.

Abrantès, Junot d'. *La Duchesse de Valombray*. Paris: Charles Lachapelle, 1838.

Allart, Hortense. *L'Indienne*. Paris: Ch. Vimont, 1833.

———. *Settimia*. 2 vols. Paris: Arthus Bertrand, 1836.

Ancelot, Virginie. *Emérance*. 2 vols. Paris: Charles Gosselin, 1842.

———. *Gabrielle*. 1839. Paris: Charles Gosselin, 1840.

———. *Médérine*. 2 vols. Paris: Berquet et Pétion, 1843.

Arlincourt, Victor d', *Le Rénégat*. 2 vols. Paris: Bechet aîné, 1822.

———. *Le Solitaire*. Paris: Le Normant, 1821.

Arnaud, Angélique. *Clémence*. 2 vols. Paris: Berquet et Pétion, 1841.

———. *La Comtesse de Servy*. 2 vols. Paris: Charpentier, 1838.

———. *Coralie l'inconstante*. 2 vols. as 1. Paris: Berquet et Pétion, 1843.

Auger, Hippolyte. *La Femme du monde et la femme artiste*. 2 vols. Paris: A. Dupont, 1837.

Balzac, Honoré de. *Béatrix*. 1839. In Vol. 2 of *La Comédie humaine*. Paris: Gallimard, 1976.

———. *Les Chouans*. 1829. In Vol. 8 of *La Comédie humaine*. Paris: Gallimard, 1977.

———. *La Femme de trente ans*. 1842. In Vol. 2 of *La Comédie humaine*. Paris: Gallimard, 1976.

———. *Ferragus*. 1833. In Vol. 5 of *La Comédie humaine*. Paris: Gallimard, 1977.

———. *La Grenadière*. 1832. Edited by Anne-Marie Meininger. In Vol. 2 of *La Comédie humaine*. Paris: Gallimard, 1976.

———. *Honorine*. 1843. In Vol. 2 of *La Comédie humaine*. Paris: Gallimard, 1976.

———. *Illusions perdues*. 1843. Introduction by Antoine Adam. Paris: Garnier Frères, 1961.

———. *Le Lys dans la vallée*. 1836. Afterword by Anne-Marie Meininger. Paris: Gallimard Folio, 1972.

———. *Mémoires de deux jeunes mariées*. 1842. In Vol. 1 of *La Comédie humaine*. Edited by Roger Pierrot. Paris: Gallimard, 1976.

Balzac, Honoré de. *Modeste Mignon.* 1844. In Vol. 1 of *La Comédie humaine.* Paris: Gallimard, 1976.

———. *La Muse du département.* 1843. In *L'Illustre Gaudissart et La Muse du département.* Edited and with an introduction by Bernard Guyon. Paris: Garnier Frères, 1970.

———. *Le Père Goriot.* 1835. In Vol. 3 of *La Comédie humaine.* Paris: Gallimard, 1976.

———. *Sténie.* 1821. Paris: Librairie Georges Courville, 1936.

———. *Une Double Famille.* 1830. In Vol. 2 of *La Comédie humaine.* Paris: Gallimard, 1976.

———. *Une Fille d'Eve.* 1839. In Vol. 2 of *La Comédie humaine.* Paris: Gallimard, 1976.

Barthélemy Hadot, Marie-Adèle. *Guillaume Penn.* 3 vols. Paris: Pigoreau, 1816.

Bernard, Charles de. *Gerfaut.* 1838. Paris: Calmann Lévy, 1889.

———. *Le Noeud gordien.* 2 vols. Paris: Béthune, 1838.

Berthoud, Samuel-Henry. *La Bague antique, Courtisane et sainte.* 2 vols. Paris: De Potter, 1842.

Bignan, Anne. *L'Echafaud.* Paris: Madame Charles Bechet, 1832.

Billotey, Elisa. *L'Agent de change, esquisse de moeurs.* Dieppe: Delevoye-Barrier, 1837.

———. *Quoi ...? Tout ce qu'il vous plaira.* Dieppe: Delevoye-Barrier, 1834.

Bodin, Camille [a.k.a. Jenny Bastide]. *La Cour d'Assises.* 1832. Paris: Arnauld de Vresse, 1860.

———. *Elise et Marie.* 2 vols. Paris: Dumont, 1838.

———. *Pascaline.* 2 vols. Paris: Ch. Vimont, 1835.

———. *Savinie.* 2 vols. Paris: Dumont, 1835.

Brot, Alphonse. *Priez pour elles!* Paris: Sylvestre, 1833.

Calvimont, Albert de. *L'Honnête Homme.* Paris: E. Guérin, 1833.

Carlowitz, Aloïse de. *Caroline, ou le Confessseur.* Paris: G. Berrier, 1833.

———. *La Femme du progrès, ou l'Emancipation.* 2 vols. Paris: Desforest et cie. 1838.

———. *Le Pair de France, ou le Divorce.* 3 vols. Paris: Charles Lachapelle, 1835.

Charrière, Isabelle de. *Caliste, ou la Continuation des Lettres écrites de Lausanne.* In *Romans de femmes du XVIIIe siècle.* 1787. Paris: Robert Laffont, 1996.

———. *Lettres de Mistriss Henley.* 1784. In *Romans de femmes du XVIIIe siècle.* Paris: Robert Laffont, 1996.

Chateaubriand, François-René de. *Atala.* 1801. *René.* 1802. Paris: Garnier-Flammarion, 1964.

Constant, Benjamin. *Adolphe.* 1816. Paris: Librairie Générale de France, 1972.

Cottin, Sophie, *Amélie Mansfield.* 1803. 3 vols. Paris: Giguet et Michaud, 1805.

———. *Claire d'Albe.* 1799. In *Romans de femmes du XVIIIe siècle.* Paris: Robert Laffont, 1996.

———. *Elisabeth, ou les Exilés de Sibérie.* 2 vols. Paris: Giguet and Michaud, 1806.

———. *Malvina.* 1801. Vol. 1 of *Oeuvres complètes.* Paris: Foucault, 1817.

———. *Mathilde, ou Mémoires tirés de l'histoire des croisades.* 1805. Vols. 8–11 of *Oeuvres de Mme Cottin.* Paris: Roret et Roussel, 1820.

Couailhac, Louis. *Pitié pour elle.* 2 vols. Paris: Charles Lachapelle, 1837.

Dash, Countess [a.k.a. Gabrielle-Anne Pouilloüe de Saint-Mars]. *Un Mari.* 2 vols. Paris: L. Potter, 1843.

Davin, Félix, *Les Deux Lignes parallèles.* Paris: Librairie de Mame-Delaunay, 1833.

Desbordes-Valmore, Marceline. *L'Atelier d'un peintre.* 2 vols. Paris: Charpentier, 1833.

Desprez, Ernest [a.k.a. Éléonore Tenaille de Vaulabelle]. *Un Enfant.* 3 vols. Paris: C. Gosselin, 1833.

———. *Les Femmes vengées.* 2 vols. Paris: A. Ledoux, 1834.

Duffeyte-Dilhan, Joseph. *Les Mémoires d'un Ange, ou les Femmes vengées, Roman Historique, Philosophique et Moral.* 2 vols. Bordeaux: Ramadié, n.d.

Dumas, Alexandre. *Le Comte de Monte Cristo.* 1844–46. Paris: Robert Laffont, 1993.

Dupin, Aurore. *Marguerite.* 2 vols. Paris: Moutardier, 1836.

Dupuis, S[ophie?]. *Tableaux de moeurs.* 2 vols. Paris: Lecointe et Pougin, 1832.

Duras, Claire de. *Edouard.* 1825. In *Romans de femmes du XVIIIe siècle.* Paris: Robert Laffont, 1996.

———. *Olivier, ou le Secret.* Introduction by Denise Virieux. Paris: Albert Corti, 1971.

———. *Ourika.* 1823. Paris: des femmes, 1979.

Epinay Saint-Luc [a.k.a. Espinay Saint-Luc], Sophie d'. *Valida, ou la Réputation d'une femme.* 2 vols. Paris: Alphonse Levavasseur, 1835.

Etiennez, Hippolyte. *Un Droit de mari.* Paris: Dumont, 1834.

Gautier, Théophile. *Mademoiselle de Maupin.* 1835. In *Oeuvres.* Paris: Robert Laffont, 1995.

Genlis, Stéphanie-Félicité de. *Adèle et Théodore, ou Lettres sur l'education.* 2d ed. 3 vols. Paris: M. Lambert, 1782.

———. *Alphonsine, ou la Tendresse maternelle.* 1806. 3 vols. Paris: Maradan, 1819.

———. *La Duchesse de la Vallière.* 1804. Paris: Librairie Fontaine, 1983.

———. *Mademoiselle de Clermont.* 1802. In *Romans de femmes du XVIIIe siècle.* Paris: Robert Laffont, 1996.

———. *Mademoiselle de La Fayette, ou le Siècle de Louis XIII.* 2 vols. Paris: Maradan, 1813.

———. *Les Mères rivales, ou la Calomnie.* 1800. 3 vols. Paris: Maradan, 1819.

Gerber, Anatole. *Rosane. Désordre, Crime et Vertu.* Paris: Eugène Renduel, 1832.

Girardin, Delphine de. *Nouvelles.* Edition includes *La Canne de M. de Balzac* [1836] and *Le Lorgnon* [1831]. Paris: Slatkine, 1979.

———. *Monsieur le Marquis de Pontanges.* 2 vols. Paris: Dumont, 1835.

Heures du soir, Livre des femmes. 6 vols. Paris: Urbain Canel—Adolphe Guyot, 1833.

Hugo, Victor. *Claude Gueux.* 1834. Paris: Livre de Poche, 1995.

———. *Le Dernier Jour d'un condamné.* 1829. Notice by Roger Borderie. Paris: Gallimard, 1970.

———. *Les Misérables.* 1862. 2 vols. Paris: Garnier, 1971.

Hugo, Victor. *Notre-Dame de Paris*. 1831. Paris: Gallimard, 1992.

Kock, Paul de. *Soeur Anne*. 4 vols. Paris: Barba, 1825.

Krüdener, Juliane von. *Valérie*. 1803. In *Romans de femmes du XVIIIe siècle*. Paris: Robert Laffont, 1996.

Lacroix, Jules. *Une Grossesse*. Paris: Eugène Renduel, 1833.

Lamothe-Lagnon, E.-L.-B., and Touchard-Lafosse, Georges. *Les Jolies Filles*. 2 vols. Paris: Charles Lachapelle, 1834.

Lesguillon, Hermance. *Rosane*. 2 vols. Paris: Charles le Clère, 1843.

Luchet, Auguste. *Frère et soeur*. 2 vols. Paris: Hippolyte Souverain, 1838.

———. *Le Nom de famille*. 2 vols. Paris: Hippolyte Souverain, 1842.

Maignaud, Louise. *Les Etudians, épisode de la Révolution de 1830*. 4 vols. Paris: Mme Vve L. Maignaud, Leconte, Pugin et Levavasseur, 1831.

———. *La Fille mère*. 4 vols. Paris: Eugène Renduel, 1830.

Marbouty, Caroline [a.k.a. Claire Brunne]. *Ange de Spola, études de femmes*. 2 vols. Paris: Victor Magen, 1842.

———. *Une Fausse Position*. 2 vols. Paris: Librairie D'Amyot, 1844.

Masson, Michel. *Vierge et martyre*. 2 vols. Paris: Werdet et Spachman, 1836.

Mérimée, Prosper de. *Chronique du règne de Charles IX*. 1829. Paris: Gallimard, 1969.

Merlin, Maria de las Mercedes de Jaruco de. *Histoire de la Soeur Inès, épisode de mes douze premières années*. Paris: printed by S. Dupont et Laguionie, 1832.

———. *Les Lionnes de Paris*. 2 vols. Paris: D'Amyot, 1845.

Monborne, Madame B. *Deux Originaux*. Paris: Corbet aîné, 1835.

———. *Une Victime, esquisse littéraire*. Paris: H. Mouillefarine, 1834.

Montolieu, Isabelle de. *Caroline de Lichtfield, ou Mémoires d'une famille prussienne*. 1786. 2 vols. Paris: Arthus Bertrand, 1843.

Montpezat, Madame de. *Natalie*. Paris: Gustave Barba, 1833.

Mystère. Signed the Baroness de T***. Paris: Desforges, 1837.

Niboyet, Eugénie. *Les Deux Frères, histoire intime*. Paris: Charles le Clère, 1839.

Pannier, Sophie. *L'Athée*. 2 vols. Paris: Librairie de Fournier, 1835.

———. *Un Secret dans le mariage*. 2 vols. Paris: L. de Potter, 1844.

Pigault-Lebrun, Guillaume-Charles-Antoine. *Les Barons Felsheims*. 1798. In Vol. 2 of *Oeuvres complètes de Pigault-Lebrun*. Paris: J.-N. Barba, 1822.

———. *L'Enfant du Carnaval*. 1792. Paris: J.-N. Barba, 1818.

Reybaud, Madame Charles [a.k.a. H. Arnaud]. *Les Deux Marguerite*. 2 vols. Bruxelles: Hauman, 1845.

———. *Mézelie*. Paris: Ladvocat, 1839.

Riccoboni, Marie-Jeanne. *Lettres de Mistriss Fanni Butlerd*. 1757. In *Romans de femmes du XVIIIe siècle*. Paris: Robert Laffont, 1996.

Robert, Clemence. *L'Abbé Olivier*. Paris: Pastori, 1839.

———. *Les Mendians de Paris*. Bruxelles: Meline, Cans et cie., 1848.

———. *René l'ouvrier*. Paris: G. Roux et O. Cassanet, 1841.

Rochoux, Armand-Ambroise. *Le Coeur et le code*. Paris: Pougin et Legrand, 1839.

Rousseau, Jean-Jacques. *La Nouvelle Héloïse*. 1762. Paris: Garnier, 1960.

Sade, Donatien François Alphonse de. *Justine or the Misfortunes of Virtue*. 1791. Translated by Helen Weaver. New York: Capricorn Books, 1966.

Saint-Felix, Jules de. *Mademoiselle de Marignan*. Paris: Desessart, 1836.

Saint-Surin, Rosa de [a.k.a. Marie-Caroline-Rosalie Richard de Cendrecourt Monmergné]. *Maria ou soir et matin*. 2 vols. Paris: Belin-Mandar, 1837.

Sand, George. *Le Compagnon du Tour de France*. 1841. Plan de la Tour: Editions d'Aujourd'hui, 1976.

———. *Horace*. 1840. Meylan: Editions de l'Aurore, 1982.

———. *Indiana*. 1832. Paris: Gallimard, 1984.

———. *Jacques*. 1834. Vol. 59 of *Oeuvres complètes*. Paris: Michel Lévy, 1869.

———. *Lélia*. 1833. 2 vols. Plan de la Tour: Editions d'Aujourd'hui, 1976.

———. *Lucrezia Floriani*. 1846. Paris: Editions de la Sphère, 1981.

———. *Mauprat*. 1837. Paris: Gallimard: 1981.

———. *Le Meunier d'Angibault*. 1845. Plan de la Tour: Editions d'Aujourd'hui, 1979.

———. *Le Péché de Monsieur Antoine*. 1845. Meylan: Editions de l'Aurore, 1982.

———. *Valentine*. 1832. Meylan: Editions de l'Aurore, 1988.

Servan, Félix. *Maria Joubert, ou les Chagrins d'une jeune mariée*. 2 vols. Paris: Roux, 1836.

Sor, Charlotte de. *Madame de Tercy, ou l'Amour d'une femme*. 2 vols. Paris: Charles Lachapelle, 1836.

Soulié, Frédéric. *Le Conseiller d'Etat*. 2 vols. as 1. Paris: A. Dupont, 1835.

Souvestre, Emile. *Riche et pauvre*. 1836. Paris: Michel Lévy Frères, 1873.

Souza [a.k.a. Flahaut], Adélaïde de. *Adèle de Sénange*. 1794. In *Romans de femmes du XVIIIe siècle*. Paris: Robert Laffont, 1996.

———. *Charles et Marie*. In *Oeuvres de Madame de Souza*. 1802. Paris: Charpentier, 1840.

———. *Eugène de Rothelin*. 1808. In *Oeuvres de Madame de Souza*. Paris: Charpentier, 1840.

Staël, Germaine de. *Corinne ou l'Italie*. 1807. Paris: Gallimard, 1985.

———. *Delphine*. 1802. 2 vols. Paris: des femmes, 1981.

Stendhal. *Armance ou quelques scènes d'un salon de Paris en 1827*. 1827. Paris: Garnier, 1950.

———. *Lamiel*. 1889. Vol. 19 of *Oeuvres de Stendhal*. Paris: Le Divan, 1968.

———. *Le Rouge et le noir*. 1830. Edited by Henri Martineau. Paris: Garnier, 1957.

Stern, Daniel [a.k.a. Marie d'Agoult]. *Nélida*. 1846. Paris: Calmann Lévy, 1987.

Sue, Eugène. *Les Mystères de Paris*. 1842–43. Paris: Robert Laffont, 1993.

Tarbé des Sablons, Michelle-Catherine-Joséphine. *Roseline, ou de la Nécessité de la religion dans l'éducation des femmes*. 2 vols. Paris: A. Jeanthon, 1835.

———. *Zoé, ou la Femme légère*. Paris: Waille, 1845.

Touchard-Lafosse, Mademoiselle [a.k.a. Louise Bury]. *L'Homme sans nom*. 2 vols. Paris: L. de Potter, 1844.

———. *Les Trois Aristocraties, roman de moeurs*. 2 vols. Paris: L. de Potter, 1843.

Tristan, Flora. *Méphis ou le prolétaire*. 2 vols. as 1. Paris: Ladvocat, 1838.

Tullie Moneuse, Madame [a.k.a. Marguerite Robert Bloum]. *Régina*. 2 vols. Paris: L. Desessart, 1838.

———. *Trois Ans après*. Paris: L. Desessart, 1836.

Vigny, Alfred de. *Cinq-Mars*. 1826. Paris: Gallimard, 1980.

Waldor, Mélanie. *Pages de la vie intime*. 2 vols. Paris: Dumont, 1836.

Primary Critical and Theoretical Texts Cited

Unsigned articles are listed by title. I list untitled review articles by the title of the book under discussion or by the author, if the title is not specified.

Review of *Adélaïde,—Mémoires d'une jeune fille* by Madame Augustin Thierry, signed H. M. *Le Siècle*, Aug. 19, 1839.

Review of *Les Ailes d'Icare* by Monsieur Charles de Bernard, unsigned. *Le Charivari*, May 30, 1840.

Review of *Albertine de Saint-Albe*, signed A. *La Minerve Française* 2, 1818.

Aristotle. *The Poetics*. In *The Basic Works of Aristotle*, edited by Richard McKeon. New York: Random House, 1941.

Review of *Auguste et Frédéric* by Madame de B***, signed A. *Journal des Débats,* Mar. 11, 1817.

Balzac, Honoré de. *Avant-propos*. 1842. In vol. 1 of *La Comédie humaine*. Paris: Gallimard, 1976.

———. "Du Gouvernement moderne." 1832. In vol. 2 of *Oeuvres diverses*, vol. 39 of *Oeuvres complètes*. Paris: Louis Conrad, 1938.

———. "Lettre sur la littérature, le théâtre, et les arts," no. 1., July 15, 1840, *Revue Parisienne*. In vol. 3 of *Oeuvres diverses*, vol. 40 of *Oeuvres complètes*. Paris: Louis Conrad, 1940.

———. "Note de la première édition de *Scènes de la vie privée*." 1830. In vol. 1 of *La Comédie humaine*. Paris: Gallimard, 1976.

———. *Physiologie du mariage*. 1829. In vol. 11 of *La Comédie humaine*. Paris: Gallimard, 1980.

———. "Préface de la première édition de *Scènes de la vie privée*." 1830. In vol. 1 of *La Comédie humaine*. Paris: Gallimard, 1976.

Review of Balzac signed "Un ermite." *La Lecture*, 1843. Cited in René Guise, "Balzac devant la presse," in *L'Année Balzacienne*, 1981.

Barbier, A. A., and N. L. M. Desessarts. *Nouvelle Bibliothèque d'un homme de goût*. 1808–10. 5 vols. Paris: Arthus Bertrand, 1817.

Barrière, F. Review of *Mes loisirs* by Madame la baronne de Montaran. *Journal des Débats*, June 23, 1846.

Biographie des femmes auteurs contemporaines françaises. Edited by Alfred de Montferrand. Paris: Armand-Aubrée, 1836.

Buchez, J.-B., and P.-C. Roux. Vol. 32 of *Histoire parlémentaire de la Révolution française*. Paris: Paulin, 1837.

Bussière, Auguste. "Les Romans de femmes." *Revue de Paris*, Oct. 1843.

Review of *Calixte [sic] ou Lettres écrites de Lausanne* by Charrière, unsigned. *L'Illustration* 5, no. 122, June 28, 1845.

Chasles, Philarète. Review of *Gabrielle* by Virginie Ancelot. *Journal des Débats*, Feb. 15, 1839.

———. "Romans de M. de Balzac. Troisième article." *Journal des Debats*, Aug. 16, 1838.

Review of *Le Château de Kenilworth* by Walter Scott, signed A. B. *L'Abeille* 3, 1821.

Review of *Le Château de Saint-Germain* by H. Arnaud [Madame Charles Reybaud], unsigned. *Le Charivari*, Jan. 12, 1837.

Review of *Le Château de Saint-Germain* by Madame Charles Reybaud, signed I. C. T. *Le Constitutionnel*, Jan. 31, 1837.

Chaudes-Aigues, Jacques. "George Sand.—Alexandre Dumas." *L'Artiste*, 2d ser., no. 1, 1839.

Chénier, Marie-Joseph de. *Tableau historique de l'état et des progrès de la littérature française depuis 1789.* Paris: Maradan, 1816.

Choiseul-Meuse, Félicité de. "De l'esprit chez les femmes." *Journal des Femmes*, Sept. 8, 1832.

Colet, Louise. "La marquise de Lambert." *Le Constitutionnel*, Dec. 19, 1842.

Review of *Le Compagnon du Tour de France* by George Sand, signed W. W. *Le Constitutionnel*, Jan. 21, 1841.

Constant, Benjamin. *De l'esprit de conquête et de l'usurpation.* 1814. Geneva: Slatkine, 1980.

———. *Principes de politique.* 1815. In *De la liberté chez les modernes.* Paris: Librairie Générale de France, 1980.

Review of *Corisande de Mauléon* by Madame de Montpezat, unsigned. *Journal des Débats*, Oct. 9, 1835.

Review of *Oeuvres complettes [sic] de Mme Cottin*, unsigned. *Le Corsaire*, July 26, 1823.

Davin, Félix. "Introduction" to *Etudes de moeurs au XIXe siècle.* 1835. In Balzac, vol. 1 of *La Comédie humaine.* Paris: Gallimard, 1976.

"De la réalité en littérature," signed J.-Jph. V...E. *Le Mercure du XIXe siècle* 11, 1825.

Review of "*La Dernière Aldini—Les Maîtres Mosaïstes*" by George Sand, signed H. L. *Le Charivari*, May 18, 1838.

Review of *Deux Femmes* by Louise de Constant, signed L. C. *Le Charivari*, July 4, 1836.

Diderot, Denis. "De la poésie dramatique." 1758. In *Oeuvres esthétiques.* Paris: Classiques Garnier, 1959.

———. "In Praise of Richardson." 1762. In *Denis Diderot: Selected Writings on Art and Literature*, translated by Geoffrey Bremner. New York: Penguin, 1994.

Dupaty, Em. Review of *Les Séductions* by Madame Jenny L.G. D. *La Minerve Littéraire* 1, 1821.

Review of *Education pratique des femmes* by Nathalie de La Jolais, unsigned. *Le Constitutionnel*, July 17, 1842.

Announcement for *Emérance. Le Siècle*, Nov. 27, 1841.

Féletz, Charles Marie de. *Mélanges de philosophie, d'histoire et de littérature.* 6 vols. Paris: Grimbert, 1828.

"La Femme libre," signed L. Cc. *Le Siècle*, Jan. 28, 1838.

Review of *La Femme du progrès* by Aloïse de Carlowitz, unsigned. *Le Charivari*, June 23, 1838.

Galerie des dames françaises distinguées dans les lettres et les arts. Paris: Dussillon, n.d. [early 1840s].

Girault de Saint-Fargeau, Pierre-Eusèbe. *Revue des romans.* 1839. 2 vols. Geneva: Slatkine, 1968.

Granier de Cassagnac, A. "*Jacques* par George Sand." *Revue de Paris*, n. s., 10, Oct. 1834.

Guéroult, Ad. "Lettre à un ami de la province sur quelques livres nouveaux." *Revue de Paris*, n.s., 20, Aug. 1835.

Hegel, Georg Wilhelm Friedrich. *Aesthetics.* 2 vols. Translated by T. M. Knox. Oxford: Oxford University Press, 1975.

———. *Hegel's Philosophy of Right.* Translated by T. M. Knox. Oxford: Oxford University Press, 1967.

Review of *Heures du soir*, unsigned. *Le Charivari*, Apr. 17, 1833.

Review of *Heures du soir*, unsigned. *Le Charivari*, May 28, 1833.

Review of *Heures du soir*, unsigned. *Le Charivari*, Oct. 29, 1833.

Janin, Jules. Review of *Une Fausse Position. Journal des Débats*, July 22, 1844.

Limayrac, Paulin. "Du roman actuel et de nos romanciers." *La Revue des Deux Mondes*, 5th ser., 11, 1845.

Loève-Veimars, François-Adolphe. *Précis de la littérature française, depuis son origine jusqu'à nos jours.* 1825. Bruxelles: Société Belge de Librairie, 1838.

Luchet, Auguste. Preface to Elisa Billotey's *L'Agent de change, esquisse de moeurs.* Dieppe: Delevoye-Barrier, 1837.

Review of *Magdeleine la repentie* by E. Guérin, signed G. *Le Siècle*, Dec. 8, 1836.

Marc, Antoine. *Dictionnaire des romans anciens et modernes.* Paris: Chez Marc et Pigoreau, 1819.

Review of *Mariana* by Jules Sandeau, signed H. L. *Le Charivari*, Mar. 28, 1839.

Marmontel, Jean-François. *Essai sur les romans considérés du côté moral.* 1787. In vol. 10 of *Oeuvres complètes de Marmontel.* Paris: Firmin Didot, 1819.

Marx, Karl. Letter to Arnold Ruge, Kreuznach, Sept. 1843. In *Writings of the Young Marx on Philosophy and Society.* Edited and translated by Loyd D. Easton and Kurt H. Guddat. Garden City, N.Y.: Anchor Books, 1967.

———. *The Poverty of Philosophy.* 1847. New York: International Publishers, 1982.

Review of *Mézélie* by Madame Charles Reybaud, signed Y. *La Revue des Deux Mondes*, 4th ser., 20, 1839.

Michelet, Jules. *Le Peuple.* 1846. Edited by Paul Vialleneix. Paris: Flammarion, 1974.

Molènes, Paul Gaschon de. "Les femmes poètes." *La Revue des Deux Mondes*, July 1, 1842.

———. Review of *La Muse du départment. La Revue des Deux Mondes*, June 15, 1843.

———. "Revue littéraire." *La Revue des Deux Mondes*, 4th ser., 9, 1842.

Nodier, Charles [signed T. L]. "*Louise de Sénancourt* par Mme de T.... " *Journal des Débats*, Apr. 19, 1817.

Pages, Emile. "Bulletin bibliographique." *Le Siècle*, July 26, 1838.

Review of *Pascaline* by Camille Bodin, signed F. T. C. *Le Charivari*, Jan. 6, 1835.

Petitot, A. "Notice." In vol. 1 of Sophie Cottin, *Oeuvres complétes.* Paris: Foucault, 1817.

Pigoreau, Alexandre-Nicolas. *Petite Bibliographie biographico-romancière ou dictionnaire des romanciers*. 1821. Geneva: Slatkine, 1968.

———. *Troisième Supplément à la petite bibliographie biographico-romancière*. Paris: Pigoreau, 1822.

———. *Dix-septième Supplément à la petite bibliographie biographico-romancière*. Paris: Pigoreau, 1828.

Planche, Gustave. Review of *Gabrielle*. *La Revue des Deux Mondes*. 4th ser., 20, 1839.

———. Review of *Jacques*. *La Revue des Deux Mondes* 4, 1834.

———. "Revue littéraire." *L'Artiste*, 2d ser., no. 2, 1839.

———. " 'Les royautés littéraires. Lettre à M. Hugo.' " *La Revue des Deux Mondes*, 3rd ser., 1, 1834.

Review of *Régina* by Madame Tullie Moneuse, signed L. D. *Le Constitutionnel*, Nov. 5, 1837.

Review of *Régina* by Madame Tullie Moneuse, signed E. S. *Le National*, Nov. 7, 1837.

Review of *Régina* and *Trois Ans après* by Madame Tullie Moneuse, unsigned. *Le Charivari*, Dec.14, 1837.

Review of the complete works of Riccoboni and Cottin, signed A. *La Minerve Française* 7, 1818.

Rodrigues, Olinde. "L'Artiste, le Savant, et l'Industriel." 1825. In vol. 5 of *Oeuvres de Saint-Simon*. Paris: E. Dentu, 1875.

"Le Roman à bon marché." *Le Charivari*, Oct. 10, 1834.

Review of *Romans historiques de C.F. Vander-Velde*, signed V. *Journal des Débats*, Oct. 20, 1828.

Review of *Le Rouge et le noir* by Stendhal, signed J. J. *Journal des Débats*, Dec. 26, 1830.

Rousseau, Jean-Jacques. *The Social Contract*. 1761. Translated by Maurice Cranston. New York: Penguin, 1987.

Sainte-Beuve, Charles-Augustin. "De la littérature industrielle." *La Revue des Deux Mondes*, Sept. 14, 1839.

———. "Dix ans après en littérature." *La Revue des Deux Mondes*, 4th ser., 20, 1840.

———. "Poètes et romanciers modernes de la France, Madame de Duras." *La Revue des Deux Mondes*, 3d ser., 2, 1834.

———. "Madame de Souza." *La Revue des Deux Mondes*, 3d ser., 1, 1834.

Salvandy, Narcisse-Achille de. Preface to Madame de Montpezat, *Natalie*. Paris: Gustave Barba, 1833.

Sand, George, letter to Angélique Arnaud, Paris, beginning of June 1843. In vol. 25 of Sand, *Correspondance*, edited by Georges Lubin. Paris: Garnier, 1991.

———. *Histoire de ma vie*. 1854. Vols. 1–2 of *Oeuvres autobiographiques*. Paris: Gaillimard, 1971.

———. *Préface générale*. 1842. In *Questions d'art et de littérature*, edited by Henriette Bessis and Janis Glasgow. Paris: des femmes, 1991.

———. *Jean Ziska*. 1843. Paris: Michel Lévy Frères, 1867.

Review of *Savinie* by Camille Bodin, unsigned. *Le Corsaire*, Aug. 3, 1835.

Review of *Savinie* by Camille Bodin and *Valida* by Sophie d'Epinay Saint-Luc, signed E. G. *Le Courrier Français*, July 9, 1835.

Review of *Savinie* by Camille Bodin, signed Ed L. *Le Charivari*, June 19, 1835.

Smith, Adam. *The Theory of Moral Sentiments*. 1759. Indianapolis, Ind.: Liberty Classics, 1984.

Southern, Henry. "French Novels." *The Foreign Quarterly Review* 10, Oct. 1832. Reprinted in *A Victorian Art of Fiction*, edited by John Charles Olmsted. 2 vols. New York: Garland, 1979.

Introduction to selection from *Souvenirs d'un enfant du peuple* by Michel Masson, unsigned. *Le Constitutionnel*, Sept. 16, 1838.

Souvestre, Emile. "Du Roman." *Revue de Paris* 34, 1836.

Stendhal. "Appendice sur le Rouge et noir [*sic*]." 1832. In *Le Rouge et le noir*, edited by Henri Martineau. Paris: Garnier, 1957.

———. *De l'amour*. 1822. Paris: Garnier, 1959.

———. Paris, Apr. 20, 1828 [Duras's obituary]. In vol. 3 of *Courrier anglais*. Paris: Le Divan, 1935–36.

———. "Walter Scott et La Princesse de Clèves." *Le National*, Feb. 19, 1830. In *Mélanges de littérature*, vol. 39 of *Oeuvres complètes*. Paris: Le Divan, 1968.

Surville, Laure. *Balzac, sa vie et ses oeuvres*. Paris: Jaccottet, Bourdillat et cie., 1858.

Review of *Teresa* by Madame Charles Reybaud, signed H. L. *Le Siècle*, Apr. 16, 1841.

Vacquerie, A. "Par qui la critique devrait être faite." *France Littéraire*, n.s., 3, 1840.

"*Valentine*, par G. Sand, auteur *d'Indiana*," signed C——r. *Journal des Débats*, July 11, 1833.

Review of *Vanina d'Ornano* by Mme *** [Lattimore-Clarke], unsigned. *Journal des Débats*, Sept. 27, 1825.

Vieillard, P. A. Review of *Agnès de France ou le Douzième Siècle, roman historique, par Mme Simons-Candeille*. *Annales de la Littérature et des Arts* 4, 1821.

Secondary Texts Cited

Alliston, April. *Virtue's Faults*. Stanford, Calif.: Stanford University Press, 1996.

Althusser, Louis. *Montesquieu, Rousseau, Marx*. Translated by Ben Brewster. London: Verso, 1972.

Arac, Jonathan. "What Is the History of Literature?" In *The Uses of Literary History*, edited by Marshall Brown. Durham, N.C.: Duke University Press, 1995.

Armstrong, Nancy. *Desire and Domestic Fiction*. New York: Oxford University Press, 1987.

Auerbach, Erich. *Mimesis*. Trans. Willard R. Trask. Princeton, N.J.: Princeton University Press, 1968.

Balibar, Etienne. "Citizen Subject." In *Who Comes After the Subject?*, edited by Eduardo Cadava, Peter Connor, and Jean-Luc Nancy. New York: Routledge, 1991.

Barbéris, Pierre. *Balzac et le mal du siècle*. 2 vols. Paris: Gallimard, 1970.

————. *Mythes balzaciennes*. Paris: Armand Colin, 1972.

Bardèche, Maurice. *Balzac romancier*. Paris: Plon, 1940.

Barthes, Roland. *S/Z*. Translated by Richard Miller. New York: Farrar, Straus & Giroux, 1974.

Benjamin, Walter. "Theses on the Philosophy of History." In *Illuminations*. Translated by Harry Zohn. New York: Schocken Books, 1969.

Bennett, Tony. *Outside Literature*. New York: Routledge, 1990.

Biermann, Karlheinrich. *Literarische-politische Avant-garde in Frankreich*. Stuttgart: W. Kohlhammer, 1982.

Bourdieu, Pierre. *The Rules of Art*. Translated by Susan Emanuel. Stanford, Calif.: Stanford University Press, 1995.

Brooks, Peter. *The Novel of Worldliness*. Princeton, N.J.: Princeton University Press, 1969.

Caplan, Jay. *Framed Narratives*. Afterword by Jochen Schulte-Sasse. Minneapolis, Minn.: University of Minnesota Press, 1985.

Chaussinand-Nogaret, Guy. *The French Nobility in the Eighteenth Century*. Translated by William Doyle. Cambridge, Eng.: Cambridge University Press, 1985.

Cixous, Hélène. "The Laugh of the Medusa." In *New French Feminisms*, edited by Elaine Marks and Isabelle de Courtivron. New York: Schocken Books, 1981.

Cohen, Margaret. "In Lieu of a Chapter on Some French Women Realist Novelists." In *Spectacles of Realism*, edited by Margaret Cohen and Christopher Prendergast. Minneapolis, Minn.: University of Minnesota Press, 1995.

DeJean, Joan. "Classical Reeducation: Decanonizing the Feminine." *Yale French Studies*, no. 75, 1988, *The Politics of Tradition*, edited by Joan DeJean and Nancy K. Miller.

Denby, David. *Sentimental Narrative and the Social Order in France, 1760–1820*. Cambridge, Eng.: Cambridge University Press, 1994.

Eisenhut, Werner. *Virtus romana*. Munich: Wilhelm Fink, 1973.

Fortassier, Rose. "Balzac et le roman par lettres." *Cahiers de l'Association Internationale des Etudes Françaises*, 29, 1977.

Fraisse, Geneviève. *La Muse de la raison*. Paris: Editions Alinéa, 1989.

Furet, François. *Terminer la Révolution*. Paris: Hachette, 1988.

————, and Mona Ozouf. Preface to *Le Siècle de l'avènement républicain*, edited by François Furet and Mona Ozouf. Paris: Gallimard, 1993.

Gellrich, Michelle. *Tragedy and Theory: The Problem of Conflict since Aristotle*. Princeton, N.J.: Princeton University Press, 1988.

Gide, André. Preface to *Armance* by Stendhal. Paris: E. Champion, 1925.

Harrison, Nicholas. *Circles of Censorship*. Oxford, Eng.: Clarendon Press, 1995.

Herrenstein-Smith, Barbara. *Contingencies of Value*. Cambridge, Mass.: Harvard University Press, 1988.

Hesse, Carla. "Reading Signatures: Female Authorship and Revolutionary Law in France, 1750–1850." *Eighteenth-Century Studies* 22, fall 1989.

Hobsbawm, E. J. *The Age of Revolution*. London: Abacus Books, 1994.

Iknayan, Margaret. *The Idea of the Novel in France: The Critical Reaction, 1815–1848*. Geneva: Droz, 1961.

Jameson, Fredric. *The Political Unconscious*. Ithaca, N.Y.: Cornell University Press, 1981.

Lefort, Claude. *Democracy and Political Theory*. Translated by David Macey. Minneapolis, Minn.: University of Minnesota Press, n.d. [first published in English by Polity Press,1988].

Le Yaouanc, Moïse. "En relisant 'Le Lys dans la vallée.' " *L'Année Balzacienne* 1987.

Lyons, Martin. *Le Triomphe du livre*. Paris: Promodis, 1987.

Maigron, Louis. *Le Roman historique à l'époque romantique*. Geneva: Slatkine, 1970.

Mann, Heinrich. *Flaubert und George Sand*. Leipzig: Insel, 1971.

Marcus, Sharon. "Disciplining Cultural Studies." Paper delivered at the Colloquium for Nineteenth-Century French Studies, Santa Barbara, Oct. 1994.

Martin-Fugier, Anne. *La Vie élégante*. Paris: Fayard, 1990.

Milner, Max. *Le Romantisme I*. Vol. 12 of *Littérature française*. Paris: B. Arthaud, 1973.

Moretti, Franco. *Atlas of the European Novel 1800–1900*. London: Verso, 1998.

———. *The Way of the World*. London: Verso, 1987.

Parent-Lardeur, Françoise. *Les Cabinets de lecture—La Lecture publique à Paris sous la Restauration*. Paris: Payot, 1982.

Petrey, Sandy. *Realism and Revolution*. Ithaca, N.Y.: Cornell University Press, 1988.

Pierssens, Michel. "*Armance*: entre savoir et non-savoir," *Littérature*, Dec. 1982.

Planté, Christine. *La Petite Soeur de Balzac*. Paris: Seuil, 1989.

Prendergast, Christopher. *The Order of Mimesis*. Cambridge, Eng.: Cambridge University Press, 1986.

Prior, Henry. "Balzac à Turin." *La Revue de Paris*, Jan.–Feb., 1924.

Rosenvallon, Pierre. "La République du suffrage universel." In *Le Siècle de l'avènement républicain*, edited by François Furet and Mona Ozouf. Paris: Gallimard, 1993.

Schama, Simon. *Citizens*. New York: Alfred A. Knopf, 1989.

Schor, Naomi. *George Sand and Idealism*. New York: Columbia University Press, 1993.

Scott, Joan. *Gender and the Politics of History*. New York: Columbia University, 1988.

———. *Only Paradoxes to Offer*. Cambridge, Mass.: Harvard University Press, 1996.

Séché, Léon. *Hortense Allart de Méritens*. Paris: Société du Mercure de France, 1908.

Serval, M. *Une Amie de Balzac*. Paris: Editions Emile-Paul Frères, 1925.

Stewart, Joan Hinde. *Gynographs*. Lincoln, Neb.: University of Nebraska Press, 1993.

Starobinski, Jean. *1789: The Emblems of Reason*. Translated by Barbara Bary. Charlottesville, Va.: University Press of Virginia, 1982.

Szondi, Peter. "*Tableau* and *Coup de Théâtre*." *New Literary History* 11, no. 2, winter 1980.

Terdiman, Richard. *Discourse/Counter-Discourse*. Ithaca, N.Y.: Cornell University Press, 1985.

Tanner, Tony. *Adultery in the Novel*. Baltimore, Md.: Johns Hopkins University Press, 1979.

Waller, Margaret. *The Male Malady*. New York: Columbia University Press, 1993.

Wallerstein, Immanuel. Vol. 3 of *The Modern World System*. London: Academic Press, 1988.

Watson, Nicola. *Revolution and the Form of the British Novel*. Oxford, Eng.: Oxford University Press, 1994.

Weinberg, Bernard. *French Realism: The Critical Reaction 1830–1870*. New York: MLA, 1937.

Wright, J. Kent. "Les Sources républicains de la Déclaration des droits." In *Le Siècle de l'avènement républicain*, edited by François Furet and Mona Ozouf. Paris: Gallimard, 1993.

Planté, Christine, 169, 170, 176n.15, 177n.16; on women authors, 187–88
poetics: of forgotten literature, 21–22, 25; gendering of, 112–18, 192n.42, 193–95; and genre, 17–18, 21
poetics, realist. *See* literary realism
poetics, sentimental. *See* sentimental novel
Pope, Alexander, 49
portrait moral, 147, 151
position-taking, 6–7, 18, 192; and influence, 7n.14; realism as, 18; realist against sentimentality, 12, 18, 85–87, 88, 94–96, 98–102, 105–6, 107, 109–10, 111–12, 113–16, 117–18, 180–81; realist against Sand, 183. *See also*, Bourdieu, Pierre; literary production
poststructuralism: genre and, 16; literary history after, 4–5, 17n.45; materialism in, 5
power: and knowledge, 110; relations of, 89, 100–101, 130–31
Prendergast, Christopher, 101n.64, 110n.82, 111n.86, 112
private sphere: in realism, 107–8, 110, 111; in sentimentality, 50, 69, 70–71, 113; in sentimental social novel, 144; women authors and, 170, 176, 181; women in, 46–48, 106–7, 137, 169–70
protagonists: gender of, 46–48, 106–7; physical body of, 54; of sentimental novel, 46–48, 50–52, 60, 62; of sentimental social novel, 131–32, 139–42, 143, 144, 153–54; sympathy for, 62, 65; tragic, 58–59
psychology: vs. sentiment, 92–93, 95–96, 105–6
public sphere: gender in, 14, 46, 47, 72, 169–70; literature's engagement with, 71, 158, 159, 181; in sentimentality, 71; in sentimental social novel, 136, 159, 160, 181–82

Radcliffe, Ann, 27, 29, 78, 79n.3; sources for, 81n.6
readers: community of, 69, 71, 75, 92, 97, 110, 156, 157; contract with, in realism, 109, 110, 112, 156; interpretive freedom of, 69–70, 159; as leisured, 83; sympathetic engagement of, 62–67, 92–93, 108–10, 145, 152, 156–57, 158–60; women, 84–85, 89, 113n.9
realism, literary, 3, 4, 5, 10, 12, 16, 103, 195; absence of women authors from, 8–

9, 13–14, 19, 23, 120–22, 124, 165, 191–92, 195; appropriation of sentimentality in, 12, 87–89, 94–96, 98–102, 105–6, 107, 109–10, 111–12, 115; contract with reader in, 96, 108, 109, 110, 112, 156; description in, 113–16, 148–49, 150; emergence of, 5, 8, 18, 23–24, 98; English, 9, 195n.53; feminine sexuality in, 108n.79; gender of characters in, 106–8; knowledge in, 112–14, 118, 153, 195; lost illusions in, 4, 99–100, 131; Marbouty on, 186; masculine viewpoint of, 12, 87, 112–18, 195; materialist criticism on, 4, 5, 12, 97n.49, 99, 100–101, 102–3, 110, 112; melodrama in, 140; political context of, 9, 11–12, 103–4; as position-taking, 18, 78, 87, 98, 102, 106, 107, 110–12; professions in, 112–14; psychology in, 95–96, 101; relationship to Revolution, 102–3; Sand on, 117, 149; Sand's use of, 127, 149, 152–53; virtue in, 100, 104n.72
reason: in sentimental novel, 42n.41, 45, 47
religion: in sentimental social novel, 137, 157
Restoration: book trade of, 26–27, 28, 85n.19; censorship under, 11; literary production during, 26; novel reading during, 83–84; preferred novelists of, 26n.2, 27–29; social inequality in, 95, 103
Revolution, French: effect on female literary culture, 14–15, 177; in fiction, 10; liberty in, 72–73, 75; public sphere as producing, 71; realism as response to, 3–4, 102; relation to sentimental novel, 33, 71–76, 102; social contract in, 111; Terror during, 72–76; virtue in, 74–75; women's role in, 72, 177n.18
Revolution of 1830, 10, 11n.23, 103; importance for sentimental social novel, 159–60. *See also* July Monarchy
Revolution of 1848, 103, 162
Reybaud, Madame Charles, 149–50, 182n.26, 193–94
Riccoboni, Marie-Jeanne, 76
Richardson, Samuel, 33n.26; *Clarissa*, 39, 81, 109; Diderot on, 68–69, 70, 156
Richard the Lion-hearted: in sentimental fiction, 40, 51, 53
rights: Constant on, 44, 73; in French liberalism, 42, 43–44, 75n.125, 91; Hugo on, 134; under July Monarchy, 10; positive